... and it's all true.

I dedicate this true autobiography to my dearly loved family Kevin, Louisa, Victoria, Christopher and Jed, who sadly live so far away...

and to my very special friend, who taught me so much about love and wanting to always give of one's best - Hyline Gentry.

Alan Potter

Hyline Gentry with his father Sir Quincy Bob winners of their Quarter Horse Colt and Stallion Halter Classes at the 1971 P.N.E. Vancouver - congratulating and inspiring each others futures!

I.S.B.N. 0-9681247-0-4

Published by Joy Dee Marketing Ltd. 1996

c.sympatico.ca

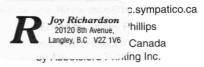

Joy Richardson
20120 8th Avenue, 'hillips
Langley, B.C V2Z 1V6   Canada

by Abbotsford Printing Inc.

-FOREWORD-

From early childhood, my parents often spoke of my ancestors; some were pioneering agriculturists, some were leaders of local communities and in politics, always encouraging me to be strong, hard working and fearless like them. My father, Everett Delanoix Cooke, whose, great great grandmother had fled France to England with the Hugenots, when persecuted by the Roman Catholics in the early 17th century, was equally undefeatable.

My childish dreams claimed the most famous navigator in the world, Captain James Cook, who surveyed the shores of Canada, America, New Zealand and Australia, discovering and charting coastlines, from the Arctic to the Antarctic, was a distant relative. I had been mesmerized from the stories of his travels, feeling an inexplicable close bonding, listening to the family stories and reading books, confident he had somehow bequeathed much of his spirit to me, and so it seems to have been.

James Cook married Elizabeth Batts in December 1762, fathering two sons and a daughter, any of whom could have passed on the requisite genes for discovery and adventure. My brother Andrew did not believe any of it! Perhaps he was right, but I know my own spirit of adventure and determination to conquer the near impossible, had to have come from somewhere very special.

My mother, Kate Elizabeth Andrew, was a direct descendent of Joseph Banks, whose family were gentry, owning large acreages in Lincolnshire and Rutland, with peerless social connections. His ancestral estate, Revesby Abbey, near Lincoln, was close to the Fens. His father had been fascinated with the enormous challenges of land drainage, initiated by the Danes and Romans, ultimately producing much of the finest agricultural land in the world. Joseph Banks had been educated at both Eton and Harrow, then Oxford, with later a Cambridge tutor instructing him in botany and natural philosophy. His father died leaving a great fortune and responsibilities in 1764 when Joseph purchased a fine house in London. He made numerous natural history tours, collecting specimens of birds and plants following in the wake of Cook's surveying.

In due course Banks and Cook arrived on board the Endeavor in August 1768, each to carry on with their unique discoveries for England. After three incredible voyages and thousands of plant, mammal and bird specimens carefully conveyed back, the Royal Botanical Society created magnificent Kew Gardens in London for their continued growth and display. My great uncle was knighted, becoming Sir Joseph Banks, while Captain Cook was killed by the natives in an Hawaiian uprising.

I choose to believe, after more than one hundred and sixty years, those intrepid explorers for England were finally united, through their descendants, by my parent's marriage. It was inevitable at least one of their children would face massive challenges with a dauntless spirit. I believe that descendent is me!

-ADDENDUM-

Three Score and ten years always seemed a very long way off, but time does rush by and I have been there, certainly having an extraordinarily varied, busy and exciting life, not to mention especial fulfillment from my family Kevin, Louisa, Victoria, Christopher and Jed.

Throughout the years commitment and strong love for my horses has been foremost. They saw me through distressing times with two husbands, giving me courage and tenacity against unethical situations and to stand up for what I believed was right.

Perhaps my strongest side has been an excessive amount of energy, bestowed through my parents whose motto seems to have been "Run don't walk". I have had far more than my fair share of accidents, mainly on the roads with others driving, with some inevitability from horse back. To no one do I lay intended harm for my sufferings, but I do claim inner strength from having to combat various degrees of pain. Sufficient to say there were always horses to be looked after, so I had to get on with their care.

I am no paragon, but wondrously have collected an abundance of friends from all walks of life within three countries in which I have lived, England, Canada and the United States. I defy the old adage which says "you can only count true friends on one hand". I claim them all around me. To list them all would be an impossible task, but I appreciate their love and only hope I am strong enough to be there if needed by them.

70 years looks intimidating from one's youth, but my lifetime has rushed by, giving an abundance of challenge and reward to me. Those years were surely guided with the love I inherited from my father for horses. The deep compassion I feel for all animals has seemed to control my daily living, so that caring especially for my horses, with all the knowledge I have learned over the years, controls my existence. The love I receive back and which I give to them, has been truly blessed I know by God.

I have tried to recall the major portions of my life, and written it down, led by the efforts of beloved Gentry. I hope this little book gives some value of how to do and what not to do with the fragments of life we are dealt. I have enjoyed putting it down, although it did take a long time with all the other things I take on. The 13 years since our return to Canada have not been idle, there is much to record from them too, perhaps with encouragement, I will tackle my continued story of Paladin, Wager, Music Man, Spirit, Comet, and beloved Gentry.

My gratitude to my family and all those who have 'been there' for me, along with the great horses I have owned and ridden who taught me so much - especially Gentry.

It is hard to separate the good from the bad - for it is all Life in the end. I will always remember the special kindnesses of Bob and Christy Avila,

Pat Alrich, Susan Holroyd, Pat Dyke, Len Cooke, Dr. Bill Saunders, Dr. John Twidale, Dr. Lisa Burgess, Dr. Marvin Beaman, Don Burt, Richard Deller, Dorothy Neville, Gerry and Grace Bryson, Shirley Phillips, John Tichnor, Virginia Fisher, Debbie Power, Viv Harder, Jan White, Annette and Ernie Kehler, Susie Taylor, Betty and Ellis Foulds, Paul and Maureen Forseth, Bunty and Ken Forsythe, Brandy Couvosier, Mavis Dayton, Joanne Dixon, Joanne Boyle, Ann Hall, Barbara Woodhouse, Jeanne and Leslie Dungworth, Robert Hall, Betty Atkinson, Anne Measures, Nancy Wherry, Margaret Evans, Winnie Cant, Robin and Betty Leyland, Leanne Petersen, Noni Franks, Jean and Fred Long, Delia Puttkamer, Rick and Jennifer Maynard, Colonel Michael Gutowski, John Stelfox, Jean Phillipe Giacanomi, John Geisbrecht, Dr. Richard Watson, Dr. John Gilray, Robert Scheres, Rich Ingram, Sharone Nielsen, Janice Jarvis, Andy Rees, Buz MacDonald, Dr. John Metchalfe, June and Charles Mason, Pat Bennett, Pam Boulter, Doug and Dorothy Denyer, Earl Brown, Malcolm Keogh, Sarah Neeld, Caryll Forbes and Brian Franks.

Joy with her trainer, world renowned Bob Avila, receiving the Hi Point Gelding Award from Ted Maynard.

Chapter One

George Elliot:
"Our deeds travel with us from afar,
and what we have been makes us what we are.".

My parents came from old farming stock whose families were large landowners in the fertile County of Lincolnshire. My father grew up at Postland House, near to Crowland Abbey, an immaculate estate of fertile green fields which were stocked with cattle in the summer months. The farm consisted of several hundred very black soil acres, which had been drained from the North Sea marshes by the Danes four hundred years earlier.

Whilst Grandpa Cooke specialized in cattle and the crops grown to fatten them, like sugar beet, mangel-wurzels, a coarse yellowish beet, rich hay and grain, the family of three boys and two artistic girls lived a carefree life, all attending good boarding schools, receiving instruction in religion as well as cultural educations.

My father was a natural born leader. He had the most outgoing nature of the family and was always into mischief at home and in school. After a minor transgression, as punishment, he was made to learn an Epistle of St. John by heart from the Bible. Luck was so often with him throughout his life, for starting at this point - the scripture exam that year was taken entirely from the same Epistle. Daddy came out with 99% and to everyone's amazement won the Scripture Prize.

His love for fine animals was instilled by his father. He learned to appreciate the value of conformation, beauty and strength. The family's cattle consistently won major County Show awards as did his heavy Shire horses. They stood two stallions at all times. A groom walked each one during the breeding season to different farms, often twenty or more miles a day, staying the night and covering the mares in season the following morning. This was repeated weekly from February until June. The magnificent heavy stallions gleamed with good health, bedecked with coloured raffia plumes in their manes and braided tails, as they proudly paraded through the countryside. The finest foals were kept to improve the breeding stock whilst the cattle were fattened for the weekly markets.

E.D., as my father was affectionately called by his friends, had

1

a magnetic personality. He was full of life, an inveterate gambler, he laughed at anything, especially himself. He was generous to those in need, and made friends everywhere. He was extremely good looking, with dark curly hair, flashing brown eyes, and meticulous in appearance. He was an outstanding progressive farmer who constantly studied the newest breeding technology and pioneered modern agricultural equipment.

E.D., being the eldest son and more capable than most young men his age, initially managed a new farm purchased by his father at the young age of twenty. Three hundred acre North Fen Farm near Bourne, on the edge of the hills leading to the higher land levels of the sought after Shires, was only thirty miles from Postland, but a major endeavor by pony and trap. His father must have had great confidence in his son's ability bestowing such responsibility.

Three miles away the Bourne market was held every week where cattle, sheep and pigs were sold by auction. Thursdays became a day out when the local people, dressed in their finest, met to purchase fruit, vegetables, clothes, fish and hardware from wooden stalls erected in the market place, whilst the farmers swapped tales of their hardworking lifestyles. The environment provided an exciting place for young people to meet away from the watchful eye of their families. This is where my parents eventually met.

Shortly after my father had been installed by Grandpa Cooke to manage the farm, World War I broke out. Farmers and their sons were exempt from military service due to the importance of growing food. However, my father would not stay at home, and joined the Lincolnshire Yeomanry the same year. He fought in the trenches of France, where he was appalled by the shocking loss of horses to gunfire, witnessing their terror from the noise and explosions. He never forgot the horror of seeing wounded and dead horses piled into the trenches to create bridges for gun carriages to cross. These agonies developed into a lifelong mission to help horses of all kinds.

The Lincolnshire Yeomanry sailed from England to Egypt later in the war. Their horses, seconded from elite hunter and racing stables, were stalled on the decks of The Mercian, a creaking freighter. Three or four miles from the Cairo shoreline, a prowling German submarine torpedoed the ship, resulting in most of the horses being drowned as the ship sank. My father, to his dying day, heard the shrieks of fear as they disappeared into the Mediterranean Sea.

The several thousand soldiers, anxious to get on with fighting the war, became very bored waiting for months in the sands of the

Sahara. For amusement they competed frequently in games of cards and sports, particularly races over assorted distances. It was an event my father spoke of proudly, years later, when he recalled winning the thirty mile long distance marathon.

And then there was my mother. Kate was the youngest of four, a brother and two sisters, of strongly Victorian minded parents. Her father farmed on a large scale living at the Manor House of Austerby, Bourne. No one had wider experience or possessed more thoroughly sound and practical knowledge than Charles Edward Andrew, educated at an elite boarding school, who was one of the most outstanding farmers in Lincolnshire, and the adjacent counties of Northampton and Leicester. He farmed over 2,000 acres in the early 1900's. He was Chairman of the Bourne Urban Council and a staunch Conservative, being Chairman of the Constituency.

My grandmother, Eliza Jane Ward, was tall, very straight, always severe, and I recall wore a long black gown from which keys to the wine cellar and storage, hung on a silver chain around her waist. She was a severe disciplinarian, very frugal, ensuring everything stayed in its proper place.

My mother was quite a small woman but strong and wiry with light brown hair and blue eyes. She loved all music, playing both the piano and banjo, enjoying the lead in local operatic performances. She had a fine sense of humour and was devoted to her dogs, poodles or smooth haired terriers, and blue Persian cats, whose coats she loved to groom.

Katie, as she was fondly called, attended Brasnose Ladies Boarding School in Stamford, ten miles away, with daughters of other prominent families. She acquitted herself well, especially with the piano and on the hockey and cricket fields, playing for Lincolnshire, where she was Captain of both teams.

Grandpa Andrew had the first motor car in the county, a Model T, so my mother was encouraged to travel with him, opening the gates to the fields as he attended his duties of running the farms. His speciality was sheep breeding, cattle raising and general farming, growing the root crops, grain and hay to support them. My mother loved spending many days with the various shepherds, riding along in a wooden float (cart), drawn by a smart pony, as they tended the flocks, and watched the delivery of tiny lambs. Sometimes she attended the Agricultural Shows where her father won many prizes with his cattle, sheep and Shire horses.

Whilst Daddy served his country in the army, Mummie became

an enthusiastic member of the Volunteer Aid Detachment, helping nurse the wounded soldiers, in makeshift hospitals near Bourne, as they were sent back from the front lines of France. Her piano playing and surprisingly lovely soprano voice made her in great demand for entertainments.

There are still a few cards written by my father to mother from his service over seas, showing their love blossoming during the ghastly war. After his safe return, E.D. took control of the Bourne Fen Farm again and his courtship flourished.

They were married in 1920 and lived happily on the Fen farm for five years, trying very hard for a son to carry on the family dynasty. Sadly it took the five years for a child to be born, who turned out to be me. After such a long wait I was named JOY to celebrate their elation, and Delanoix to continue on the French family tradition. My brother Andrew was born twenty months later.

Daddy and I were both Libras, October born and very alike in temperament. However, my brother Andrew was a different matter. He arrived twenty months after me, in August, 1927 the same astrological month Leo, as my mother. Throughout our lives the similarity of father and daughter, compared to mother and son was extraordinarily evident.

I was brought up to always give the best of myself. As a tiny child, my strong willed, successful parents would say whenever I had to go anywhere "Run, don't walk", there was never time to dawdle. As a result, I became hyper-active which has never left me, and for which there are no regrets as I have lived life to its fullest!

As a eight month old child being pushed in a perambulator along an English country lane by my nurse maid, we stopped to talk with a horseman bringing three of my father's Shire horses home from work in his fields. I was enthralled by the gentle giants, begging to be lifted up on one. That moment was to cement my all consuming passion for horses.

My father, always devoted to his farming heritage and thoroughbred horses, hoped his family would have the same dedication. Before my first birthday, he purchased a Shetland pony on which I was regularly taken for fresh air rides. When I was three our family moved into the Manor House, after my grandfather had a double stroke, and could no longer take care of his farming pursuits. E.D. soon began leading my pony and I beside his thoroughbred hunter as he daily rode around the 1000 acre home farm. Impatient by nature, energetic and brave, he soon tired of the slow pace we created. An extra long girth was fitted to my felt saddle pad, enabling him to place it over the mare's withers, at the front of his saddle.

Thus our morning rides moved into another phase. The little girl wrapped securely in her father's arms, sat tall and proud as they rode around the fields overseeing the workmen ploughing, harvesting, or shepherding cattle and sheep. It was not long before E.D. tired of dismounting to open the gates dividing the fields. At first our trio popped over little ditches and low hawthorn hedges, but soon advanced to jumping the five barred wooden gates! My poor mother turned white within a week upon learning of the adventures and jumping exploits of her little girl. Taking the gates with my father instilled within me a fearless courage toward danger, along with total confidence of horses and the capacity to respect and love a good one beyond all possible horizons. Those feelings, gained so early, have governed my life, which I have never lost.

All of my childhood hours were not spent with horses. I loved playing in our kitchen garden - an acre of fertile ground surrounded by protective shelter hedges. A variety of tender vegetables thrived, including the asparagus beds whose thick, but delicate ferns afforded wonderful camouflage in games of hide and seek.

The garden game I enjoyed most was fitting a pony halter on one of our Golden Retrievers. I fashioned clotheslines into harnesses, hitched up a rake or hoe and 'plowed' the garden, as the workmen and the Shires ploughed the fields. Unfortunately, we sometimes wounded tender roots, and I was ultimately persuaded to slow down my farming and banished from the garden.

My hyper-active state, unrecognized by the medical profession in those days, can now be controlled with planned diets. In my day fed on home-grown fruit, our own Jersey cow milk, cream and golden butter, vegetables, fat chickens and plenty of rich red meat, I found it impossible to remain still, physically or mentally. I must have been a torment to those around me.

In 1930 I was subjected to Miss Chamberlain's private nursery school, conducted in her home a mile through the town of Bourne. Twenty-four boys and girls, between four and seven years of age, were taught basic reading, writing, arithmetic and french.

Because of my French ancestry it was presumed I would master French with ease. I hated it and eventually rebelled against going to school. Mother solved the problem with a bribe.

"I see no reason why you shouldn't ride your pony to and from school. Sandy will lead you."

5

Sandy was my father's old army batman. He had been gassed in the French trenches and had little lung power left, but was able to ride his bicycle happily alongside my pony and me. I loved this kindly man, my pony and those delightful treks mornings and afternoons. In return for such privileges, preparatory school was tolerated... even French. However, we were sure of one fact: French and I would never be compatible. I had learned some basics but seemed unable to progress beyond them.

Each summer gypsies passed by our Manor House in Bourne on the way to Stowe Green Horse Fair, some asking to stay overnight in one of the grass fields. My father never refused them. There were ten to fifteen brightly painted caravans pulled by coloured ponies, with suckling foals at their sides. The women's golden dangling earrings fascinated me, along with the vibrant charm of their tousled black hair and flashing smiles. Their menfolk were incredibly dashing, with glowing swarthy skins and the same black curly hair. Most of all I was enchanted by their animals, the ponies, horses and dogs. They were gentle, confident creatures, obviously loved and treasured.

I was six years old when the gypsies arrived during the summer of 1931, en route to the Annual Fair, eighteen miles away. Daddy and

My parents, house staff, Joy and Andrew in front of the Manor House, 1931.

I drove over in his rumble-seated car. He was always in the market for good work horses and found several prospects. While he engaged in the age old horse trading game, I wandered around petting the ponies on display.

"I love them," I told Daddy when he came to fetch me. "Let's take them all home with us....please."

Rather than explain why one does not buy a penful of ponies just because of love, Daddy struck a deal with his gypsy friends. Seven of the ponies I fancied most, would be taken to The Manor along with the young work horses Daddy had purchased.

"You must decide which of the ponies you want to keep until the gypsies return later in the week" he said "Keep two, one for you and one for your brother Andrew, letting the others go."

None had been broken, but they were gentle and, once in a paddock by The Manor, followed me around taking care not to nip my fingers when they accepted carrots or apples. Although Daddy had said we would keep only two, I thought he would come to love the ponies as much as I.

The day of reckoning came when my father said "Which ones do you want to keep? The gypsies will take the others early tomorrow morning."

I was unable to choose. "I want them all, Daddy!"

His eyes were firm and dark, at odds with his usual warm and tolerant gaze when directed at me. Not so on that day. He held up two fingers, the same gesture Sir Winston Churchill later used as a symbol of victory.

No victory for me in the pony selection. Only sadness, knowing five would be leaving forever. I finally chose a pair of grays, the colour my father favoured for his horses, and named my favourite Daisy. Next morning Daisy and her companion Fritz were alone in the paddock. I cried for the ones taken away and promised myself never to take on more animals than I could keep, or fall in love with any I did not own.

"Your job now," my father told me, "is to concentrate on the two you've chosen. Along with buying them comes accepting responsibility for them."

"Well" I said "the first thing is to break them properly, who will help me?"

"You can handle it yourself with Sandy," Daddy said. "After all, you were riding astride before you were one year old."

Patting me on the back he walked away. Wide eyed I watched

him go. What did I know about breaking ponies?

"Sandy!" I shouted. The old army batman appeared cheerily, somewhat out of breath.

"We have to break the ponies," I panicked.

Neither of us had any idea of what we were doing, but we did manage the job, if somewhat haphazardly. In a few days they were very quiet under saddle, loving us as much as we did them. After all the gypsies had treated them as friends all along, there was nothing to it.

One morning I was playing with Daisy in the farmyard when Daddy rode past on his thoroughbred, Lady. His shooting dogs - Red the setter and Goldie, the golden retriever, bounded near the mare's heels. Wanting to show him I knew what I was doing, I clambered onto Daisy attempting to follow. But Lady was already in a gallop, so the pony had little chance to catch up.

As I breathlessly followed to the nearby potato field, where a gang of pickers toiled, and thought about riding past them at a canter to show off my new skills, Daisy gave a cheeky buck towards Lady. I fell off within a few feet of my father. He dismounted, grabbed Daisy's reins and scooped me from the earth. Plunking me back in the saddle, he thrust the reins in my hands, giving Daisy a spank on her quarters so she bounded forward.

"If you fall off again," my father called "I'll sell that pony this afternoon."

I did not fall off. I knew enough to keep my heels well down, but my pride was terribly askew. How could Daddy have shamed me so, in front of those potato pickers!

That was the first and only time I came close to being angry with my father, but I remained on board which was his intention!

Many children are sent off to boarding school in England when they are only seven years old, and so was I in September 1932. My mother believed me to be rather spoiled, precocious, and much too close to my father. When she told me what was to happen I cried - that daunted her, but she remained firm.

"I know you don't want to go now," she said, "But it's a lovely school and you will enjoy the other girls. You'll understand when you grow up."

Daddy appeared to take my mother's side when he said: "Your mother knows best, don't worry, you can handle it. After all you were --"

"I know" I interrupted. "Riding astride before I was one year old!"

Frustrated I ran away from him, my supporter and leader into adventure. Feeling somewhat betrayed, I had to accept their decision and get on with it.

Although my parents seemed to have all they wanted, in reality, there was a shortage of cash. My mother strove to find some school expenses by making cream cheeses, which involved a complex process of separating the Jersey cow's cream in a hand cranked machine and maturing it in the airing cupboard for a few days. The cheeses were formed into 1/4 lb blocks. My mother then hitched up Daisy into a pony trap, placed home grown tomatoes and cucumbers inside, and drove around the neighbourhood selling her produce. I believe her efforts went towards purchase of my uniform.

The school my mother chose was Felixstowe Ladies College in Suffolk, a handsome old stone mansion set high on the cliffs overlooking the North Sea, ringed by old world gardens. Several smaller houses served as dormitories for the hundred and twenty girls. All were older than me, few sharing my simple country background. They boasted of fine city homes, theatres they attended, museums they visited, and the number of cars their parents owned. My accounts of farm life, the workhorses, my beloved Daisy and Lady, bored them. Even the most exciting event of my life did not impress those city girls.

During my first holiday from boarding school, after I had just turned eight years old, my father decided I was capable enough to ride in my first foxhunt at Kirkby Underwood, a well cultivated farm area with tidily maintained woodlands, just five miles from our home. The Master of Fox Hounds, was Lord Burghley, an Olympic Gold hurdling medalist, who later became the Marquess of Exeter.

Riding my spritely grey pony, Daisy, it had been drummed into me I must always keep my heels down to ensure a strong balance, to sit up straight, and to stay quietly beside my father. Previously I had watched him hunt his thoroughbred mare, Lady, from the security of my mother's car and could barely control my excitement, that I too, would be joining the hallowed Field.

How proud I felt when we arrived on the morning of the never-to-be forgotten day for my first proper hunt! Daddy, of course, wore his black hunt coat and velvet cap with its ribbon tips sewn pointing upward to denote he was a landowner. I had on new beige jodhpurs, a tweed jacket and of course the regulation black velvet hunt cap. With unseen excitement, my heart thumped wildly.

Lady's mane was braided into nine plaits, tradition for a mare. Daisy's white mane had been roached off as it was too thick and shaggy to braid. When hounds arrived, led by Lord Burghley, his sleek hunter dancing beneath him, all the horses, including little Daisy, trembled with anticipation. The huntsman's horn rippled through the crisp air as we moved off through a nearby woodland, behind hounds, to search for a fox.

Cold, frosty weather had exposed the ditches by flattening the taller grasses, but by then I had learned to jump such potential trouble spots with some confidence. A fox left the wood quickly, having profited by his early cub education. Hounds swiftly followed under the huntsman's control, with the Field of nearly 100 riders in close pursuit. The rush over ploughed fields and ditches, with a few small hedges, was invigorating. Lady, longing to move ahead, was held back by my father to match Daisy's exuberant, but much shorter strides.

Unexpectedly the fox doubled back to his woodland home, and as he backtracked, Daddy and I found ourselves near to the front of the Field. We stopped with respect for the Master and hounds to pass by. Gathering our reins we cantered in pursuit.

Often the fox escapes, but a quarter of a mile further this one was quickly rolled over by hounds and killed. He died instantly, but I never forgot the agony I felt in the loss of his life. The huntsman blew his horn, melodiously announcing a kill. We, being near the front, arrived with mixed emotions. A lovely creature had been killed after a brave run through the fields.

"Foxes have to be kept down" my father explained, "they steal chickens, little lambs, cats, pheasants and ducks. We do not hunt them to extinction, but to keep their numbers under control."

After a brave fox is hunted and killed by hounds, it is usually the prerogative of the Master to present the mask to the riding landowner, the brush to the lady who has ridden especially well, whilst the four pads are awarded to the children who have arrived in one piece, and shown good manners and sportsmanship.

When this fox had been plucked from the hounds by the First Whipper-in, Lord Burghley spoke with Daddy, then summoned me to ride forward whilst holding his hand behind his back. I nudged Daisy along. As I drew rein, he grasped my arm, gently pulling me towards him. With the entrails dragging, he slid the blood soaked, severed mask across my face!

Strangely I felt no horror, only pride. A most sought-after accomplishment in a fox hunt those days was to be bloodied by the Master. A person is only bloodied once, but forever regales friends with the story. I survived. I do not remember getting home, only that Sandy rode Lady leading my pony alongside.

Tradition demands the one who has been bloodied leaves the gory evidence on for twenty-four hours. Later that afternoon I attended a birthday party wearing a red velvet dress with a white guipure lace collar and dried bloodstains on my face. The girls were disgusted, but I was very popular amongst the boys. To me it had been a vividly triumphant day. How sad when I had to wash my face the following morning!

I was only eight years old. I learned what a strange breed we are, we English country folk.

During school holidays I rode with the local Burghley Pony Club in Stamford, attending Saturday lectures on grooming, basic riding, tack cleaning and the myriad of techniques which were to be so essential in my future horse lifestyle. There were two other close Pony Clubs, the Fitzwilliam near Peterborough and the Cottesmore in Leicestershire. We combined for Rallies in the summer and instruction in stable management and fox hunting etiquette during the winter holidays. I lived for these events.

The Pony Club, initiated in England, became a yardstick through a series of tests, similar throughout the world, where children learned the proper way to ride the English disciplines and to care for their animals. Few even today ascend to the top levels with an "A" Certificate, and "B"s have to be very accomplished all around. I recall an ambition of wanting to earn my "D" levels quickly and pass onto "C"s before I was nine years old. I passed the written and hands on test quite easily, but then came the final qualifying as a rider.

During the Christmas holidays, my mother drove her Rover car, towing our rather heavy wooden Rice trailer, with Daisy and I carefully ensconced, to the magnificent home of Lord Burghley just outside of Stamford. The parkland, consisting of several thousand acres, was awarded to the first Lord of Burghley by Elizabeth I. It was a crisp day, the sun trying to shine though the leafless trees as we unloaded onto brittle, frosty ground.

About eighty children on ponies varying from Thelwell Shetland types, cheeky clipped part thoroughbreds, and mixed Heinz varieties, assembled around the District Commissioner as she instructed us on how to behave for following hounds. Lady Romayne Cecil, the District Commissioner, told us to be very quiet whilst we watched the huntsman and whippers-in, on big Irish hunters, encourage hounds to find a fox, allowing it to flee away across the fields. Under no conditions were any of us to ride in front of the Huntsman or the Field Master, and on this day, Lady Romayne herself.

Parents and friends pooled together in their cars to form a support group, staying well away from the hunt, lining up on a road outside of the park to catch glimpses of the children. Lady Romayne assigned the more accomplished riders, of which I was one, to ride with the hunt servants, whilst she led the rest in orderly fashion behind us.

Hounds were brought out from The Kennels, the Huntsman piloting them proudly through the manicured green fields ringed with fir and deciduous trees, keeping control of us as we skirted past a herd of several hundred fallow deer.

Soon to the rippling sounds of "Gone Away" from the Huntsman's horn, hounds tore off in hot pursuit of a deep red fox, flicking his glorious brush as he galloped away towards the seven foot stone wall surrounding the park, children excitedly struggled to control their impatient ponies, tucking in behind Lady Romayne.

My mother was in the first car on the outside road.

After a brief wait, imagine her consternation upon seeing the huntsman, behind his hounds, jump through a 4 foot high broken down part of wall, closely followed by a child on a grey pony, negotiating with every confidence. Knowing how determined her daughter had been to obey instructions and respect hunt etiquette, she was horrified to recognize me. What on earth did I think I was doing?

At the close of the hunt, she was ecstatic to hear I had been the one chosen to ride with the Huntsman! I also passed the final riding element of the "D" test with flying colours. Just another challenge on my pathway along life's journey.

After two years of unhappiness at Felixstowe, my mother relented, agreeing she had chosen the wrong school. She researched other boarding schools at a London agency, deciding upon Malvern Girls College in Worcestershire. I was outfitted with a pretty mauve and pink uniform and sent off to meet a totally different group of girls with similar background to my own.

Twice a term we were allowed out on Sundays with our parents, to be treated to sumptuous meals at one of the local hotels. We were allowed to take two other girls with us, but by careful scheduling, and by collecting a group of loyal friends, we managed to escape from school many more times than two Sundays apiece.

Part of attending a girls only school was to ensure attention was paid to lessons with no distraction from boys. However, each holiday, boys were in abundance at the Manor. I had more fun with them than with girls because they were braver and more adventurous than my girlfriends at school. My home friends and I excelled in playing tennis, game shooting, or competing in swimming, or especially, riding our horses. I was a tomboy through and through, loving every minute of it.

Sometimes we accompanied my father on his lunchtime visits to various farms. While the men rested we were allowed to drive the tractors, pull corn binders, spin out potato rows and harrow newly plowed fields. Brief as the lunchtime sessions were, we did learn a lot about good farming.

Outdoor amusements were not our sole diversion. In the wintertime, Saturday afternoons were reserved for attending movies in nearby Spalding or Peterborough. We travelled either by bus or by car with my father as chauffeur. It was around 1938, when I came to prefer the bus trips, when I could sit close to a favourite boyfriend and perhaps hold hands with him.

My friendships with these boys were warm and innocent, keeping in contact through letters during school terms. I have often measured the degree of loyalty of these boys, against other friendships. I have also entered into friendships with individuals whose principles were far short of the boys of my youth, who accepted me for myself, as one of their own. Perhaps my expectations were too high, but I seldom escaped without emotional bruising.

Like most siblings, my brother Andrew and I quarreled sometimes. My father hated to hear us argue and purchased authentic leather boxing gloves for each of us, handing them out firmly when our voices rose too loudly in discord. For a short time I won those little bouts, but Andrew grew stronger, which was to prove my regular defeat in the end. However, I was still the courageous one on a pony which led to jealous hostilities when we were riding. To encourage his son to enjoy riding Daddy gave him a very gentle bay cob, Brownie, who looked after him for several years as we pursued our accomplishments with the Pony Clubs.

Andrew and I were encouraged to take part in farming ventures, with perhaps one of the most enjoyable responsibilities on our ponies, helping to drive 60 or 70 head of cattle from one farm outside of Bourne to the other, through the centre of the 5,000 population market town. The streets were lined with glass fronted shops. Before reaching our teens we helped three or four drovers, with their shepherd dogs, quietly drive the animals several times a year from one farm to the other. Often with a heavy bull leading the way with his cows and their calves at foot, listening to the mellow mooing as they trudged quietly along, made us feel somewhat like the Canadian cowboys who had always been my heroes.

However, we discovered, after picking up a discarded horn in a field, it could be put to extraordinary use. The point of the horn was sawn off, creating an unusual musical horn if we blew down through the narrow opening. This made a noise somewhat like the bull bellowing, which enticed the rest of the herd to follow. It was not long before one of us, at the front of the herd, blew into the horn with all the rest following the leader. Thus we became Pied Pipers enabling we two children and one man to safely drive 50 - 60 head of cattle quietly, without help from drovers, or collie dogs, right through the middle of town. None of us even thought our bull might turn raucus and tear into a china shop!

After the holidays, Andrew and I remained, on the whole, fond and supportive of each other, writing weekly during the school term. Our letters spoke of sports, various friends and plans for the next holidays, the contact remaining firm. After I left school I visited Andrew at his Oundle School, just forty miles away, some Sundays with my parents, where sisters were in special demand for the afternoon ballroom dancing sessions.

Holidays on the farm with my family were very special. Andrew and I rode each morning, playing tennis on our hard court on the weekends with the children of other farming families, when my mother would invite six or eight for tea and supper. We accompanied Daddy around the farms, Andrew being especially encouraged to learn the business, for one day he would be managing them. It must have been difficult for our parents, for I was definitely the Tomboy. I was into everything, constantly seeking adventure, sliding down from the tops of the straw stacks, shooting game during the winter months with my father's friends, whilst Andrew, for many years, preferred to remain in the house with his toys.

So often my parents said "Joy should have been the boy!" which must have hurt Andrew and brought out a longstanding resentment. Especially when Daddy was frequently heard to say "Joy was conceived on whisky, Andrew on lemonade."

After Andrew left Oundle he returned home to learn more farming from my father. It would have been better had he attended Cirencester Agricultural College, but Daddy had been disappointed in his results from school and thought he could teach him better himself. Andrew hated getting up in the mornings, whereas my father was out in the yard by 6:00am supervising the men for their day's work as they arrived. When Andrew did show up my father had sometimes left in disgust, or scolded him in front of the remaining farm workmen, which certainly did nothing to encourage their respect.

Andrew did inherit my family's love for animals. We were both given a couple of calves to look after to rear for profit. I later sold mine and purchased twenty lambs. Andrew bought a fine young Lincoln Red bull. He was wiser, or luckier than me at this stage, my purchase netting me little to reinvest, but Andrew's bull became a major part of the founding stock of a fine herd of purebred Lincoln Red Shorthorns. He and my father, years later, as partners in E.D. and A.D. Cooke, shipped 13 fine young bulls to Australia which became a paramount part of their selective cattle stations.

School holidays were not without catastrophies. My first occurred one hot summer day at the beginning of grain harvesting. Daddy took Andrew and me to the Bourne Farm where the workmen had been stacking the wheat sheaves, in orderly stooks for loading onto horsedrawn wagons, for carting to the nearby yard, for threshing and stacking.

It was unusually hot and clear under a a bright blue sky, the sun beating down unmercifully on the stubble field. A green background of tall woodland beckoned enticingly for shade, but there was no time in the lunch hour to experience its cooling benefits. The men were resting on the stooks, drinking the customary cool lemonade their wives had sent along earlier in the morning.

Several horses stood between the shafts of their carts, quietly dozing, as I walked among them. Thinking surely they would be happier if they could be free from the weight of the wagons for a while, I decided unhooking them should be simple enough. I was not quite in my teens but fancied I could do all I had seen the farm hands do. The cart shafts were held in place by a chain running over the horse's back housed in a padded leather saddle. I had so often watched the men remove a horse from a cart by taking the weight of the shaft on one shoulder, unhooking the chain, lifting and holding it, whilst urging the animal forward. Simple enough.

Wrong. I managed to lift the shaft and unhook the chain, but I had not reckoned on the tremendous weight of the wooden shafts once they were not supported. My right thumb was hooked in a link of the chain when it flew across the horse's back, taking the top of my thumb from the first knuckle with it.

Hearing me scream, my father ran quickly to my side. He shed his cream silk jacket, wrapping it around my bleeding hand. Retrieving the bloody thumb top, we made haste to the Bourne Butterfield Cottage Hospital. Intricate surgery was performed by Dr. Alaistair Gallatley, a newly qualified surgeon from London's famous Middlesex Hospital, successfully reattaching the top of my thumb. Five days later, with my arm supported by a sling, I was released from hospital.

During the following few days I was not allowed to ride my pony, but accompanied my father in his car as he directed his workmen in the fields. I had invited a school friend to spend a few days with us on the farm and was happy when Barbara Lehman arrived. Daddy saw no reason why we could not go for a few quiet pleasure rides with Daisy and Lady, knowing how it would restore my happiness.

"Just remember your arm must remain in the sling, so you will be riding with one hand. Be sensible and go quietly" "We have had enough excitement with you for one summer" my mother added forlornly.

"I understand and I'll be careful" I nodded, meaning every word.

Barbara was a novice rider, and old Lady now was a perfect babysitter for her. I, of course, sat on cheeky Daisy. We rode to the North Fen Farm, three miles away on the slipe beside the meandering River Eau. It was a dreamy, quiet ride in the bright sunshine, the horse and pony calmly jogging along beside the sparkling water, with Barbara quickly picking up my few instructional tips.

As we arrived at our farm, the workmen were loading the wheat sheaves onto heavy wooden carts for hauling along a gravel road to the farmyard for threshing. My father had an uncanny way of being around when I needed him, and this day was again to be no exception.

We rode over for a friendly chat as he appeared in his car, overseeing his workmen. He was as usual wearing one of his unending supply of freshly hand-laundered cream silk jackets, and a wide brimmed panama hat. He admonished me to be careful; I promised I would, and would have done so, if Daisy had not been so anxious to play.

Daisy had noticed the stooks of drying corn sheaves, recalling the good times we had jumping them in other fields, and was ready to be off. They were placed for easy loading in rows down the length of the field. Throwing my parents' words to the wind, I asked Barbara to remain safely near my father, as Daisy and I trotted off for a spin. Shortening my reins for the return to the old mare, finding it difficult since I had only use of my left hand, we turned back towards the tempting row of stooks.

We were more or less under control for the first few jumps, but the joy felt by child and pony was not to be denied as we skimmed over more stooks, faster and faster. Soon the reins were virtually useless, since with each leap Daisy pulled them further through my left hand. Still, I was not alarmed until I noticed an empty cart, drawn by a grey Percheron, returning for a another load. I could hear the heavy, wooden iron bound wheels make a crushing sound on the gravel road.

There was no time to think as Daisy was running happily away with me. The last jump would put her onto the road in direct path of the cart. The driver, sitting on the front, did not see me and even if he had, with the rumbling cart behind and a big ditch on the other side of the road, it was impossible to avoid us.

Barbara and Lady were down the field to the left. Desperately, I leaned towards them assuming Daisy would go toward the mare, her friend. Instead, for a reason known only to her and to God, she veered right. Unbalanced, I shot directly over her head landing on the gravel road immediately behind the big horse's hind legs, but in front of the huge cartwheel. It rolled over me.

I remember looking up to see Barbara, wide-eyed with shock, while behind her, my father and several workmen were running toward me. Daddy was shrugging out of his jacket and had it off when he knelt down. As he wrapped me with it I remember thinking "Oh dear, I've made him ruin another one". That is all I remember.

I was taken to the Cottage Hospital for the second time within three weeks. My insides were displaced. My right hand, still in a sling, had received no further damage, but my left hand was a mess. The iron-rimmed heavy wheel had gone right over it, pressing and splitting the young flesh and bones into the hard gravel.

Back again to the operating table, to undergo further intricate surgery by Dr. Gallatley, to realign the tendons and bones in my hand, to clean out the gravel and stick me back together. Courtesy of his skill, I retained use of both hands eventually, but in cold weather the thumbs still contract like claws unless regularly massaged, and neither thumb pad has much strength or thickness.

I wore both arms in slings for most of the holiday, receiving constant painful dressings of the left hand, using gallons of hydrogen peroxide for cleansing.

E.D. wearing a silk jacket and straw panama hat
summer farm uniform!

In the middle of November I returned once again to the Butterfield Hospital for an unexpected appendectomy. Whilst performing the surgery Dr. Gallatley untwisted part of my intestines, result of being run over by the heavy cart wheel. I had missed over half a term from boarding school, so was far behind with my lessons. Threatened by the possibility of having to repeat the year I summoned every bit of determination to work harder, catch up on what I had missed, and passed the final exams.

To help strengthen my hands I began violin lessons at my new school Malvern. I was not a promising linguist, my French heritage never helped those studies, so I chose German as an alternative. My interests spread to drawing, with art added to my schedule. There was so much I craved to learn — I wanted it all.

Malvern was a culture haven for we girls, often attending Philharmonic concerts in the Winter Gardens Hall, given by London and Liverpool Orchestras, listening to soloists such as famous pianist Dame Myra Hess. Sometimes I did not particularly care for the heavier classics but we were taught "if you do not like it, think why not" by our Music Appreciation teacher, Miss Jackson, which so often did make us come to understand and listen more.

Miss Jackson had a most unorthodox way of ensuring our mouths were open wide enough when practicing singing scales. We wore around our necks, a cord with a section of 1.5" narrow bone attached, which we inserted between our front teeth, at her command, to keep our mouths wide open. It paid off as Malvern girls were renowned for their clear voices, winning many festivals.

My hands did strengthen as I practiced the violin daily, with twice weekly lessons, and I was chosen to play in the forty member school orchestra, rising to be Leader of the First Violins after three years.

In the May of 1939 my father led a Deputation of twenty leading British farmers to Germany. They had been sent by the Ministry of Agriculture to compare methods and exchange ideas. Their reception had been overwhelming, which included escorted tours of major agriculture centres, often passing huge military bases. Evenings were full of dinners and gala events given by Goering, Goebbles and Hess from which they were invited to witness miles-long military parades, as well as the flourishing German modern farms.

During the visit my father was summoned to meet Adolf Hitler for dinner, where with the help of an interpreter, they spoke for several hours. Daddy was asked to use his influence on the British Government to form an alliance with the Germans in the inevitable war with Russia. Upon returning to England he did try to convey the seriousness of the military might he had seen, such as the ten thousand soldiers standing to attention outside of the Reichstag for a parade honouring Hitler, and the hundreds of aeroplanes hidden in the Black Forest, to senior members of the British Government, and the Prime Minister, Neville Chamberlain, but his words fell on deaf ears, being assured Britain was fully prepared, there would be no war!

Shortly before the war began my father received a cordial letter from Hitler, saying in appreciation, he had shipped some of his favourite sparkling burgundy wine which they had enjoyed together. It had been shipped, but due to the imminent war it was stocked somewhere en route. It did not arrive until after WWII! It was a vintage red wine, superbly bottled and we used it for many family special celebrations.

By July of 1939 most of Europe was aware of, and concerned about, Germany's ever growing military strength. But in England we blindly refused to allow dark thoughts to interfere with plans for long anticipated summer holidays. My parents and another couple whose surname was, coincidentally, Holiday, had planned a trip to northern Scotland in August. Andrew and I, the Holiday children, Tony and Elizabeth, along with their cousins, John and Nadine, had been looking forward to the adventures for months.

Due to uncertainty regarding the course Hitler might take, my father was naturally dubious about us driving so far from home. We children were upset. Not go! Our country teetering on the brink of a disastrous war was not in our sphere of understanding. We wanted to go to Scotland! Our mothers, who were also looking forward to the trip, decided to go ahead with it, leaving the husbands behind. If war did break out, we would be little more than two days drive from home.

We drove through the low purple Grampian Mountains, visited forbidding Stirling Castle, and on past Loch Lomond without sighting the Lochness Monster. Continuing north, we found our destination, Helmsdale, a charming Sutherland fishing village.

Later that evening, playing tennis on the hotel court, I met a handsome youth, James MacKay, son of wealthy owner of a trawler fleet. We both loved the game of tennis, playing often until midnight with the heavenly Northern Lights dancing above us in dashes of purple, pink, green, yellow and blue giving more than enough light.

During the days we swam, climbed the surrounding hills, later dining on delicious Berridale grilse, young salmon, caught fresh from the North Sea just hours before. We viewed the wildness of John O'Groats, Scotland's northern point, and the Orkney Isles. Between family tours, James tried to teach me the rudiments of golf, but I could not be too enthused. It was too slow, although I was experiencing my first love, always tender and special. I was entranced by James. His soft spoken burr and charming good manners were irresistible. He was twenty-one and assumed I was sixteen. I was thirteen but saw no reason to tell him so.

Scottish tradition says when a boy gives a girl a bouquet of white heather it is an invitation to marriage. I received such a token from James. It was my first proposal, and the kiss he gave me after a village dance one night is still one of the sweetest I remember.

With war rumblings thickening by the hour, we cut the holiday short journeying back to Lincolnshire. So ended my first romance and what I have always thought might have been a beautiful union. Dreams are made of this.

My childhood ended the day we arrived home — September 1, 1939 — the same day Germany invaded Poland. Two days later, Sunday morning at 11 am, Prime Minister Neville Chamberlain declared war against Germany and fear hit all our hearts.

Chapter Two

Psalms 30: v5
Weeping may endure for a night, but joy cometh in the morning.

England was unprepared for war in 1939, inspite of E.D.'s pleas to the Government after his Farmer's Tour in Germany during May. For two years Chamberlain's historic statement, "Peace in our time," had lulled the world into believing no one would defy us. Yet Czechoslovakia had been overrun, Poland invaded, England now had to commit herself. We British have always come through best with our backs to the wall, this was no exception, we rallied surprisingly fast. We had no military arsenals in readiness, but our Navy was certainly the best in the world, and we depended on it to protect us until we gathered forces.

Civil Defense and the Home Guard were quickly formed, though weapons were virtually non-existent. Had the Germans invaded immediately, all we had to defend ourselves with were pitch forks, other farming tools and limited private collections of hunting guns.

My father was swiftly appointed Chairman of the Agriculture Executive for the East of England, whose primary objective was to utilize every possible square inch of productive land to the fullest. His powers included taking over fields or farms and allocating them to more capable farmers, to maximize their output.

The Women's Voluntary Services (WVS) led by Lady Reading was rapidly extended to cover the whole country. Center Organizers, such as my Mother, recruited many members. In my Mother's case, she took the responsibility for Bourne, with a population of 6,000 and about thirty nearby villages.

Instruction was given under the "1 in 5" pyramid scheme whereby one woman instructed five, and those five in turn instructed five others, in first aid and many basic means of survival in case of invasion. One I remember, was how to warm a baby's bottle by standing it, from one feed to another, on an earthenware flower pot with a burning candle beneath.

The WVS also kept a roster of services to be rendered by the Volunteers, serving meals-on-wheels to the elderly and disabled, chauffeuring people to hospitals, offering training in all kinds of survival techniques and teaching first aid.

My capable Mother was appointed Billeting Officer also with these duties involving her most poignant challenge. At twenty-four hours notice nine hundred children, under the age of twelve, wearing labels around their necks providing names and home addresses, arrived by train from the big seaport of Hull on the east coast. The evacuees came to the comparative safety of Bourne, prior to anticipated air attacks on Hull.

The bedraggled little mites had to be quickly housed on arrival in Bourne. WVS members magnificently succeeded in finding immediate homes for every one of the children, sometimes transferring misplaced ones in succeeding weeks and maintaining constant surveillance on the foster homes and children, some needing medical attention. Most were suffering from home sickness, with many of those becoming inveterate bed wetters, causing extreme problems to their hosts.

The fear of poisonous gas was paramount. Through the WVS, all civilians were fitted with gas masks, carrying them with us in cardboard boxes throughout the war. I remember going with Mother and some of her WVS ladies to the local mental hospital. We took a supply of the masks to fit on the patients, a difficult job as most of them could not understand why those ugly things should go over their faces. One girl gazed at the mask for awhile and rightly quipped, "It makes us look like cows."

Regardless of the war Andrew and I, and other children in the area, were packed off to boarding school as usual. Life does go on. The new term took me from Junior to Middle School. I was transferred to The Mount, one of seven large older homes, housing girls from thirteen to sixteen years of age. We already fancied ourselves self reliant, and to make us more so, our teachers instructed us in the essentials of darning our own socks, sewing on buttons, along with knitting balaclava wool helmets for our servicemen. Classes were held in a handsome five-storey building that had once been a major hotel. With only blackout material securely fixed over all windows to remind us of the war, and the beginnings of food rationing, our education continued undaunted.

The old wine cellars of one Middle School House, Ivydene Hall, across the road from The Mount, were deep and large. We were told, in case of enemy bombing, to seek shelter in the cellars, although no one expected it to happen in rural Malvern, the virtual center of England. For what possible reason would the Germans bomb us?

One October night the wailing of air raid sirens roused us from sleep. Teachers rushed to our dormitories, anxiously commanding us to dress in warm day clothing, take the blankets from our beds and follow them. We trailed, in blackout darkness to the Ivydene cellars. Mattresses had been laid on the floor on which we huddled. Songs were sung, prayers said, and biscuits handed around. Through the thickness of the night, we heard the heavy drone of many German planes, a drone persisting for hours, accompanied by shock waves and shudders of bombs striking in the distance. Sleep was impossible. We were apprehensive, but we were British and knew we must survive.

In morning's early light we were permitted to peek outside. To the east brilliant reds and oranges filled the sky, making it seem on fire. We had experienced the first major bombing of the war, in which the lovely city of Coventry, including its ages-old majestic cathedral, were destroyed, and thousands of lives were lost.

The destruction of Coventry acted as spurs to the Britains, who were already moving swiftly to build forces, relying on Civil Defense, Air Raid Wardens, the Home Guard and the WVS to man front lines in the meantime. Yes, Britains were frightened, but we were growing angrier all the time. How dare that pipsqueak exhouse painter, with his tiny moustache and slanting forelock, taunt us so!

One could see and feel the ancient might of England arising, as munitions factories scheduled three shifts, and workers toiled around the clock seven days a week. Volunteers for the army, navy and air force came from everywhere. All we needed was a bit of time to put Hitler in his place. No one expected seven years to elapse before peace returned. No one in the beginning understood how close we were to oblivion. Perhaps that is why we endured.

The ancient town of Bourne, in which we lived, is on the edge of the fertile Fens producing some of the finest agricultural land in the world. In Medieval times, the site of a stone castle had been home to such leaders as Hereward the Wake, all long since disappeared, but the free running deep supply of water ran from the Wellhead Field. This still runs through the little market town, where it joins other drainage waters known as the Bourne Eau, as it wanders to a river through the farms of grain and root crops of the Fens to the North Sea.

From the northern bank for several miles runs a narrow grass field, perhaps only 300 feet wide, providing especially rich grazing for cattle and horses of the adjoining farms. This area is known as a slipe where horse and rider could enjoy about four miles of galloping

25

stretches, especially precious to my family who owned much of the nearby land.

In the summer of 1940 a preteen girl friend, Margaret Tinsley, and I had been told by our parents we could ride on the slipe by the river to check our cattle and horses grazing, but not to stay away too long. Constant fear of a German invasion was always with us knowing how dreadfully unprepared we were.

We cantered for nearly a mile, and were walking our ponies beside the river when I noticed a young Shire horse in some kind of distress, standing on the banks of a raw smelly sewage drain about twelve feet wide, on the outer edge of the slipe. Riding over to see what was wrong, to my dismay, I saw another young horse, one of my father's percherons, lying in the drain, covered in the slime, except for its neck and head. Judging from the signs of struggle on the slippery bank, it had been there quite some time, exhausting itself trying to get out.

I shouted for Margaret to gallop to the nearest farm for help, gathered some long grass and taking a deep breath, slid down the bank into the slime. I was there a long time, with the colt's heavy head supported on my shoulder, cleaning his face and nostrils as best I could with the grass, crooning encouragement to him.

Eventually farm men arrived with ropes and a very large horse, who managed to pull the weary young one to safety. He recuperated from the near tragedy, but I awoke two mornings later with a very sore throat and terrible taste in my mouth. The doctor, called to the house, noticed a collection of white spots in my throat, correctly diagnosing diphtheria. I was speedily removed to the nearby Isolation Hospital, and totally segregated from visitors. I had of course contracted the serious disease from bacteria in the filth of the open sewage drain.

During the following six weeks in the Isolation Hospital, my only food was small bowls of fresh raspberries from our garden, with thick Jersey cream. My throat was too sore to swallow much else. Diphtheria, like rheumatoid fever, often leads to a weak heart, as it did in my case. Since then I have had to take care, as often mine beats twice as fast as it should if I am over stressed or tired.

Most Bourne market days, Thursdays, my father brought six or seven farmer friends back to the Manor for a game of cards, no one begrudging them the amusement, for their day had been spent in Agriculture Executive meetings discussing ways and means to increase farm production — helping those who needed loans of equipment, repairs to broken ploughs and tractors, and seeing crops were planted and harvested on time. Even roadside verges were planted with potatoes and cabbages, as every ounce of fertile ground was to be utilized to the fullest.

The card games generally took place around our game table in the lounge, with a cosy wood fire burning in the wintertime. A Persian Khermin carpet, a gift to Mother from my father, covered the lounge floor. It was most unusual in shades of teal, peach, beige and soft blue green. Many years later, I inherited this rug and still treasure it. It's color scheme remains my favorite saving to remind me of my days back home.

My father and his friends played poker or solo whist. Their favorite fare during the early evening was Stilton cheese, purchased that day from a market stall, and chunks of the fresh country bread washed down with black market whiskey, or tea when no liquor was available. Andrew and I would pull up stools and watch for hours. Sometimes if a player won a big pot we were given a pound note for counting his paper money.

As the war progressed, with petrol strictly rationed, few girls at school expected visits from their parents. I was among the lucky ones. Being a farmer, my father was granted all the petrol he needed, to be used judiciously. It was necessary for him to visit his produce stand in the Birmingham Wholesale Vegetable Market to ensure his Lincolnshire potatoes and other produce were properly distributed. Sometimes he took a detour, thirty miles out of his way, to visit me, time I treasured.

In 1941, Malvern Girls College was commandeered by the Admiralty for the purpose of taking Naval Headquarters away from London. Parents had to make speedy decisions, to allow their daughters to evacuate down to Somerset, and stay in a quiet country estate, or return home and attend their local High Schools.

My home in Bourne, near the east coast, was in the front line of attack if England were invaded. Somerset, much farther south, was perhaps safer, but if the Germans invaded they would cut off Bourne from Somerset. The enemy would be between my family and me, for how long and under what circumstances, no one could say. My parents decided the family should be together come what may.

I went home, where I wanted to be, though I found the Manor routine had changed considerably. Three army officers were now billeted with us, as were two young evacuees.

My own routine also changed where I attended Stamford High

School. Every morning at seven, I caught a bus near the house which took me eight miles to Market Deeping, where two dozen other students waited half an hour on the roadside, regardless of the weather, for another creaky bus to take us into Stamford a further seven miles. The last leg was by foot. We walked a mile uphill through the ancient town to the school. Obviously, it was a problem continuing our education. Sadly I was unable to continue with my violin studies as there was no one to teach me, apart from which someone sat on my violin and broke it!

In April of 1940 Germany invaded Denmark and Norway. In May they blitzkreiged through Holland, Luxembourg, Belgium and France. Winston Churchill became Prime Minister after Neville Chamberlain resigned and, in his acceptance speech to the House of Commons, offered the famous lines, "I have nothing to offer but blood, toil, tears and sweat."

We became accustomed to planes flying overhead, ours en route to bomb major German industrial cities, while the enemy, with their easily recognizable drone due to the kind of fuel being used, plodded toward our Midland towns. Often we witnessed our brave fighter pilots attacking the enemy planes. Strangely oblivious to our own danger, we watched in fascination, cheering when an enemy plane was destroyed or a pilot floated to the ground by parachute.

The Summer of 1940 was grim. In June, Italy joined Germany against the Allies, and France surrendered. The Battle of Britain began August 8. More than one thousand planes attacked at one time. The Blitz on London lasted eighty-four nights, killing 12,696 civilians.

The huge Shire horses I had always loved were diminishing in number. Most able bodied men had gone to war, and with less farm labor to depend on, grooming and caring for the giant horses was a problem. In addition, more and more crops were being planted in rows closer than usual in order to utilize all productive land. The tremendous weight of the shires and their large feet, seriously wounded root crops. To replace the gentle giants, smaller lighter Percherons became popular. My father owned at least sixty, all grays.

E.D. had an intrinsic knowledge of many animals. He began assembling a modern piggery, being one of the first to use computer technology, on one of our farms. Chatterton & Cooke, Counter Drain, which had an annual contract with the vast grocery chain of Sainsburys, to produce ten thousand bacon pigs.

The Cooke companies controlled twelve farms, several

specializing in sheep breeding. I remember in the cold months following Christmas, the shepherds, with several of us helping, delivering upwards of two thousand lambs. I loved visiting the farmyards, which had many warm pens built undercover from the wind and rain. I could not resist the small woolly lambs cavorting together, so happy just to be alive. Those dependent, trusting animals gave me a special strength. When I was with them, or especially my horses, the war seemed far away. Even today, in moments of stress, I receive immeasurable support when hugging my favourite horse.

Half a dozen top farmers established the Lincolnshire Red Shorthorn Society to promote interest in the breed. Unlike Herefords, the Shorthorns had no white on their faces. They were red in color and, carrying heavy infusions from Scotch black cattle were stocky in conformation with no wasted long legs.

Cattle bred in Lincolnshire grew straight and strong, particularly on the Limestone Wolds in the northern section of the county. Our own herd quickly multiplied with selective breeding. In order to record the age of an animal they were accorded registered names beginning with a specific letter, starting with A for the first year. Andrew chose many from the Bible, which meant our cattle were easily recognized.

My father and Colonel Bowes, a major breeder from Reading, Berkshire, chose to cross outstanding members of their herds to strengthen the breed. On one occasion, I went with my father to supervise the unloading of several young bulls he had purchased, that had travelled by train to Bourne. Two beautiful young horses were unloaded with them — Footprints, a 4-year-old gelding, and his sister, Footsteps. They had won their yearling classes at the last Olympia Horse Show in London, early in the war and had spent the time between roaming in Colonel Bowes' parkland. The beautiful pair, to my delight, were purchased for Andrew and me! Wonderful, straight moving conformation horses with intelligent heads.

Old Lady, who had been so patient with my youthful exuberance, produced a foal by the Hunter's Improvement Society Premium Lincolnshire stallion. Lady's foal had been given to me. He was a long legged chestnut thoroughbred, and I promptly named him The Duke of Windsor, after the abdicated King Edward VIII, constantly in the news at that time, but I always called him Dukey.

The three young horses were to grow up together, and I was delighted to be in charge of them, though Dukey would give me cause for alarm more than once. Playing with the other young horses, he was kicked, severely damaging a knee. It was badly swollen. We knew the problem had to be resolved quickly. Portable X-Rays were not available in those days, so my father and I, with old Sandy's help, loaded Dukey in a lorry and took him carefully to the Butterfield Hospital, where so much had been done for me.

The hospital staff balked at taking Dukey inside, but were cooperative in rigging up a platform on which we climbed, gently holding him whilst his injured leg was slowly manipulated through the X-Ray lab window. X-Rays revealed joint oil escaping from the knee casing. In veterinary terms, synovial fluid was leaking from a ruptured bursa. With much careful nursing, cold hosing, and gentle daily rubs, Dukey was able to function normally again, although he always had a square knee. It remained enlarged, but he was never lame, and I was able to ride him. I turned to him more and more as the war progressed.

In spite of the war, local horse showing continued in England, although in a much more reduced way. In July, the East of England Show at Peterborough scheduled a gypsy flapping race — eight laps to the mile at a flat out gallop. I entered Dukey and was surprised when friends told me conventional horse people never indulged in flapping races. In fact, it was frowned upon. Most of the participants were gypsies and protocol was seldom observed. Not to be daunted, we trained seriously, schooling up and down the long hills in the Bourne Forestry Reserve of 3,000 acres every day, building up his muscles and lungs.

Dukey and I entered the race. The ribald shouts of the gypsies must have put a temporary wildness in his spirit, for my horse galloped as never before. We were in the lead at the finish and the only girl jockey! The gypsies and all the spectators were shouting their heads off. In return for our efforts, we were awarded the First place Silver Cup, marking my initial win in the horse world other than Pony Clubs.

The win lifted my spirits considerably. I connected it to England's winning the war. The gypsies, Dukey and I had outrun, were the enemy. I, the British Empire. A girl's fantasy, I suppose. Ever after I never doubted England would survive despite any devastation wrought on her.

After a year, the Navy, who had taken over the main school building at Malvern and installed 800 telephones, decided in their 'wisdom', not to move in but remain in the thick of the war's battle in London. Consequently, we girls were able to return.

Happily back again, I resumed my weekly riding lessons, which included jumping, cementing my confidence over fences for the rest of my life. We did hours of gymnastic exercises, trotting over poles placed four or five feet apart, riding with arms straight out from the shoulders for balance, and taking small fences without reins. When approaching a jump it is natural to balance by pulling on the horse's mouth, so we were taught to ride over them with closed eyes so as not to anticipate our horse. I learned this lesson so well, when fox hunting years later, I often closed my eyes if a fearsome obstacle came in our path, giving my horse as much rein as possible. It is important when riding to never pull on a horse's mouth unnecessarily as they are very sensitive and soon become inattentive to the rider's hands.

One of the reasons my riding improved at Malvern was because of the strict disciplinary system. We received stripes for especially good work in gymnastics and dancing, being proud to wear them on our tunics. A stripe was taken away if we were ever caught slouching at our desk, and marauding teachers were alert in spotting lazy postures. Consequently, we grew up with ramrod backs and riding straight backed became second nature to me.

Although I enjoyed boarding school to a large degree, I still lived for the holidays at home, where my friendships with neighbouring farmer's sons persisted. When not engaged in outdoor sports, we played cards or sang around the piano, there were no televisions at this time. We travelled in groups, no couples. We were aware of the difference between the sexes, hormones were no different then than now, and teasing was strong if anyone caught us winking or flirting. Also, our mothers were very strict. The last thing mine said every time I went out was, "Promise not to do anything I wouldn't like." That helped keep me pure for a long while, but not necessarily from having special feelings for certain boys from time to time.

One of my friends, Peter Francis, was my tennis tournament doubles partner. He lived in Pinchbeck, ten miles from Bourne. We played tennis together when we were home on holidays, on our hard court or Peter's grass one. On occasion, Peter's friend Hoagy visited. His real name was Peter too, but we called him "Hoagy" because his surname was the same as Hoagy Carmichaels'. the popular American composer and piano player. Since 'our' Hoagy's parents lived in South Africa, he usually spent the shorter holidays with Peter.

I found it difficult to resist Hoagy's crinkly smile and stopped trying to after awhile. Sometimes after tennis, we would still play our old childhood games of hide and seek and sliding down the strawstacks. The higher they were, the better we liked it — especially me, with Hoagy to catch me with a hug.

Both Peter and Hoagy were on my correspondence list, and as time passed by, the letters between Peter and I remained on the brother-sister level, but my correspondence with Hoagy was much more exciting, for we spoke of our affection and made sketchy plans for a future together.

During his visits to Pinchbeck, he would phone me five or six times a day, especially if we were unable to meet in the evenings for lack of transportation. Fuel for cars was so short because of gas rationing, and often we could not get to see each other. Occasionally I stayed overnight at the Francis home, travelling via Spalding on a creaky one-a-day train linkage. Like other young people, we would not let the war get in our way. We knew the war was still there, but we tried to put it from our minds. However, even the ostrich has to pull its head out of the sand sometime.

The war changed the world around us, and it changed us. Before the war, news of a friend's death or relative was heart wrenching and cause for extended mourning. In wartime, news of old friends killed in battle or missing in action, was a regular occurrence. We never forgot our friends, but our grief was momentary. War does that to you.

The dreaded hum of enemy planes overhead became commonplace. We watched the Heinkels flying in formation on their way to bomb a city where we more than likely had friends. Our hatred for the Germans was intense. We could identify the fighter planes, the Messchersmitts, our Spitfires and Hurricanes, as they engaged in their deadly battles. We never ran to hide. We stared at the sky, our anger building, cheering when an enemy plane went down, mourning briefly when one of our own fell.

The youth of my day had heavy feelings to combat. We could not get away from the war. All of our homes had heavy blackout curtaining, using low voltage bulbs in electric light fittings. It was dangerous to show a glimmer of light, even if walking down to the stables or along a country road. Vehicles had shaded hoods over slotted headlamps to shield any light from a plane above. Radio broadcasting came through, but sounded squeaky and rough.

Farmers' sons were exempt from service call up as food production was at the top of the priority list for the home front. England, being an island, was in a vulnerable position if blockaded.

However, most of the farmers' sons I knew volunteered and went to war as their father's had during WWI. Peter and Hoagy said nothing, but I sensed they were coming ever closer to making the same decision as their school days finished.

A month after I returned to Malvern again, Hoagy joined the Fleet Air Arm. Usually, we were not allowed to take personal telephone calls at school, but somehow Peter managed to get through by pretending to be my father.

"Hoagy's being sent to the States for fleet air arm fighter pilot training," Peter told me. "He wants to see you to say goodbye. Can you think of a way to manage it?"

"Yes," I said quickly. "They already think you're my father. Speak with Miss Brooks again, the headmistress, and tell her it's all right for Hoagy to visit me here!?" It was a daring gamble.

It worked.

The next day Hoagy and I met in a small room in the Senior House — a first for the school I am sure, but war brought about many changes in timeworn patterns.

Hoagy was excited as he told me he was going to receive his training at the Pennsacola Naval Base in Florida, but neither of us wanted to think about the perils which might befall him between England and the United States.

"Will you marry me, Fiddlesticks?" Hoagy asked, using his term of endearment, "Let us be engaged now and you promise to wait for me until I return?"

"Oh, yes, Hoagy, yes of course!", I said breathlessly, not knowing what I was doing.

We sealed our betrothal with tender kisses, and he gave me a Fleet Air Arm enameled broach, with the center "A" encircled with diamonds. I wore the brooch proudly every day. It was my engagement token.

My vicarious introduction to Florida and America was through Hoagy's letters, written on colorful stationery depicting palm-lined beaches, white sand and blue water. Oh, how Hoagy loved the challenge of learning to land those nippy planes on aircraft carriers. He qualified brilliantly and later shot down the first MIG 3 fighter in the Korean War and received many accolades for his daredevil flying.

While in Florida, Hoagy was exposed to the elite Powers models, glamorous in a way I could never be, country bumpkin that I was. Many of those sophisticated, enchanting girls lived close to the naval camp, and one eventually filled Hoagy's eye.

So ended my first wartime romance.

It seemed unpatriotic to be languishing in school while the war escalated everywhere else. I abandoned dreams of training at the Slade School of Art in London, playing tennis on an international level, joining Ivor Novello's Theatrical Company or becoming a veterinarian.

I longed for my horses back home, but more immediate priorities had to be considered. I begged my parents to allow me to join the WRNS (Women's Royal Naval Service). They were against the idea at first, but when they understood how much I wanted to make a contribution for my country, they relented slightly and suggested a compromise.

Though never enthusiastic about my secretarial courses at Malvern in the 6th Form, I had fared rather well in them. My parents agreed I could join the WRNS if I completed a year's extensive training at Mrs. Hoster's Secretarial College in London, which educated students to the highest levels.

The timing was right. The College had moved from London, escaping the bombing, to nearby Greatford Hall, only seven miles from Bourne. I enrolled in January of 1942.

The objective of the course was to prepare students as secretaries for Government Cabinet Ministers. My typing was reasonable when I started but it improved considerably, since we typed to gramophones playing fast marching band music. Government procedures, shorthand, accounting and social studies were all part of the curriculum.

I was given an auto-cycle, a small motorcycle, on my sixteenth birthday, which eliminated any worry about petrol rationing. On a pint of gas I could scoot along for at least a hundred and twenty miles and was able to make frequent visits home to ride. Sometimes I towed a couple of girls on their bicycles into Stamford for an egg and chip meal, or daringly, to a local pub for a glass of beer.

I left Mrs. Hosters in June of 1942 with an armful of graduating certificates after only six months, but could not actually serve in the WRNS until I was seventeen and a half. I returned home, helped a little in my father's office and began seriously training Footprints. He was a cheeky horse, bucked a great deal, and I finally sent him to an experienced trainer, Vin Toulson, for a month of intensive schooling, to remove the worst kinks. Idling away the hours with my beloved horses was wonderful, but I longed to be part of the war effort.

England had formed a Home Guard staffed by local men who

were too old, too young or physically unfit for active service, or were exempt because their civilian work was essential to the war effort. The South Lincolnshire Kesteven Headquarters were in Bourne, and I went to work as secretary to the Adjutant, Captain Tim Tinsley, for the princely sum of three pounds a week.

I was fitted into a khaki battle dress uniform, and rode my bicycle from home through Bourne to the headquarters, about a mile away, each morning. There were a large assortment of military orders and instructions I had to process for our six companies, of mostly older men, or those awaiting their own calling up. Every able bodied man, many farm workers, volunteered to defend their country and needed constant training.

At this time the Home Guard were disciplined to toughen up with constant marches and map reading sorties through the local countryside. It had not been long since these volunteer soldiers had only pitch forks and broom handles to defend their homes and country, all ammunition and guns had been directed to the armed forces.

There was constant apprehension we might be invaded at any time. To that effect, one of my tasks was to cycle around the local lanes, changing the road sign posts to point in different directions at the end of the day. Eventually we removed them altogether, but I am sure had the Germans arrived they would have followed their own maps and my small efforts would have been useless.

Back in Bourne, I waited for my call up papers, to be forwarded in six months. I was impatient with the waiting, though the days passed quickly. My main pursuits, beyond my secretarial Home Guard efforts, were riding my horses Footprints and Dukey, and playing tennis as 1st couple for the Bourne Tennis Club with my cousin, Annie Furneaux, a fine athlete who, had the war not intervened, surely would have made the Olympic Team as a sprinter. Many hours were also spent writing chatty letters to my male friends in the services.

My only intentions, in writing those letters were to cheer up my friends. I did not know that almost all servicemen, when engaged in warfare, sustain their morale and courage by dreaming of home, hearth and family in a future where peace reigns. The regularity of my letters incorporated me into the future dreams of seven dear friends, all of who proposed marriage, with three happening to come home on leave at the same time.

My father chuckled, watching me cope when one came visiting, another called in unexpectedly, and a third rang me on the phone. I made light of it too, and must admit the multiple pursuits for my hand in marriage boosted my ego. Yet underneath, I regretted having unintentionally toyed with the feelings of young men risking their lives to save Britain, and in the end I was able to make each understand I had wanted to help, not mislead. We remained friends, but never quite like before.

November 7, 1942, Eisenhower landed in French North Africa. We did not know it at the time, but the landing was prelude to the tide turning in favor of the Allies. On the home front in England, however, times were still grim as food was in short supply, though we always managed some diversion to take our minds off the war.

Raymond Mays, a World Champion race car driver, brought much needed brightness to the Manor when on weekends he invited leading theatrical artists to Bourne, to give them peaceful respite from the eternal bombing of the city where they head-quartered, entertaining troops whenever and wherever they could.

Some of his friends were famous Ben Lyon and Bebe Daniels, glamorous American revue performers who refused to return to their homeland at the outbreak of war, preferring to remain and entertain servicemen. Barry Sinclair, a handsome musical comedy actor, Ivor Novello, the premier composer of romantic operettas such as The Dancing Years and Glamorous Nights; Sybil Thorndyke, superb actress, later to be made a Dame of the British Empire; Noel Coward with his wonderful song, "Keep the Home Fires Burning," and more.

My mother's youthful musical talent continued, but apart from a few local concerts in aid of wartime efforts she enjoyed her piano and sang only at home. She always played while Ray and his theatre friends joined us in song fests at our home Sunday evenings.

E.D. had purchased a beautiful Bechstein piano for her at the beginning of the war. It had been stored in Waring and Gillow's London warehouse which was bombed, but fortunately the piano had not been damaged. It had been played before many kings and queens of Europe, with each Royal name inscribed in Olde English script beneath the strings — Queen Wilhemenia of The Netherlands, King George V and Queen Mary and the Kings, Olaf of Norway and Leopold of Belgium, to name a few.

We were prey to awe, as if in the presence of past majesty, when we gathered around the Bechstein to sing the old songs whose sweetness gave us courage and helped carry us through the war — Tiny Old Town; I'm Stepping Out With A Memory Tonight, Safe In

My Heart, That Lovely Weekend, Beautiful Dreamer, You Made Me
Care, A Nightingale Sang in Berkely Square, Only A Rose from The
Vagabond King, 'Til We Meet Again, Now Is The Hour…

My voice was developing, and the composer/play-wright, Ivor
Novello, fulfilled one of my longstanding dreams by inviting me to
enroll in his singing and dramatic school. What a different life I might
have led had I taken advantage of his offer, but I was determined to
follow through on joining the Wrens at that time, and did not want to
be far away from my horses.

In February of 1943 the Germans surrendered at Stalingrad.
That was the day my cousin, Paul Tointon, in celebration of the
event, swung me into a lively spinning dance in the Manor lounge
hall. We twirled so fast my vision blurred, and the familiar teal,
peach and beige pastels in the carpet blurred into a warm, rosy blur.

Paul was the middle son of my father's sister, Nan, and her
husband, Jim Tointon, who tragically died within six months of each
other in 1938. The elder son, Peter, joined the Royal Air Force as a
navigator, and was in the first raid the British made over Germany,
the Kiel Canal. When his plane was shot down, he parachuted into
enemy hands and remained a prisoner throughout the war. Their
youngest son, Maxwell, went to live with Grandpa Cooke, while Paul
came to live with us.

He became like a second brother to me, and I loved him dearly.
He called me "Fiddlesticks" or "Joykins." He had a marvelous sense
of humor and was a hard worker on the farms, always up before my
father and willing to attempt any task. I remember Paul once threw
out a challenge to anyone in Bourne to beat the weight he could
carry away from a heavily loaded cart of grain. He carried five
hundred pounds, a quarter of a tonne, on his back for more than fifty
feet with no one meeting his challenge. Needless to say, since then,
he has had a weak back throughout his life.

Paul joined the RAF in April of 1943 and served valorously as an
air gunner throughout the remainder of the war. E.D. favoured Paul
over my brother Andrew because he rose earlier in the mornings,
working far harder with considerably less reward. He was later
made an Executor of my father's Will.

Lincolnshire has had a tumultuous history. Invaders from
across the North Sea, Normans, Danes and Romans were constant
from Medieval times, reclaiming land from the sea, developing some
of the richest farmland in the world, claiming it for their countries.
Many castles had been built by successive kings to hold off attacking

marauders. Perhaps one of the strongest, set in an exquisite park of oak trees and green pastures, where deer roam freely, is Grimsthorpe Castle, just five miles from Bourne. It had been built by Henry VIII for one of his wives, Kathryn of Aragon.

During the war different military regiments were stationed in the stables and grounds, with officers living within the castle walls. Much of the valuable art collection had been stored in the cellars, although some of the antique furniture and carpets remained retaining part of the earlier magnificence. Surprisingly the officers respected the artifacts and the Castle remained much as it had prior to the war.

In 1944 the 1st Airborne Division stationed their elite 1st Parachute Regiment at Grimsthorpe Castle. It was a final training phase before the anticipated invasion into Europe against the Nazis. These men had parachuted into Sicily from North Africa and were some of the finest the army had produced, fearless and well skilled in battle. The officers and men had earned the nickname of "Red Devils" in honour of their red berets and courage.

Each weekend my parents invited three or four young officers from the Regiment for a home cooked meal. To an extent I enjoyed playing the hostess to those brave young men, carefully taking care not to become involved with any of them, at least for a while.

When the Bourne Tennis Club planned their summer dance I chose to spend a quiet evening at home for a change. I did not have any inclination to meet more young men, I was kept constantly busy writing letters to all of the young friends I had grown up with. It had become a kind of duty cheering them on, which I enjoyed. I, for once, was tired and did not feel like dancing.

My brother Andrew seldom directed me in my pursuits, however, this evening he became quite indignant when I made clear my intentions to stay at home.

"The "Red Devils" will be coming over from Grimsthorpe Castle" he said. "It is your patriotic duty to be at the dance, a highlight for the summer." He shamed me into going reluctantly.

Shortly after we arrived I saw a tall, fairhaired lieutenant across the room talking with several other officers. He looked up and our eyes met. He was by far the most handsome man there, immaculately turned out. As the music began for a foxtrot he walked across and asked me to dance. He courteously introduced himself as Robert Feltham, Rob for short. Inspite of myself I was intrigued with his commanding appearance.

We were magnetically attracted to each other, and a romance began. Surprisingly we had both been reluctant to attend the dance, but fate intervened. From then on Bobbie, the name I gave him, either drove to our house in an army jeep or rang me, daily. We took long walks around the countryside or rode the Delaine buses into Peterborough to the movies, reaching home prior to curfew time, 10:30pm, imposed not by the war, but my father.

There was always the dark shadow over us, knowing he would shortly be called into battle. Like many other sweethearts in wartime, our philosophy was simple. There may not be a Tomorrow, lets live for Today.

During our courtship the tempo of the war was quickening, and at Grimsthorpe Castle tension mounted. Gone were the days of fearing Hitler's conquest of England. The tide had turned in favour of the Allied Armies, and the elite troops were anxious to be off bringing the war to a final conclusion.

Most of the men in the regiment had already seen combat. Bobbie had been the first man to jump from a plane over Sicily when the paratroops dropped over the Catania bridge after the North African advances. Having been through combat, the troops knew what was in store for them once they received their orders. From the moment they parachuted from the planes they would be targets for enemy anti-aircraft bunkers below. Fear had to be in all their hearts, but they showed none.

Bobbie proposed to me, but with the wilderness of uncertainty stretching before us, we had no idea of when a wedding could take place, only that perhaps one might. With the tenuous days before us, no one knew if we would even be alive 24 hours later. It was easy to make a commitment to give hope for the future. Like all young couples we made dreamy plans too.

Out of the blue, my Naval call up papers arrived, summoning me to report for initial training at Balloch near Glasgow, in Scotland. This was as a result of travelling on my seventeenth birthday to Queen Anne's Mansions, WRNS HQ, in London, with girl friend Audrey Lyall, to volunteer for the Navy. I was told I was too young, but that my application would be processed six months later.

My call up was not what we had expected. I had 48 hours to quit my job, pack my brief belongings and say goodbye. The days ahead were unpredictable for us both. Would I get a leave to cross the country to see Bobbie before he went off to war?

I had assumed he would receive his call for battle before I did —

perhaps I was surprised because traditionally it is the girl who stays behind while her soldier goes to war. In my case I said goodbye to Bobbie, and my parents, at the Peterborough Great Northern Railway Station, arriving in Balloch, Scotland, eight hours later, from an overcrowded, stuffy train filled with servicemen.

It was all business at the Naval intake station. No time for tiredness, regrets or fears. We new recruits were given uniforms and soon initiated into a standard geared for the Senior Service facing the long established rivalry between the Army Trained Service, Women's Auxiliary Air Force and the Women's Royal Naval Service.

While being measured for my uniform I met a girl about my own size. Her name escapes me now, for soon after we became friends the nicknames of Tweedledee and Tweedledum were bestowed upon us. Our short curly hair and diminutive size reminded others of the fairytale story, and we were never called anything else.

We were kept busy from morning until nightfall. During the first two weeks we marched at all hours, polished our shoes interminably and pressed our new uniforms several times a day. Before dawn, on my knees, I daily scrubbed the men's ablutions — naval jargon for toilets. We received two sets of painful inoculations, the ones for typhoid leaving us with sore, swollen arms and high temperatures. This was the Navy!

At the end of two weeks we were interviewed for allocation into service categories. Many of us chose the exciting MI5, security work, but it was oversubscribed, and other tasks had to be considered. Because of my training at Mrs. Hosters, it looked as though I would be stuck behind a desk throughout the war. Not what I had in mind at all. Since I was too young to go abroad, the minimum age was twenty-one, I volunteered for motor transport driving, along with Tweedledum, only to find we had to be at least five feet two inches tall. Tweedledum and I both missed the mark by half an inch.

We saw no reason why a mere half inch should stand in our way. To correct matters, that night we broke into the office, found the appropriate files, and altered our records to meet the minimum height requirement. The following day we were informed we would travel immediately to Headingly in Leeds, Yorkshire, for Motor Transport Training!

Life became more exciting. I did not have time to worry about myself because a major turn in the war took place.

Since mid August we had known the Allied Army commanders were waiting for the right weather to drop our soldiers somewhere on the Front — France, Belgium or even Holland, all under German Occupation. As the weeks passed by, radio silence regarding invasions by our forces became ominous. Then on 17th September, England stood still. Even the birds were silent.

German spies had intercepted Allied plans to launch "Operation Market Garden" in which the 1st Airborne Division, supported by the U.S. 101st Division, would be dropped over Arnhem and Einhoven in Holland. Swiftly and silently the entire German Panzer Division were moved in before the drop. Our "Red Devils" who parachuted silently to earth that moonless September night, had no way of knowing what awaited them on the ground. A slaughter took place, killing many brave men before they hit the ground. "Operation Market Garden" is remembered as one of the most tragic battles of the war. For nine days they fought and held off the enemy in one of the most glorious exploits of the British Army. General Eisenhower described the action as one of the finest exhibitions of valour in all the history of war, and even the Germans paid spontaneous tribute to their prowess.

Those of us who had Airborne lovers and relatives had no immediate way of knowing who had survived and who had not. I was numb, in a state of suspended existence until October 6th, the day after my eighteenth birthday, when I received a telegram from good friend, Major Tony Jessop, stating Bobbie had been wounded, and was a prisoner of war. I thanked God he was alive, but my fears increased. How would the Germans treat him?

Two hellish months later the red Cross contacted his parents to say Bobbie's shrapnel wound in his back was healing. He was relatively safe in the Stalag Luft VII prison near Spangenberg on the Rhine River. An old castle, impregnable from all sides, had been converted. Escape was impossible, only the most important prisoners were kept there. Bobbie and a friend, Lord George Lascelles, cousin of then Princess Elizabeth, later to be Queen, were held as hostages, for possible trading, should the war reverse badly for the Germans.

A short letter I received from Bobbie eased my anguish a little. He bravely assured me he was recovering from his wound. He told me none of the prisoners were mistreated, but food was in short supply. I made arrangements to send packages through the Red Cross and prayed he would receive them.

In the meantime our M.T. training course carried on for six weeks. We learned to manoeuvre navy blue vans with blackened out back windows, solely using the near side mirror. Instructors patiently taught us to drive safely, do three-point turns without touching either curb on the narrow roads, drive with minimum lights, and double declutch the gears. Passing the driving test was relatively easy.

Learning the maintenance of the vehicles and how to pinpoint what was wrong in case it failed, was another matter. Climbing down in a sump, squirting oil onto nipples was not my idea of heaven, and it was dirty work. Although we wore protective overalls and gloves, the oil stained us anyway. By persevering, however, we learned about distributor heads, how to change a wheel, fix a flat tire, tighten brakes, and to start a cold engine from jump leads.

Earning the driving certificate and badge put us into the official ranks of Motor Transport drivers, allowing us to wear the traditional bell bottom blue serge trousers to match our jackets. We had never felt so smart or saucy, and somehow developed a new sense of maturity...

Tweedledum and I were separated in January 1944 when we received different postings. We never met again. I was sent to the Nore Holding Depot, Rochester, near to the high security major port of Chatham, Kent.

At this time the Germans had about perfected the V1 and V2 buzz bombs, the first weapons propelled by rockets, which were directed towards London in colossal numbers, over a thousand in one day. They resembled small planes with very short wings with long streaks of flame jetting from their tails. We grew accustomed to seeing the black monsters in our skies overhead aimed for London, forty miles away, often flying little more than tree height, blowing up suddenly or falling into the dockyards. They made an irregular fearful sound. As long as we heard it we were unconcerned, when they suddenly became silent, we dove for cover, in a ditch, doorway or lay flat on the ground for the tremendous explosion which shattered the immediate neighbourhood. The explosions were frightening initially, but became so frequent we just picked ourselves up, dusted off and carried on with whatever we had been doing.

I was at the Nore Holding Depot to be mobilized into the most suitable posting. In the meantime, winning the war was not all battle. From the tiny railway station of nearby Rochester to London took little more than half an hour, providing the line was not under current repairs from a bomb hit. Regardless of continuous air raids, London was our mecca for needed entertainment. The Windmill Theatre never closed and performances continued around the clock.

Glamour girls in brief costumes cheered our service boys, and all of us loved the musicals produced in theatre land at The Palladium or Haymarket, Ivor Novello's "Dancing Years", Cecily Courtnidge and Jack Hulbert comedies, along with Americans Ben Lyon and Bebe Daniel's revues. Sometimes I went backstage to meet the well known entertainers who had graced our Sunday night musical evenings at home, to be greeted with warmth and encouragement.

Why did we make trips to London under threat of buzz bombs doing away with the city and ourselves at any moment? Who knows — perhaps because we might be dead on the morrow, or perhaps it was defiance to the Germans. Whatever it was we felt no fear. London was the heart of England, our homeland, we would support to the bitter end. We felt extreme closeness to the friends we were with from moment to moment, yet we lived with an ever present tightness in our chests. We laughed at every possible opportunity, refusing to entertain fear. An indominatable courage perhaps.

I had been hoping for an exciting posting, but my father had recently developed diabetes and was seriously ill. Nevertheless, he would not abandon an ounce of his agricultural committee work and was increasingly stressed. We were all worried about him.

I was offered a choice posting to Rosythe on the west coast of Scotland, a submarine base, but being so far away from my sick father, it was out of the question. Wrens were able to choose from three postings, one of the perks for the Senior Service. I secured my posting to H.M.S. Royal Arthur, situated in an old Butlins Holiday Camp, two miles outside of the east coast town of Skegness, only 45 miles from Bourne via country roads.

HMS Royal Arthur was the initial naval intake. Many British boys were now being conscripted for service, as well as young men who had escaped from their occupied countries — Dutch, Norwegians, Belgians and Free French. Sadly, most were suffering from extreme malnutrition, especially those from the larger cities where rations had become very scarce.

One of my favourite morning tasks was to drive the Duty Supply Officer to the meagre storage depot to weigh flour, dried fruit and margarine, which we delivered to the sick bays and the foreign intakes, billeted on neighbouring farms the navy had taken over for the duration of the War. The duty I hated most was driving the garbage truck through the camp. I had found double declutching whilst training difficult, but now appreciated the necessity to change the heavy gears. Few disinfectants were available, and the stench and flies were horrendous as I toured the many smelly mess halls.

A duty I performed frequently was delivering officers to and from the railway station, driving them the two miles in a small Hillman car, considered a plum job. The camp was situated on low land, close to the beach, with a high broad dyke serving as the road into Skegness. One frosty morning I accelerated too strongly through the Guard Gate, shot up onto the bank, and was unable to turn swiftly enough on the icy top, tipping down the other side. We landed upright, my passengers and I unhurt, but the Commander I was to deliver to the Station, requested a more experienced driver!

The ratio of 10,000 men to four hundred women at HMS Royal Arthur put each Wren in great demand. Nightly curfew was stringent, however, for we had to be in our quarters by 10pm, unless by some special arrangement, or we were on duty. There was never a question of breaking it.

Being right on the coast, there were frequent enemy machine gun strafings from very low flying Messerschmitts. We learned to recognize the screaming engines and dart for cover. The fuel used by the Germans was of a higher quality than our own making their planes sound different, and we were easily able to identify them when they zeroed in over our station.

HMS Royal Arthur was never meant for winter living. We were put two to a cabin in two-tiered bunks. The cabins were cheaply built plywood structures with no insulation or heating. condensation resulted in icicles, often six to eighteen inches long, hanging from the ceiling with ice caking the walls. Leading Wren Bunny Carter, my cabin mate, and I, pulled the bunk into the centre of the tiny area, piling all our clothes on top of us each night to keep from freezing.

By March our walls and ceiling were free of ice, and Great Britain was gearing up to enter its sixth Spring season at war. Allied troops moved in to occupied zones mingling with the ghosts of young soldiers, sailors and airmen, many of them friends of mine, who had forfeited their lives in defense of England.

Nazi Germany had built gruesome concentration camps to carry out Hitler's "final solution". Auschwitz one of the many on the Polish border was perhaps the most horrendous, where more than 4 million Jews from across Europe were killed, along with gypsies, homosexuals and political prisoners. Auschwitz had been partially destroyed by Germans when the last prisoners were liberated by the

Red Army on January 27th, 1945, but our advancing troops made grim discoveries of past atrocities. Horrible photographs and accounts of torture flooded the newspapers.

By now we were under severe food rationing, although families like mine grew their own farm produce. Although it was illegal due to lack of food supplies, we shared our bounty with neighbours and friends as we could.

I was able to get home on periodic 36 hour leaves, becoming adept at hitch hiking in a variety of vehicles, including farm tractors, standing on an iron bar behind the driver. People in uniform were always picked up. I could be with my horses during these visits, but war or no war, I wanted at least one horse nearby day by day. Daddy agreed to pay the board on my Duke of Windsor, as my 15 shillings a week pay packet went nowhere.

Mother and I hauled Dukey to a boarding stable in Skegness. When I could manage a few hours off, I hitch hiked the two miles from camp to groom him, saddle him up and ride along sand dunes to the beach, whilst other off duty friends found small homes which had been set up as black market cafes, to purchase egg and chips meals.

The seabed was flat, tides sliding out twenty miles or so leaving vast hard beaches ideal for riding at ebb tide. With invasion imminent, barbed wire entanglements were threaded throughout the many miles of The Wash, the inland marshes between Norfolk and Lincolnshire, much of which had been developed further inland into some of the finest farming land in the world. Since the beach was heavily mined, I was only permitted to ride down a narrow strip, about four miles long, monitored by the Coast Guard patrols. Dukey loved those leg stretching rides. One day during a gallop I spied a dreaded mine propped against a sand bank, rolled in by the tide.

After exercise, Dukey and I usually returned to the stables at a sedate canter, but this day we raced flat out as we had in that winning gypsy flapping race, direct to the Coast Guard blockhouse to report our discovery. The mine was subsequently blown up, and I felt worthy and useful, knowing my find probably saved some lives.

Jutting from the coast a mile north of camp, an outcrop of land, known as Gibralter Point, was pitted with our mines and strewn with massive barbed wire entanglements visible only at ebb tide. Obviously the sailors were forbidden anywhere near the water.

Nevertheless one warm spring evening the Norwegian contingent, bored and tempted by sun sparkling on the water, disobeyed orders and took a swim.

The sailors placed wooden planks over the barbed wire off the Point, climbing swiftly over, to frolic in the low tide sea, amazingly avoiding the mines as they swam strongly several hundred yards from the coastline. I was on duty later that night, when an emergency call came through ordering the ambulance and rescue crews to Gibralter Point immediately.

The tide had turned quickly, the waters rushed back over the long flat seabed, streaming across the firm sands, over the barbed wire. The Norwegians, used to their deep fjords, were unaccustomed to the contrariness of such a tide. All of the 67 young sailors who had gone for a joyful escapade, were drowned, being caught up in the barbed wire tangles. A tragic ending to their wilful adventure. Throughout the night I drove mutilated young men to a makeshift morgue.

Our mess halls adjoined the butcher shop. No doubt initially this seemed a good idea, to get the meat to the kitchen quickly. Meat was in very short supply, with rumors we were eating horse. Anathema to me of course. When the weather warmed up, the smell from the hanging carcasses was powerful. Blood flowed out of the shop, down a slope to the gutter, trickling over the mess hall entry, flies settling in the red ooze. Worst of all, was wondering if perhaps the blood flowed from a horse I might have once known. Such thoughts soon convinced me I never wanted to eat meat again. I would become a vegetarian!

The following day I visited the Medical Officer, saying I had always been vegetarian, and had attempted to comply with naval meals, but was finding it increasingly difficult. I did not feel I could do my best duty without a proper diet. What would I have to do to be put on a vegetarian one?

"No problem" the M.O. told me. He prepared a written order to the mess hall cooks. For the rest of my stay in the navy I received special cheese allocations, an occasional poached egg, salads and milk. I was soon the envy of many, who in their turn spoke with the M.O. trying the same tack. He turned each one down. I was as false as the rest, my advantage being the first to make the request. Away from camp I ate an occasional rasher of bacon, or meat as before, if any available.

Bobbie's intermittent letters confirmed he had received some Red Cross parcels, which was comforting. I knew the young officer I had said goodbye to when I joined the navy, was not getting much food from the Germans.

The war at last was turning in our favour, but England was pathetically weakened. We were still taking recruits, but many were too malnourished for the rigid training necessary to complete a fighting force. Some died in camp of tuberculosis, other weakening illnesses or physical exhaustion. Although we were on the road to peace in Europe, the Japanese were still in control of the Pacific, forcing us to continue with the conscripted intakes.

Our Motor Transport drivers, including me, numbered four. Bunny went on some special course, Sheila Neale Green went off on leave from which she chose not to return, knowing WRNS were the only service personnel who could not be penalized for desertion, and the other driver was taken ill.

This left me to hold the fort for about two weeks when the sun over the mountain came in early May of 1945. It was apparently not considered necessary to send more drivers to the camp with peace being just around the corner. We knew the German Army had folded, surrender was imminent to Eisenhower's forces within hours. I called home to hear victory parties were already under way everywhere.

As peace drew closer hour by hour, I continued driving the supply van each morning and the odorous garbage truck or ambulance the rest of the day. I was asked to chauffeur officers to the various farms where the foreign sailors were still in training, and worst of all, still delivered coffins containing the bodies of young men to Skegness Railway Station, departure point for shipping them to their loved ones for proper burial.

Hour by hour I knew little relief. I was only eighteen, exhausted mentally and physically, but never thought of giving up. There was always a skeleton guard at the gate to check anyone coming or going, and I should imagine my signature was on that roster as much as any other and probably more than most.

When the Germans surrendered May 7th, I was dispatched to drive officers for a series of victory parties in Skegness. Each time we arrived at one, they bade me to wait for them outside. I could hear the cheers, singing and laughter inside and wondered why I too should not be included in the celebrations. Why must I sit outside? Had I not been a part of the war effort too?

Such thoughts built within me a strong measure of indignation, resentment and surprising anger. Bolstered by my disillusions I pulled away from the curb, after yet another delivery of frolicking officers to their third or fourth party, driving rather recklessly back

47

to camp, ignoring the brakes until I swept through the gates, where I skidded a few yards, but no one seemed around to witness the derring-do. Even the guards were off celebrating.

I ran into the Guard Room, intending to leave the keys and then walk off to I knew not where. A lone sailor appeared. I tossed him the keys and proceeded to tell him what I thought of navy protocol. Before the end of my onslaught, he picked up the phone, called someone, while I paid no attention to what he was saying. When he rang off he took me by the hand, pulled me back to the car, guiding me into the passenger seat.

We drove to Sick Bay, where a lonely nurse was sitting around with nothing to do. I was told to lie down and rest. I wanted to protest, but realized lying down and forgetting all of it was precisely what I most wanted to do.

I awoke later that afternoon to find two naval Commanders, doctors, standing beside my bed. Having left some celebration party, I am sure they were not pleased to find me. They murmured comfortingly and, after examining me, my heart especially, administered a tranquilizer which put me out until the following morning, when I appeared before the Senior Medical Officer for an intensive examination. Within hours I was processed to leave the WRNS, discharged with a nervous breakdown and permanently disabled weak heart, a throwback to my diphtheria and surprisingly not spotted during the medical exam prior to my signing up!

My mother, hastily informed of my serious state, arrived early in the afternoon hauling a horse trailer. I was discharged into her care and later told I could have died at any time within twenty-four hours because of my heart condition.

So it was goodbye to the navy. We collected Dukey and drove home to Bourne, where old Sandy waited to unload my patient horse and lead him to a comfortable stable.

My father, wearing one of his eternal cream silk jackets, appeared in the doorway and walked to hug me. He looked much older. So, I suppose, did I.

Mother, with an unusual tender expression, watched us meet and embrace. Never was the love for my parents and England more precious than at that moment of homecoming in 1945.

I was ushered into my pretty bedroom. The following day summoned by my father, a heart specialist from Harley Street in London, examined me, recommending bed rest for at least four months. No stress, no stirring around of any kind. Our modern day heart medications were not then available.

After the specialist left I tried persuading my parents I knew what was best for me, and staying in bed was not the answer. They did not listen. I had to settle into the quiet routine, slowing down my double active heart beats.

Three months of inactivity found me begging to be allowed to leave my bed briefly each day. The doctor initially allowed two hours each afternoon visiting with the family downstairs. I was not permitted to walk back up the stairs, but had to go backwards from the sitting position one step at a time, so as not to stress my heart!

Each sojourn, Dukey and Footprints were brought to the lounge windows to say hello. Everyone noticed how my spirits brightened when we had our window talks, and within a month, after much pleading on my part, I was allowed to ride Dukey each day for half an hour so long as I never left a walk. We were into late summer by then, and how glorious it was to feel the warm sun on my back as Dukey and I ambled sedately around our fields.

One morning when we returned to the stables after a happy ride, I noticed my mother had moved her regular Women's Volunteer Services knitting team outside. Their needles had not stoped clicking with Germany's surrender. The Japanese were still the enemy. Among the team members was the wife of our bank manager. She stared at me for a moment or two, then loudly intoned; "We all know your father bought you out of the navy! The least you could do, while other young folk are still out there trying to finish the war, is do something more than ride a horse!"

My mother was horrified, but smoothed things over rather than make a scene. The woman was the best knitter. However, my father's resentment matched mine when over over lunch he was told of the outburst.

"We will go to the bank this afternoon" he said.

I assumed we would face the manager, Mr. Morrison, together, but Daddy only accompanied me to the main door.

"Go in and tell him what you think. I'll wait for you there" he said, indicating a pub across the street.

He took most of my confidence with him when he strode away, but I retrieved enough to confront the manager and explained what had happened that morning.

"I was invalided out of the navy," I told him. "I'll not tolerate your wife's vicious untrue remarks. I have come to close my account". I had learned how to stand up for myself quickly.

He disappeared into another room for a little while and then returned saying I was twenty pounds overdrawn!

It was my turn to disappear. I fled from the bank over to my father in the Angel Hotel bar, trying to remain haughty, and wondering what should I do next.

Very angry by it all, Daddy gave me thirty pounds. "That will settle your account in this bank and give you enough to open one in another."

I ran back across the street to give the money to the manager. He knew where it had come from, and I reminded him if the account to be closed had been one of my father's, the bank would have been facing a much larger problem.

"Daddy and I both think it would be right for you to tell your wife of her unkindness. She had her story all wrong." I added indignantly, being rewarded by a flicker of anxiety in his eyes.

Many years after, when remembering the final victory of the Allies in 1945, I would wonder if perhaps I had not suffered an odd sort of defeat during the same month. Remembering my father standing strongly behind me, advancing funds necessary to close my meager bank account with dignity. I might perhaps have developed a better awareness of money, and been prepared for the unexpected, if he had not always been there to quietly fulfill my needs.

Chapter Three

I have to live with myself, and so, I want to be fit for myself to know.

During the Summer of 1945 advancing American troops liberated Bobbie's camp, and he and other prisoners of war were returned to England, thin but jubilant, some having been in prison six or seven years. Many of the homecoming veterans wore the high-peaked, heavily badged caps of German officers, which they had picked up as souvenirs. The only men who would not exchange their own headgear for any other were the Red Devils taken at Arnhem. I am sure Bobbie was wearing his red beret at the same jaunty angle when, emaciated but still proud, he touched English soil again, but I was unable to be there. Security would not allow civilians to welcome them or attend their brief hospitalization. Bobbie returned to his parents' home in Hereford, and I boarded a train to visit him shortly after.

Our meeting was emotional. So much had happened to both of us since the day I joined the WRNS and he left to make the jump over Arnhem. He was pathetically thin and exhausted. We were far too young and immature to become engaged. I was in love not so much with Bobbie but with romance. He was a hero wherever we went, and I was so proud to be at his side.

Our personalities were not at all alike. I was excitable, anxious to enjoy peace and plenty with my horses. Bobbie wanted only to gain strength enough to return to army life and make it his career. Our future and all of England's were still uncertain, yet when Bobbie asked me to marry him, I could not refuse.

My parents consented, and Bobbie bought me a beautiful ruby and diamond ring which I loved to flash about. The announcement of our betrothal appeared in the Daily Telegraph Court Circular September 21st, 1945. Telegrams of congratulations came from everywhere.

We were unable to plan our wedding date with any exactness. For when Bobbie regained his health, he was recalled to his regiment and sent to Palestine, a dangerous zone due to the ever present battle between religious factions, often involving barrages of sniper's bullets and car bombings in residential sections and no military dependents were allowed. In February of 1946 Bobbie wrote to say he would be home on leave in May and wanted us to be married then. My parents became involved in arranging the wedding, the first fashionable one after the war in our part of the country.

The entire populace of Bourne was elated by the impending event. Mother, as usual, was making plans. By then I knew everything was moving too quickly, knew in my heart I should not walk down the aisle, but did not feel secure enough, or did not have courage enough, to call off the wedding. I comforted myself by remembering I was deeply attracted to Bobbie, and he to me. With that advantage we should be able to make our marriage work, premature though the wedding might be. Much had happened to us both, yet we really did not know the other at all.

Meanwhile, Mother forged ahead with elaborate planning for the Manor garden, especially the marquee — a large tent with a portable oak floor for dancing, decorated with flowers around the sides and climbing up the supporting poles. A hundred small round tables, with chairs covered in pastel chintz would be scattered around the edge of the dance floor. Eternal conferences with caterers, concerning a four-tiered wedding cake and the wedding menu were discussed. The guest list was virtually endless. A tea for one hundred of Mother's WVS supporters the afternoon before the wedding, four hundred to attend the ceremony and reception, two hundred of my father's employees to be entertained and fed the day after... on and on.

Mother took me to Adderleys in Leicester, later to become the celebrated Marshall and Snelgrove, to purchase a trousseau. By then I was caught up in the rushing splendor of it all, and what fun it was to choose fine sets of dainty underwear and negligees plus clothes for all occasions.

Leicester was forty miles away, but we somehow managed petrol for weekly visits. I was given the traditional dozen sets of pure linen sheets and pillowcases, a dozen huckaback hand towels in pastel colors with matching sets of soft velour towels, all sent to Ireland for hand embroidering with my monogram.

The leading model of Adderleys, Barbara Pym, was responsible for my trousseau. We were to become close friends. She was able to find beautiful fabrics hidden during the war years, including a delicate French crepe for my wedding gown. It had a square neckline to which fresh lilies of the valley would be fastened before the ceremony.

There were two senior bridesmaids in a soft printed cream silk, and three children, all in white satin and silk taken from parachutes. The men were to wear dark grey morning dress, with Bobbie, his Best Man and some ushers, in their service uniforms.

My parents were dedicated to giving me a superlative sendoff, and everyone in the county was devoted to making the ceremony and attendant activities a cause for celebrating, not only a wedding, but also the end of many grim years of war.

Bobbie arrived home on schedule in May and called me from his parents' home in Hereford. Excitement in anticipation of the wedding captured both of us. We did not meet.

Early in the afternoon the day before the wedding. May 21st, I drove to Peterborough Station, sixteen miles away, to collect my fiance and his mother. They were not on the train I met, or the one afterward. I waited another hour. No sign of them. Was he jilting me in the final moments?

I drove home disconsolately to be met by my mother, who was frantic.

"Where have you been! Bobbie and his mother are waiting at the Great Northern Hotel in Peterborough!"

I had gone to the wrong train station. Was it an omen?

That night Bobbie and I retreated to the garden to be alone and spend some time getting reacquainted. I really did not know him as well in person as by his letters. That built shyness between us which was compounded by the splendor of the Manor dressed for the wedding on the morrow. It was bedecked with flowers throughout the interior. The gardens were meticulously manicured and resplendent with colorful blooms. The drawingroom had been turned into a showroom for hundreds of gifts displayed on long trestle tables covered in white cloths — groups of crystal, linens and vast amounts of Georgian antique silver. A detective had been arranged to watch over the gifts for three days.

I recall Bobbie's still thin face as we strolled in the garden and later admired the array of gifts. I could not tell what he was thinking. Did he have doubts to match mine? I will never know.

May 22nd, to become an extraordinary milestone as the years rolled on, the hottest day of the year, had a wilting effect on wedding guests garbed in their finest, but the heat of the day had no effect on my father. He looked crisp and handsome in his grey top hat and morning dress, with grey spats on his shining shoes. A limousine decorated with white ribbons waited to take us to the church. As we climbed in, Daddy grasped my hand.

"You're so young, I don't think you are ready for marriage yet!" he sighed. "Why don't we drive past the church and just keep on going. Forget the whole thing."

"It's far too late now. I can't let all those people down waiting at the church." I defied. "I know what I'm doing." Typical twenty year old!

The ceremony was to be performed in the Abbey Church of St. Peter and St. Paul in Bourne, a scant mile away from our house. Hundreds of townsfolk gathered on both sides of the road to watch the procession of cars moving slowly toward the church. I had been their little princess throughout my life, and they did not want to miss the scene. The wedding was beautiful. The church was filled with flowers. The chancel rail covered by the delicate white keck that grows wild in the countryside. Only one hitch occurred. At the last minute my little page boy, John Atkinson, refused to follow me down the aisle. He was three years old. I heard him say to his mother, "I don't want to marry her anyway."

I gazed into the eyes of my handsome young bridegroom as we exchanged vows and thought myself a fool for having doubted our future together.

The Abbey bells pealed melodiously as we walked out of the church, to be greeted by hundreds of townsfolk who cheered and threw confetti as our motorcade began the return trip to my home for the reception.

Champagne had been scarce during the war and still was in 1946, but corks were popped out of more than two hundred bottles during the reception all the same. Much of it was purchased from some of my father's wealthy horse racing friends, who had kept their stock replenished during the war, by tapping the expensive black market.

Two bottles of the champagne were put in the trunk of my father's wedding present to me, a maroon Hillman car, and long before the reception ended, Bobbie and I were on our way to a honeymoon in Yorkshire. Our final destination was The Black Swan, a charming old inn in Helmsley, but we checked in for an overnight stop at a picturesque roadside inn outside of Doncaster. Once settled, we chilled one of the bottles of champagne. When Bobbie opened it later, it was flat. We ordered more ice, and once that bottle was chilled, Bobbie opened it with much ceremony. It was flat too, not one bubble appeared.

Neither of us thought we believed in portents or presentments, but one's wedding night is not the time to be confronted by flat champagne. We feigned laughter but were both daunted nevertheless.

In spite of our worries about not knowing each other very well, it was a perfect honeymoon which ended all too soon. For three weeks we explored the Yorkshire Moors by day and each other by night, and by the time Bobbie returned to Palestine and I to the Manor, we had developed a warm, caring relationship.

With the end of the honeymoon came the end of glamour and excitement, the doldrums moved in. I was to remain with my parents until the army decreed it safe for wives to follow their husbands into war torn countries. My horses were once more great solace, but I had been awakened. I was no longer the single daughter of the largest landowner around, to be courted by aspiring young blades. I was soon horrendously bored.

My salvation was to ride Footprints who was only '15.3 hh, but what he lacked in size he made up with superb conformation and action. I worked hard with him every day, teaching him to balance and move off his hocks which, in the lengthening of the trot, made him dramatic with long daisy cutting strides. We had a remarkable partnership with instant action from my light aids. In the gallop he out moved all the other horses. Invariably as we cornered, after the faster pace in front of the grandstand, the watching crowds held their breath, expecting us to fall, but he reacted to my inside leg supporting him so firmly, he moved like a motor cycle with my foot nearly grazing the ground. Into the bargain he had a very soft mouth enabling me to ease him to stop quietly and straight. Hunters are expected to move strongly and fast as if in the fox hunting field.

John Ashton had replaced Sandy when he retired, looking after the more mature horses. He was part gypsy and taught me many herb remedies and conditioning ways. He gave me a leather bound book "Every Man his own Horse and Cow Doctor", with 160 ancient recipes, the like of which today's veterinarians would be horrified. One of the cures for bog spavin suggests using two quarts of old urine, 6 ounces of soft soap, boiled together till they acquire the consistency of an ointment, and put in a pot for use. Then to add 2 ounces of pure ammonia to 4 of the liniment, and shake well, applying twice daily for two weeks. Sadly the majority of the ingredients in the old recipes can no longer be found.

Ashton was at his happiest when accompanying me to County shows with Footprints, grooming my little horse into peak condition. We had a new wooden Rice trailer which was pulled by an old army jeep, whose covered top had been built by my father's carpenter, Smith. It was made of thick plywood painted bottle green, a far cry from the luxurious trailers I was to become accustomed to years later.

I won many awards with Footprints as a Lightweight Hunter, the weight determined by the National Hunter Society for horses to carry under 13.7 stone, during which time we built an endearing relationship. On Saturday mornings I would sit on Footprint's back, reading aloud from Horse and Hound magazine, our bible of the time, the show comments regaling his wins. During the winter months we hunted with the Belvoir Hounds a few times, my little horse showing incredible bravery over the big fences. I was so proud of him when clipped out, everyone remarking how beautiful he was. I was never happier than being together and I vowed never to part with him.

The top showman in the hunter and hack divisions was Count Robert Orrsich, a quite remarkable rider with endless grace and talent. He could win a class with practically any horse, and being a professional trainer intimidated the rest of us showing beside him. However, the judges that year consistently placed Footprints and I higher than the Count, and his various client's horses, when it came to the Championships. He did not like it of course. Initially he tried to train me as one of his paying pupils, but as he lived at Winkfield near Windsor it was out of the question. Then he approached me to sell my lovely horse to one of his clients, strongly hinting there must be something wrong with Footprints, as there is with every horse, and he would have to make it known to judges everywhere. I was horrified, but when a very large sum was offered, through Count Orrsich, by Ann Dowley of Biddenden, Kent, Daddy convinced me it was the highest price for any show horse in the country at that time and I should accept. It broke my heart. I spent three days in my horse's stall apologizing to him, telling him I would buy him back if he was not going to be happy.

Footprints was loaded into a deluxe horse box on a train to Kent. I ensured he was securely bandaged, had deep straw bedding, hay and water for the day long journey, and gave him a final hug, tears streaming down my face. Later that afternoon I received a telegram "Footprints arrived safely - delighted with him, many thanks, Dowley".

That should have been the end of the story and my horse would live a fine new life. However, we had a telephone call later that night. The Dowley's had turned Footprints out in a paddock to gallop and stretch his legs. He raced excitedly about, bucking in glee, learning his way around the perimeter. They called proudly to him, and he raced up to where they stood. He was going much too fast, as he skidded up to the gate one leg shot through the rails, breaking it. The telephone call confirmed Footprints had been shortly after put to sleep. I vowed never again to sell a horse. Nearly fifty years ago there was never any question of mending a broken leg.

Amateur dramatics had always appealed to me, probably because my genes were attracted to anything sensational. But, other than participating in a few school plays and some amateur productions in the early war years when I joined the Girls Training Corps prior to enlisting in the Navy, I had no acting experience and certainly no training. Nevertheless I joined the Bourne Players, a vibrant group meeting once a week.

When the Players put on J.B. Priestly's "Laburnham Grove," a three-act comedy, I was chosen for the lead role, Elsie Redfern. Our amateur efforts resulted in a hit, as our performances were sold out for a week. Once more, on a visit to Bourne, Ivor Novello asked me to join his musical school, as did Dame Sybil Thorndyke, her drama one. But I had to refuse. I was, after all, a married woman now. I later took the lead in "Miranda, Tale of a Mermaid." That was really me!

I was the wife of Captain Robert Harold Bruce Feltham, and I missed my handsome hero husband very much. Saturday nights were lonesome. Petrol was becoming more available, and our crowd usually met in Grantham for a few drinks, beer for the boys and gin and tonics for the girls, before dinner at the Angel or George Hotels. My parents did not think a young wife should participate in those excursions sans husband. I watched my parents leave to visit their friends, watched my brother and Paul Tointon, home from the war at last, drive off to comraderie and fun with our friends. My own lonely evenings were spent writing long letters to Bobbie. He must have sensed my unrest, for he told me to go out with Andrew and Paul on Saturday nights and also suggested I resume playing poker with the three Franks brothers — John, Henry and Brian, on Sunday afternoons.

One such Sunday the Franks brothers, Andrew, Paul and I, entered into a poker game in the lounge hall at the Manor. Our betting units were shillings, which could make the game quite exciting if a strong pair of players decided not to fold at any cost.

I drew a full house topped by three kings and continued raising until only Brian was left in. He was a cheeky player, the most consistent winner among us.

"I'll raise you five," he said, looking me straight in the eye. I stared firmly back, unable to tell whether he was bluffing, but raised him another five showing shades of my father's courage.

The table was quiet as Brian and I continued to stare at each other. None of us had much money, and most of it was on the table.

"I fold," Brian finally said, for he had been bluffing all along. But that was not the point. During the period when we were trying to stare each other down, a wild streak of chemistry linked us. For the rest of the evening neither of us paid much attention to the card game, as we exchanged many more long and lingering looks before he and his brothers left.

Brian and I had known each other all our lives. Our fathers had served together in the Lincolnshire Yeomanry during the First World War. I had no idea what had passed between us, and neither did he, but the excitement generated during that card game was not to be denied, and Saturday nights became much more exciting.

Brian was always waiting for me at whichever pub we chose as the starting point for the evening. Each time he directed his welcoming smile toward me I was prey to a feeling of sensuality far greater than any created by my husband.

Our circle of friend's routine was to move from one pub to another as a group, and Brian, anxious to be alone with me, soon found ways to manouever me into his car separating me from Andrew and Paul. We moved in auto caravan from pub to restaurant and to pub again and were never without friends in cars ahead and behind. We tried to control our feelings, but they were difficult to hide if even our hands happened to touch. I am sure the looks passing between us were remarked upon later, though few of our friends said anything. But as time passed by I was frequently the subject among the farmers' cattle market gossipers, much to my mother's horror.

On several occasions Brian and I agreed nothing could come of our apparent infatuation. Our feelings for each other did not diminish, but we finally decided it would be best for our families if we stopped seeing each other. We were in a no win situation.

During my school years at Malvern I was particularly friendly with Pauline Holden, an extremely pretty blonde whose parents came from nearby Wolverhampton. They knew me well, of course, from a variety of school outings and asked my parents to combine with them in introducing us to Society as Debutantes after we left school. This would involve our being Presented at Court.

This could be an extremely costly luxury, entailing numerous parties, dances, dinners, days at Ascot Thoroughbred horse racing and on the Thames for the Henley Regatta in the Royal Enclosures. Apart from being Presented it would enable us to meet a whole new circle of young people. Now being married there was no point in the official year for me. My friend Pauline, two years earlier, had been named the Debutante of the Year with a marvellous formal photograph in The Tatler, the leading society magazine.

The Countess of Ancaster was on very close terms with the Royal Family and she was also an influential friend of my mother and father. She wanted to Present me, since I did not have the opportunity because of the war. It was arranged for Bobbie to come home on leave so that he could accompany me too, as it would enhance his military career, ensuring invitations to Diplomatic Levees.

The Countess applied through the Lord Chamberlain's office and an invitation soon arrived from Buckingham Palace for us to attend a Garden Party there in June. No elaborate white dresses, but pretty afternoon gowns with long gloves and hats of course.

The Countess invited us to an elegant luncheon in her townhouse, served appropriately by her butler and footman. We were then driven to Buckingham Palace in a chauffeured limousine, lining up with the many other vehicles waiting to discharge their passengers.

Bobbie wore his navy blue dress uniform, resplendent with wartime medals, topped by his distinguished beret. I wore a burgundy red and cream tiny check taffeta dress, navy silk jacket with matching taffeta collar and cuffs, with a model straw hat. We climbed slowly out of the limousine at the Palace gates, where our identification was checked, and we were saluted by a Grenadier Guard. Bobbie escorted the Countess and I through the small side gate where we paused to sign the Visitor's Book. Buckingham Palace is a most imposing structure, very stately and formal. We passed on through the inner courtyard to the main entrance. Our invitation cards were checked again, after which we were ushered up a fine marble staircase to the Blue Gallery, which runs the length of the Palace overlooking the gardens. There seemed to be hundreds of us,

Outside Buckingham Palace as Bobbie and I approached prior to
my Presentation to King George VI and Queen Elizabeth,
the Queen Mother and Princesses Elizabeth and Margaret.
I was presented by Lady Willoughby d'Ersby, Countess of Ancaster, 1948

along with escorts and presenters, as we stood waiting midst the
throng. Suddenly, huge doors were opened at the end of the Gallery
as Heralds appeared sounding their horns. The Beefeaters, dressed
in their scarlet and gold costumes, entered carrying long staves and
slowly, but solemnly, cleared us all towards the back walls, leaving
an empty pathway for the Royal Party.

Awed silence. Everyone was thrilled to see King George VI and Queen Elizabeth graciously walk through with the Princesses behind them. I was spellbound as I stood on tiptoe to get a better view. Every few strides the Royal Party paused and a young lady was brought forward, introduced and made her curtsy. It was not too long before the Royals approached our position. Her Majesty looked up, caught the Countess' eye, mouthing "What are you doing here?"

With the recognition, it was inevitable I would be one of those chosen to be Presented. The Countess stepped forward, introducing me. I made my curtsy correctly to them in turn, and was so glad I had practiced properly. The Countess and the Queen chatted for a little and I, seeing the King silent and forlorn, asked how he was feeling as this was his first outing after his very serious thrombosis illness. I found him easy to talk with, although I was later told I had broken protocol, addressing him directly!

After the Presentation Ceremony, we filed back through the gallery to Buckingham Palace gardens for an informal tea consisting of dainty cucumber sandwiches and petit-fours.

Fifty years later there are still formal introductions into Society, but much reduced in grandure. Signing of the Palace Registry still entitles recognition for diplomatic functions, but never to the degree of pre-war lavishness.

Bobbie returned to the army in Malaya, I to the Manor and horses.

My dear friend, Peter Francis, recently demobbed from a distinguished career in the Royal Air Force, came around to see how the world had been treating me during the last four years we had not seen each other. There was much to talk about. I had missed his companionship whilst he served overseas. We both sensed an urgency to get back our old roots. There was no need to be fully explicit about the horrors we had both been through, it went without saying. We needed to put it behind us and carry on.

Peter had served as a pilot with Transport Command, taking part in many epic flights. Conveniently for me, I had been unable to travel with Bobbie to Malaya because of terrorists and army regulations, to several post war postings — apart from which I did not want to leave my horses. The dedication I had to my horses then, and even now, sadly removed what should have been from me, loyalty to my husband.

The Blankney Hunt Ball was scheduled for October 24th at the RAF Officer's Training College, Cranwell, less than thirty miles away. Peter suggested we renew our close friendship by escorting me to this festive gathering. Being a married woman, for appearance's sake, it would seem more proper if we made a foursome out of the evening by including my cousin, Josephine Cooke and her steady boyfriend, Major John Smith.

Of course I longed to go to the ball with Peter. My life was flat for entertainment, with my husband stationed so far away. I feared my mother would disapprove. She seldom approved of any of the things I did, a result of her own severe Victorian upbringing. Instead she surprised me. For once she relented, perhaps feeling sorry for my restricted existence. Mothers are so often an enigma. "You should go. You and Peter have known each other all your lives. Your friendship was always as a brother and sister, renew your old relationship. Anyway I know I can trust you, you would not do anything I would not want you to. What have you got to wear?"

The choice for a fabric presented no problem. We could either cut volumes of silk from a parachute left behind by a German flyer who had been shot down over our house, or a delicate French yellow silk fabric, patterned with white and blue iris, hoarded by my fashion designer friend, Barbara Pym. My dressmaker fashioned the hauntingly beautiful and weightless material into a classic gown, full and flowing. It deserved perfect slippers, so white ones were dyed the same shade of yellow as the gown. After the years of war austerity this was to be an evening never to be forgotten.

Josephine and I chatted frequently on the phone during the days leading up to the Ball. She was as excited as I, but in those days she was travelling on her own special cloud anyway. She was deeply in love with John, and although he had not proposed, she was certain he soon would.

How happy the four of us were on the way to the Blankney Hunt Ball that Friday night. Josephine and I in our new gowns, the boys so handsome in full evening dress. We danced the hours away to such songs as "The Moonlight Waltz", Jerome Kern's "You Were Never Lovelier" and "My Devotion". I was young and full of life again, life was just a continuing melody of romantic tunes. I wanted it to never end.

Nothing lasts forever.

We had agreed to meet in the car park at two a.m. Peter and I arrived first and he smiled, helping me into his car, watching as I settled in the front seat.

"All the years I have known you, you've ridden in a car with your legs tucked under you," he said.

"Being so small, it is more comfortable and I can see where we go," I answered.

"I don't think so," he teased. "I think the habit began when you were very tiny. You wanted to look grown up but couldn't in a car because your legs were too short to reach the floorboard — I'd say they still are," he laughed. "You've not grown much you know."

"But I have grown," I told him. "Maybe not in size, but in other ways. We both have. We've seen so much, been through too much, never to be the same again."

"I know," he sighed, reaching for my hand. Holding it on his knee, contemplating the starlight sky. "Perhaps we shan't ever be the same, but I'd like everything else to be, the world as it was before the war. I want all that again, our tennis tournaments, and family closeness. I'm twenty-four and for the first time feel ready to settle down. After tonight, I wonder if you really do want your husband home again?"

He drew me to him. Our hearts beating faster, we kissed with new found awareness. He held me tightly until Josephine and John arrived. We sensed a very special excitement in the air, and our own tender feelings were eclipsed by something far more poignant. They were glowing and quickly told us why.

Josephine whispered excitedly, "We have just become engaged!"

The romance of the story tale evening had encouraged John to reveal his feelings, so eagerly desired by my cousin.

We considered returning to the Officer's Mess for a champagne toast to the betrothal, but realizing the late hour, decided against it. We were all in a state of euphoria, but pleasantly tired, and ready to go home. They all lived in Pinchbech and would have a further eighteen miles to travel after taking me home, thirty miles away.

"There will always be another Ball and another day," said Peter.

As we left the car park Josephine and John nestled contentedly together in the back seat. I leaned my head on Peter's shoulder. Lulled by the calm drone of his car, I half dozed during the next couple of miles. Suddenly, I was jolted wide awake by a frightening lurch of the Wolsley car, and Josephine's terrified scream.

Instinctively I froze, as Peter struggled fiercely with the steering wheel.

"Damn grips!" he muttered.

Little did we know, road maintenance had only that morning dug the grips — draining trenches — on both sides of the two lane road. They were possibly eighteen inches wide and more than a foot deep. A front wheel had struck deeply into one as Peter pulled the car around an uphill curve.

The car was dangerously out of control. Peter, being an excellent driver, had not been speeding, nor had he had too much to drink, but matters were now out of his hands.

The car seemed to leave the ground, landing with a thud and skidded, culminating with a terrible crash against a double telephone pole on the opposite side of the road.

I was catapulted forward, my face smashed against the dashboard, knocking me briefly unconscious. A mist of dust was still rising in the headlight beams when I opened my eyes. Fearing fire, my first automatic action was to reach and turn off the ignition.

"Peter, are you all right?" I blurted out through a mouthful of blood.

He was draped over the wheel with his head bent and did not answer. Nor did Josephine or John when I called their names. Silence. I looked at them, in the moonlight, sprawled in the back seat knowing immediately they were dead. As I moved towards Peter and gently grasped his arm, he breathed a gurgly sigh, and I knew he was dead too.

I passed into a state of shock for I remember little of what happened during the next few hours, but can reconstruct the triple tragedy by relying on newspaper clippings.

The crash occurred near Leasingham, just above Blackthorn Hollow at 2:30 am on Saturday, October 25th. There was no other traffic on the road. The first people on the scene were friends, Bob Earl and his wife, also returning from the Ball. They stopped when they saw me beside the road, blood streaking the front of my gown.

Behind me, a blanket of shattered glass, like a thin coat of snow, spread sixty feet across the road and verge to Peter's car smashed against the telephone poles. I had lost my slippers in the crash but had stumbled through all the glass without even tearing my stockings. My Guardian Angels had been busy that night, working overtime as usual. Had I been sitting normally I would have lost my legs.

Moments later other motorists arrived. Ambulances and police were summoned whilst I sat shivering on the grass verge. One by one my young friends were removed from the broken car, their mangled bodies laid on blankets beside me. Eventually they were taken home to their distraught families.

Because of the severe danger of shock, and needing to keep me warm, while the police ascertained who I was, the Hall's volunteered to take me to their nearby home. I could remember the names of Peter and John, but not my own. I did not remember if I was Jo or Joy Cooke, terrible dilemma for the police in contacting our parents.

The Halls, however were able to tell the police who I was. My poor parents, unaware of their daughter's plight, were awakened with the horror of the accident, quickly giving permission for me to be taken by ambulance to the Stamford Infirmary, forty miles away.

While propped up in the ambulance to keep the blood from blocking my throat, my distress continued as I spat out two front teeth. The ambulance attendant rescued them, placing both in my hand. At the Hospital, x-rays revealed I had received double compound fractures in my upper jawbone when I was catapulted against the dash board, with glass fragments penetrating many areas of my face and arms.

I awoke from a general anesthetic to find my jaw wired. The teeth I had lost were replaced in an attempt to hold the broken jaw immobile. The surgery was unsuccessful. The teeth, which were pushed back into my jawbone to hold it in place, dropped down. Black and blue bruises suffused my face.

Two days later I received more surgery, and the wires were removed. A fibre glass splint was cemented in place, my old teeth still there to keep the bone in line. Not a pleasant experience without an anesthetic, but the doctors decided I could not have one so soon after the first surgery. I wore the ugly splint for six months.

Investigators found no skid marks before we hit the grips at the scene of the accident. They deemed no mechanical failure had occurred, but for some reason Peter had left the road, and the car lurched onto the grass verge. Tire marks in the grass extended a hundred and sixty feet and continued sharply across the other side of the road, at which point they grew deeper and sharper, revealing Peter had struggled to avoid the telephone poles, a scant two feet from the roadside. Unavoidably the car had crashed into the poles, being totally demolished.

An inquest was held. The verdict was Death by Accident. The coroner's reports later confirmed my friends were sober and had all died from fractured skulls. No one wore seatbelts in those days.

During the first hours in hospital after the accident, the doctors persisted in assuring me my friends were in separate private wards just down the corridor, which confused me horribly. My parents later told me I was so badly shocked and injured the doctors lied thinking it in my best interest. In fact it was the worst thing they could have done. I knew my friends were dead. I was devastated, and I would have to miss their funerals.

I remained in the hospital for nearly two months. I did not understand then why I was spared. I grieved without tears, turning against the people who loved me, my mother, my brother and my husband. I felt they condemned me and held me partly responsible for the tragedy, that somehow the accident would not have occurred if I had not been at the Ball. I would not be influenced by them, refusing to feel guilty for wanting to have a life of my own. Consequently I received counselling for the following six months, with little effect, being unable to reconcile to myself that my friends had all died.

"There will always be another Ball and another day", Peter had said.

Yet he was to have none, nor would Josephine and John. I could find no reason why my splendid young friends were gone while I remained. They had fought bravely in the war, why were they taken like this? Why was I still alive?

I had no answer then and have none now.

God does not make mistakes, it was time for my friends to be taken, yet I had a lifetime to fulfill, lessons to learn and to give. My character was strengthened; I was determined to always give of my best, never to have enough time for all the things I must do. I would not be a victim. In memory of my friends, I would move heaven and earth for them, and achieve for myself, all that they could not.

As usual my horses were my solace. Unable to forget my friends and the terrible night, I turned to them more and more. I spent hours just sitting in the stalls with Dukey, stroking and hugging him, receiving the deep comfort which came through with his warm nudges and understanding. In times of loneliness, it is still a special comfort I treasure to be quietly with my horse, arms around his neck, he always understands. During the quiet months at the Manor following Bobbie's return to Malaya, I noted Daddy was back in excellent form despite his diabetes. He and Mother were seemingly more compatible. No one viewing them in the rosy post war era would guess they had declared their own war, of sorts, when the big one was at fullest pitch.

Running the WVS during the war had been stimulating for my mother. She was a great organizer, but in throwing herself headlong into the war effort, sacrificed much of her home life.

A maid cooked our meals, a cleaning lady daily ensured the

house was spotless, but my father did not like being left alone when my mother attended evening Council meetings. Consequently he pursued a maid or two and had a rather long affaire with one in particular until friends, who should have been doing something else, apprised my mother of the situation.

Ever the clever one, she arranged to come home unexpectedly, finding Daddy and the maid, Linda, together. The affair ended there and then, but for once in her life, my Victorian mother lost her rigid determination to be proper and decorous. Her shouting tirades against my father could be heard throughout the grounds of the house and beyond. Altogether shocking, since she threw in words I had never thought she would admit knowing, much less use.

My father's pecadillos in the amorous department must have disturbed my mother's complacency alarmingly. She did not surrender any of her extra curricular responsibilities, but did a tolerable reworking of her busy schedule, leaving some time to devote to my father, and her children.

As far as any of us know, Daddy's flings with housemaids during the war were his first and last, but he was prey to another type of yen beyond appreciation of bonnie lassies. In fact, Mother had the same yen but to a much lesser extent. They both loved fast horses, particularly thoroughbreds.

Mother did not attend many races, but she listened to them on the radio, watched them on television, wagering with bookies by phone. On occasion she bet a bit too much but Daddy was another matter. He knew no limits. His wagers could be shipsinkingly heavy.

My father's thoroughbred racehorses were his passion, he owned only greys, and most of them were winners at a mile and a half, though his favorite mare, Valsand, could go two miles with ease. I often accompanied him to various tracks, thus having the opportunity on several occasions to speak with one of his racing cronies, Sir Winston Churchill.

Sir Winston had a fine grey horse, Colonist II; he and Daddy freely swapped information on their horses in the saddling paddocks prior to races. Robert Morley, the British actor, especially remembered for his portrayal of The Man Who Came to Dinner, was another cohort.

Much to Mother's consternation, Daddy returned to his old habits as soon as horse racing picked up after the war. During the summertime of 1947 I often chauffeured Daddy and his friends, Frank Measures and Jack Thurlby, in our Silver Cloud Rolls Royce.

We attended all the major races, Lincoln, the Doncaster St. Ledger, Ascot Gold Vase, and Newmarket, where entries were some of the most beautiful thoroughbreds in the world.

E.D. had an excellent trainer, Percy Alden, and both were well known in the owner/trainer circle. My father received valuable tips from favorite jockeys on race day as to which horse was most likely to win, but most of the time he followed his usual system, betting on favorites, with a cover on the second favorite.

He was magnificent in his approach to gambling, master of the poker face. When he stood by the winning post, in the Members Enclosure, no one knew whether he had won or lost thousands. Heavy wins were always cause for merry celebrations in the Jockey Club lounge or in charming hotel restaurants on the way home, when he slipped a considerable number of notes into my pocket after he collected from the bookies.

Whether Daddy won or lost, the dominant subject in conversation on the way home, with the smooth humming of the Rolls accompanying our voices, always concerned the conformation and courage of the winners. He spoke, with much fervor, of the anatomical attributes of outstanding horses. From him I learned how to assess a horse by its walk and how the parts of the body must balance and fit to give the horse maximum physical supremacy in different disciplines.

I knew something was dreadfully wrong when we left at the end of the third day of the Newmarket July races. Obviously he had lost, for my pockets were empty. It must have been a bundle, for he said hardly anything on the way home. The little he did say had nothing to do with horses.

As soon as we arrived home, Daddy retired upstairs, ostensibly to change clothes. Minutes later, he summoned Mother, Andrew and me to his bathroom, always the favorite family meeting place. It was a big warm room with a green fitted carpet, a seven-foot pale blue bath, an antique inlaid satinwood Dutch armoire, and a deep, softly cushioned window seat.

Once we were gathered, Daddy sat on the edge of the bath, and sadly told us he would have to sell a few of our farms to pay off the Newmarket bookies from the three days racing. Mother was hysterical, immediately embarking on a monumental tirade, striding about the room, ending it all with, "What will everyone THINK of us!"

Daddy stared at the floor remaining coldly calm.

"I know this is a serious family problem," he said. "It requires a vote, with me abstaining of course. Our alternatives are clear. I have picked six horses I feel might win tomorrow. I can go back and wager on them, or I can stay here and sell off farms until the bookies are paid in full. So take your vote and tell me what I should do."

I was outvoted two to one. Mother and Andrew, who always sided together, felt going back would add to our predicament rather than erase it.

The following day all six of the favorites Daddy had picked came in to win at Newmarket.

As a result of Daddy's wagering, we lost six farms, about 2,000 acres, half of his life's work, during the Summer of 1948.

Chapter Four

There is a past which has gone forever,
but there is a future which is still our own.

Courageous as ever, my father quietly set about selling off farms to pay his gambling debts. I never lost admiration for his strength during this difficult time, for he was selling off the dreams he had worked towards all of his life, but knew there was no one to blame but himself. The farm he regretted losing the most was Knaptoft near Leicester, wonderful vegetable growing land, and economically close to Midland produce markets, situated right in the middle of fox hunting country. Dreams for raising his family out of the Fenlands up to the hills, away from mere cultivators of land, faded.

Neither Andrew or my mother ever ceased criticizing my father, never letting him forget he had let them down. I was so sorry for him; he had made a colossal error in judgment, and now he needed the help and encouragement of his family to help him through this difficult time. However, my mother was so beholden to the gossip mongers, constantly aware of what others would think of her and her family, she could not give to my father the support he needed. Her perfect life was falling down around her ears and everyone knew about it. My father's affairs were well known, and now disgrace was befalling the family once again. Her desire for money and status were in jeopardy and she wasn't going to let father forget he was responsible for her loss.

My brother's allegiance to my mother's position only served to alienate us further. By hurting my father, he hurt me and he knew it. Jealousy gripped his heart, for I was my father's favourite child, usurping his rightful place as the only male child. True to the rights of inheritance, Andrew would inherit my father's fortune, but I had something much more powerful, much more compelling in my possession than Andrew could ever have — the undying love and respect of my father.

After the car accident, and my slow recovery while I lived with my parents, Bobbie applied for a transfer from Malaya to his old Dorsetshire regiment, providing us with an opportunity to live together again as husband and wife. He received a posting working as Aide de Camp to Major G.G. White, as liaison with the committee running the 1948 Olympic Games in London, organizing the pentathlon. I was included in some of the preparations, for each competitor had to complete a ride over a difficult steeplechase course on horses supplied by The Games. Needless to say, the horses had been carefully chosen for their talent, but needed regular exercise and fitting for the August venue, along with consistent work over fences. I was in my glory helping with the horses, and enjoyed reacquainting myself with my husband again at the end of each day, where we lived in the Warminster Arms, a charming old hotel situated in the little town of Warminster.

England was privileged to hold the Olympic Games, and I was honoured to be involved. For participating, I received a bronze commemorative medal in recognition of my small part helping train the horses.

After the Games were over, we moved into Dorset to be near the Regiment for a short period awaiting Bobbie's entry into Sandhurst Military College, a necessity for all regular Serving Officers seeking to attain higher ranks. We created our first home there together, renting part of a house, where we entertained other officers and their families from time to time. I enjoyed this, being able to bring out some of our lovely wedding presents for the first time, making our little home warm and welcoming, and using the old Georgian silver to add an air of gracious elegance.

I did not appreciate the army tradition, however, of senior officer's wives inspecting the housekeeping of the wives of lower ranks. I outwardly rebelled to my husband, my upbringing providing me with skills and knowledge far outweighing theirs, so much so, I should have instructed them instead. Bobbie was in no position to help, except to lend a sympathetic ear, and remind me of my status as an Army wife. Frustrated, I buried my indignation, seeking solace in the fact I was supporting my husband in his quest to further his career.

I had become pregnant while Bobbie and I stayed at the Warminster arms, preparing for the Olympic Games. In celebration, Bobbie decided to take some leave, providing us with an opportunity to cement our marriage to put aside the many months of separation, and renew our commitment to each other. We chose Ireland for our second honeymoon, a country I loved because of the fond memories I had of attending the Ballsbridge Horse Sales with my father.

We flew to Dublin, rented a car to drive us into the Wicklow Mountains, and stayed at the beautiful Glendalough Hotel for two weeks. Climbing the hills each day we tired ourselves out whilst breathing the soft country air, falling in love again. Across the loch we could see a cave part way up the high rock face, and were told it was once the home of St. Kevin, the patron saint, who lived as a hermit, praying there for many years. We decided to call our first born after the saint, thus establishing Kevin, an unusual name in England at the time, for ourselves.

Upon return we moved into a tudor style home in Farnborough, close to the airport. A pretty district, with sandy hills covered in golden gorse during the spring, which made for lovely picnic spots by the many lakes nearby.

It was here, in the midst of all which was lovely, calm, and serene, I was thrown into violent spells of morning sickness. My stomach revolted at the merest whiff of fish, which I usually loved, but whose odor I could smell from a fish shop several hundred yards away. Determined to keep myself fit and healthy, I steered a power lawn mower over two acres of immaculate lawns, and taking long walks through the beautiful countryside.

My son Kevin was born on January 3rd, 1949, and after ten days I returned to the home of my parents, where I had moved temporarily, when Bobbie finished his course at Sandhurst, as the doctors at the Stamford and Rutland Infirmary knew me so well from all my various accidents. I adored my little boy, loving him with all my heart.

Bobbie, now a Major, received a dismal posting to Command the Royal Military Police in Walsall, near Birmingham. After his Far East posting, he suffered a tremendous culture shock, moving into the Black Country named for its eternal coal mines and dirty air. I know I did, away from the fresh country to which I was accustomed.

I kept busy with my young son, learning to be a good mother in this very urban area, pushing his perambulator out each afternoon to amuse him, somehow coping with the air tainted by the heavy smoke stacks all around. Our little rented house did not take much looking after, though we worked hard laying a lawn over the patch of mud in the front garden.

After a year, as dictated by the army, Bobbie was transferred, this time to Korea, where wives again could not go due, once again, to post warlike conditions. I returned to my patient parents, and of course, the horses.

My father's card playing friend, leading solicitor Dr. Jack Hunt, suggested we make a claim on the insurance from the accident. I was not at all interested as it meant further pain to the Francis family, but Dr. Hunt believed since I had not been at fault, and since I had received so many injuries, I should have some compensation. Neither Daddy nor I wanted to pursue the matter, but Dr. Hunt went ahead with the claim on my behalf anyway, and shortly thereafter I was awarded two thousand pounds for my injuries. Not much by today's standards, but in 1950 it was quite a fortune.

I decided to build myself a house, as it was becoming obvious I would never be able to rely on a permanent, settled home while I was married to a career Army Officer. I chose to stay in Bourne, close enough to my parents but far enough away to give me independence. A wonderful idea, for I would still be able to ride my horse which was kept on my father's home farm, and attend major horse shows.

I purchased half an acre on the North Road, a little over a mile from the Manor, and built a four bedroom stone mullioned house with the help of my architect friend, Parky Parkinson. I was determined to have a beautiful home, and an old carpenter employee of my father helped me dismantle a complete ballroom floor from Stretton Hall, an estate which had fallen under hard times because of the war, and was now being demolished. Smith and I struggled for days, gently pulling out long wooden dowels which pinned the eight foot lengths of oak together, sending it, along with the two inch deal floor below, to be cut and readied for The Mullions. Every floor in my house was to be of oak. My funds were short so I completed the finishing myself, making the beeswax and turpentine paste from an old recipe, and applying it on all 2,400 square feet on my hands and knees with a four inch brush, borrowing a friend's electric polisher to finish with a brilliant gloss.

Whilst the house was being finished, Kevin and I continued to live with my parents at the Manor House, where I was subjected to constant supervision from my mother. She did not trust my ability as a parent, ceaselessly giving advice on how my young son must be fed and raised. Kevin was a notoriously finicky eater, causing much consternation at meal time. He lived entirely on scrambled eggs, home made fish and chips laced with a mixture of tomato sauce and mayonnaise, bananas, and deep dish apple pie with our own Jersey cow cream. He grew well on his chosen diet, refusing anything else.

Finally, after an interminable wait, baby Kevin and I moved in together into our new home happy to be independent and away from my mother.

My days were filled, pushing Kevin in his pram down to the Manor where he was looked after by his Grandmother, whilst I rode for a couple of hours. I attempted to seed a lawn and create flower beds at the back of our home, but my father, trying to be helpful, sent one of his tractors down to plough up the area. It soon rained and the ground turned hard making it very difficult to plant anything. This was not a bad time for me, but I missed my husband. We were losing touch again, and in my case, distance does not make the heart grow fonder.

Although Brian Franks and I had agreed not to pursue our attraction for each other, the flesh is weak. After Kevin and I moved into our home, Brian and I could no longer deny we were deeply in love. The chemistry and thrill of adventure I felt when he was near was impossible to control. He called me 'Jezebel', and I suppose I earned the handle, but when the song was played, or Brian softly spoke the name, I could not hide the depth of passion I felt for him.

He wrote beautiful letters, and from the beginning he let me know we could take our feelings as far as I wanted to and no farther.

"...any time you say the word, we're back on a solid, unshakable basis of friendship until then, how grand and gay the world is...," he wrote.

Our personalities, looking for daring fun, gaiety and gentleness, melded perfectly. He was a farmer's son, and we shared much more in common than Bobbie and I.

Mothers are more aware of their children's foibles than anyone else. Mine was certainly aware of my digressions. I felt her disapproving shadow lurking everywhere, but she said nothing. My father only chuckled, for in me he saw himself. He liked Brian, and the friendship between him and Brian's father, E.J., had continued after the years they served in the Lincolnshire Yeomanry during the first World War.

Our fathers were dismayed by the way things were going for they knew nothing good could come of it, yet understanding how well suited Brian and I were, they did not interfere.

In 1951 I wrote to Bobbie asking for a divorce, a time when a divorce for a serving officer meant certain career suicide. He was doing well in the army, and sure to be promoted further as long as his private life remained in order. Through my Presentation at Court and his successful passing of the Sandhurst Military College exams, he was accepted on top diplomatic levels and a divorce would be severely detrimental to his career.

My mother and Bobbie were in close communication. She wanted the marriage to succeed, not caring what I wanted, and stubbornly insisted Bobbie not give in to me, that Brian was only a passing whim. She used Kevin as a weapon, determined to manipulate me with guilt, declaring we must stay together for his sake, if nothing else.

I continued to beg for a divorce anyway, so desperate was I, that I agreed to any conditions Bobbie set to prevent endangering his career. I admitted my affair with Brian, stating all I wanted was to live on a farm with him for the rest of my life, with Kevin and my horses. I would never join my husband in any future posting, and he could use that as grounds for desertion.

Bobbie would not agree to a divorce under any circumstances, thus beginning an agonizing period of going nowhere. Brian and I continued to see each other, hoping he would change his mind and want some happiness for himself also. I was not the dutiful army wife he needed. I did not share his dreams for the future, in a country where I did not belong. I loved my horses far too much to leave them behind, and I would not settle for a life without them, I was as stubborn about my horses as Bobbie was about the divorce.

In the meantime, life continued for myself and Kevin at the Mullions. The income I received as a Major's wife did not go far in furnishing, carpeting or curtaining our house. We still needed furniture to complete our home, so I had to find a way to earn some money. I took in a boarder, a school teacher, to help with the finances, and for whom I cooked meals. In return she kept an eye on Kevin whilst I was away in the early mornings, cultivating a patch of land where my father allowed me to harvest rhubarb. A friend of his had made a small fortune growing many acres of it and became known as the Rhubarb King; he hoped I would do the same. It was hard physical work cutting and selling the succulent pink stalks to the local green grocers, paying well but lasting just a few brief months.

My father then suggested I should go into the mushroom business by picking them from the fields on his Bourne Farm each morning. I picked five or six baskets daily, rising before dawn and bicycling two miles to the farm, and once again selling them to the local green grocers.

One morning I arrived in the fields to find not one mushroom in sight, nor were any there the following day or the next. On the fourth day I arose even earlier, made my way to the farm and discovered a poacher in the form of a brittle old man. Keeping out of sight, I learned he was stowing baskets of mushrooms in a ditch. For several days I poached on the poacher, pilfering all his mushrooms. Eventually he caught me and we called a truce. I agreed not to pick in certain fields, as did he, and we both made a little money.

The two horses Daddy had purchased at the Ballsbridge Horse Sales, Dublin, in 1947 were now ready to be broken. Lady Tartan was a black filly and Dusty Prince, a dark brown gelding standing sixteen-two hands high. Kevin showed no fear of the horses, enjoyed sitting on their backs but was not born loving them, as my father and I had been. I put him in good hands while I worked with Lady Tartan and Dusty Prince, Kevin going under the wing of one of my father's old shepherds, Mason, as they wandered along country lanes during my training sessions. I won many in-hand classes at the hunter shows with both horses, deciding to take Dusty along the road Footprints had so gallantly travelled. Many hunter championships came our way at the Country agriculture Shows, but the prize I treasured most was the Horse and Hound Perpetual Challenge Cup which we won for the Best Novice Hunter in England, at the East of England Show in Peterborough, beating many other outstanding horses from all weight categories. It was the most sought after award of the time, and I was proud to have competed against these illustrious challengers and come out a winner with my light weight horse.

Offers to purchase Dusty Prince poured in, but remembering Footprints, I would not put a price on him. He eventually became a fox hunter for Andrew, who took him hunting in Leicestershire. Andrew overrode him however, causing Dusty's legs to break down and be pinfired, a cruel and archaic remedy which could have been prevented with proper care.

Dusty Prince was never sold. He was retired to pasture and lived outdoors year round under my brother's direction, never bringing him into a stable during the bitter cold winter nights. An inhumane existence after Dusty's pampered youth.

On New Year's Day, 1953, my mother was awarded the MBE (Member of the British Empire) by Her Majesty, Queen Elizabeth II in recognition of her many years of public work. This was a banner day for my mother and we were very proud of her. I was happy for her, but discouraged regarding my own life. Bobbie continued to refuse to give me a divorce, whilst Brian's love and mine persisted.

Sometimes we knew moments of immeasurable joy by making plans to emigrate to Australia or Canada, where my parents had visited in 1950, to begin life all over again. At other times we were prey to depression, as it seemed the years were slipping by and

In Brian's jacket resting after
a game of tennis at his home
Leasingham Hall, 1948

At the Belvoir Hunt Ball
with Brian Franks, 1954

never would I be free. My mother constantly pleaded with Brians',
asking for her help in separating us. She accused Mrs. Franks of
encouraging the romance when she did nothing to stop her son,
causing severe disagreements between the two. If loving me made
Brian happy, his mother would accept it. Even my father would not
interfere, arguing incessantly with my mother over the situation,
creating an impossible atmosphere at the Manor.

Brian spent as many evenings with me as he could, as well as
managing his father's home farm, Leasingham Hall. The stress of
travelling back and forth each day and being caught up in our
impossible situation eventually took its toll. Brian contracted
pneumonia and nearly died. His doctors recommended a holiday on
the southern coast where he could breathe fresh salt air and rest in
a comfortable hotel. His mother, needing respite, took him to
Bournemouth to recuperate. While there of course, mother and son
discussed our dilemma, especially the seemingly impossibility of my
divorce. Brian's youth was being wasted and his future threatened,
as a result of our pathetic situation.

When Brian returned fully recuperated in October, our love
resumed but with a difference. The light at the end of the tunnel was
no longer there. My dependence on him as lover and friend

intensified. I was afraid Bobbie would never let me go, realizing Brian had to leave me, if he was to have any sort of life at all. He knew that too, and one day he made the heartbreaking decision to begin a new life in Canada without me. My desperation was exhausting, unable to beg him to stay for I loved him too much to deny him some happiness.

How lonely were our hearts. Mine left behind, his travelling from the eastern to western Canadian coast, working on farmsteads. We had agreed to cease all contact, including letters, and we fulfilled our promise. I did not see Brian again for many years, and by the time I was finally granted my divorce, he had married someone else. And I, so anxious to find happiness after my many years of marriage to a man I did not really love, was swept headlong into a current of circumstances, that had I been able to see into my future, I would surely have stopped dead in my tracks.

Looking back on this time in retrospect, forty years later, I am reminded of a passage from "Illusions" by Richard Bach. It brings me comfort when I think of all Brian and I shared, our hopes and dreams of a brilliant future together unfulfilled, and the distance which still separates us.

> *Don't be afraid of goodbyes*
> *A farewell is necessary before you can meet again*
> *And meeting again, after moments or lifetimes,*
> *Is certain for those who are friends.*

In December I received an invitation to visit Ireland. Barbara Pym, the model who helped me with my trousseau, had married a jovial Irishman, Barney McNamee. They lived at Ennis near Limerick. The McNamees invited Kevin and I for an extended visit, beginning with the Christmas holidays, extending through Easter. Their invitation was a lifesaver, as I could no longer tolerate living in limbo in Bourne.

Knowing I needed to keep busy, Barbara told many hunt people of my anticipated arrival and my abilities as a successful rider, volunteering my skills to ride and hunt their young horses. In true Irish fashion, I was generously offered a three year old gelding to school, who did not know much but had a heart of gold. On our first meet together, I eyed his unclipped body, not used to mounts being turned out so casually. I rubbed his neck, quickly making friends, expecting to have a quiet ride. We soon found a fox and moved off in a sharp canter towards a stone wall, something I had never jumped before, but presumed my horse would go along with the others. I steered towards a lower section of wall, not wanting to overface this young horse and risk frightening him. It was a mistake, for initially we could not get a clear take off with large fallen stones confronting us. My horse dropped to a trot, skipping through the grey confusion before pouncing up in the air over the three foot area of wall I had chosen. As we soared, the saddle flipped up, hitting me hard in the lower back, and I tumbled ignominiously to the ground midst toppled stones on the far side. Little did I know, I had been riding on a broken treed saddle. I was certainly put in my place, the fancy rider falling at the first wall! The Irish though thought nothing of it, a kind man catching my horse. I remounted and carried on, knowing to sit differently as the other walls came along.

I had received my christening, perhaps it was intentional, we will never know, but after that I had wonderful rides across country.

I continued my Christmas through Easter visits with the McNamees until Bobbie finally agreed to a divorce in December 1956.

Time spent in England continued to be painful. After Brian left England, I wanted to date again, but my mother was vehemently opposed. I might be separated, but I was still married, and until I was divorced, dating was out of the question. Visits to the Manor became unbearable due to my Mother's scolding. She criticized everything I did. Nothing made her happy, either I was not gardening enough, or I was not doing it correctly. Why did I think I had built my house in the first place if it was only to keep me from my husband, she wanted to know, and so on.

My father found himself between two women, one his wife, the other his daughter. It was a no-win situation. He refused to take sides openly, but often came alone to visit me at The Mullions. How dear he was.

The passing of time did not erase Brian from my heart but dulled the pain of losing him. Regardless of Mother's thoughts on the subject, I began dating casually before my divorce was final, but my happiest times were spent with Andrew and my cousin, Paul Tointon.

In May of 1955 we were invited to a wedding at nearby Market Deeping. Two wealthy young people were united, Captain Tim Tinsley, my Home Guard Adjutant, and Joy Koninenberg, a wealthy bulb grower's daughter from Spalding. It was a splendid occasion with much champagne and banquet fare. I had purchased a new dress, cherry pink and white taffeta with a tight bodice and wide, flaring skirt, and was feeling cheekier than I had in years. I was twenty-nine.

After the bride and groom left for their honeymoon, a few of us visited a nearby country club. Being quite small, I like to sit on a high bar stool whenever possible. I managed to sequester one that evening against a wall I could lean against. We ordered a round of drinks, and Paul, ever the wit with a sense of the ridiculous, kept us laughing with his anecdotes.

At the far end of the bar I noticed a young man sitting alone. He was clean-cut, goodlooking and well dressed. I saw him ask the club manageress for the visitor's book. He wrote in it, asked her a question, and returned the book to her. Gesturing in our direction, he spoke again to her, she nodded, and they came toward our party where he was introduced all around. It was not long before he stood beside me, and I found him most charming, showing a great deal of interest in me. In fact, within the next twenty minutes, he asked if he could take me to dinner the following evening. My brother, Andrew, overhearing the request, was immediately concerned and attempted to warn me against this person, six years my junior. His reputation as a wild car driver and an eccentric, was not what he had in mind for his only sister.

And so John Richardson entered my life. Months later on a visit to the club, I asked the owner to show me the book in which he had written. He had scribbled a few lines saying "I, John Richardson, am going to marry...", after which he had added my name and dated it. I was flattered by his certainty.

All the same, a foreboding swept over me. Words of my father flashed into my mind "She has always been brilliant when choosing horses, but a total disaster when it comes to husbands". Little did I know, I was about to prove him right once again.

John, was a determined suitor. He knew I was not yet divorced, but it did not matter. He lived on a large farm in Deeping St. Nicholas, eleven miles away. His mother, Frances, had been a hectic socializer in her younger married days, spending extravagantly on dinner parties and clothes. Her husband, Tom, was a strange man, destroying the stone stork in front of their house when John was born. He was disappointed a girl was not added to the family following their first born child, Michael. In spite of two sons, or perhaps because of, the marriage was a disaster. Frances was a severe manic depressive, committing suicide by jumping from the top floor of their three-storey home, to the terrace below.

Michael and John were both sent to expensive boarding schools. Michael, grieving for his mother, his personality anything but predictable, was expelled from several institutions. John, a brilliant individual, completed requirements for graduation from the renowned boys' school, Repton, at the young age of thirteen, sixteen being the average.

John had to be at least sixteen before entering university, but when the time came for him to enroll, his reclusive father refused him further education, putting John to work on the farm, laying to rest John's dreams for becoming a lawyer or politician.

Frances Richardson left an inheritance for both her sons. Michael purchased a farm, and John purchased a few acres of greenhouses, close to his father's main farm. Not much time passed before the little nursery produced fine tomatoes, lettuce and luxury vegetables. John bought a lorry, and each night drove his produce either to Covent Garden Wholesale Market in London or Birmingham. He enjoyed good profits, turning them back into his business, adding forced tulips and daffodils for the luxury market trade.

He sold the small nursery to his father, who owned an adjoining farm, and purchased a larger one, with three acres of greenhouses. His flower business was extremely lucrative, as John made every effort possible to learn the business from the successful Dutch peers of his trade.

When John met me he was riding on the crest of his success, no longer subjugated to his father's domination, and no longer regretful he had been denied a university education. He needed someone to share his success, and he knew my family was reasonably affluent and respected.

Andrew and Paul were increasingly worried by John's courting. They told me alarming stories about his family's mental health problems and his wild reputation. He had once boasted publicly his ambition to make love to women from every nation in the world.

"You've gone through one unhappy marriage," Paul told me. "Get your life in order. Marry a wealthy farmer, or Master of Foxhounds, who can support you and your horses."

Foolishly I ignored the good advice. Nothing Paul, Andrew or anyone else said, mattered to me. I paid no attention. John was a gentleman at all times with me, never trying to stay when he took me home after a date, never trying to press me, always trying to please. To celebrate my thirtieth birthday, October 5th, he took me to the Savoy Hotel in London. He was well known in the Grill, where we were given a table close to Sir Winston Churchills' and other well known personages. I fully enjoyed the celebrity status.

After dinner, John suggested we go for a walk in the theatre district. When we passed by the Cafe de Paris we paused to see who was performing that night. John knew of course. He had planned all of it. The star that night was Marlene Deitrich, my favorite actress.

Although all tables were taken, John passed a few bills to the maitre d', and we were led to a stage-side table. The room was crowded, and one could feel the expectancy in the silence. Deitrich would soon appear. The stage was not large. Rising from its center was a curving staircase with a landing above, edged by a delicate balustrade. The lights dimmed, a spotlight focused at the top of the stairs, and my idol appeared in a flesh-coloured chiffon dress with sequins spiralling across her breast and descending to her pelvis. What a consummate actress! So beautiful, with blond hair and still a gorgeous figure. Applause burst forth with men of all ages seduced by her movements when she came down the stairs to a standing ovation.

Her first song was "Lily Marlene", rendered in her world-famous husky tones "Underneath the lamp post by the garden gate, Darling I remember the way you used to wait."

I was elated by her performance and could not believe John when he suggested we visit her in her dressing room.

"We haven't a chance of getting in!" I said.

"Oh, yes we do," he smiled.

Indeed, we were taken backstage and asked to wait briefly, as she already had visitors. Moments later Lord and Lady Louis Mountbatten left her dressing room, and we were ushered in. I had thought awe would render me voiceless. but Deitrich was so charming I was soon chatting easily. We even talked about cooking, and she told me how she put walnut-size knobs of cheddar cheese in her scrambled eggs just before removing them from the pan.

My thirtieth birthday was a memorable one, entranced I was, by the treats John was bringing my way. He was interested in politics, especially in representing the Conservative Party. Thoughts of what his future might be intrigued me.

John was anxious to be accepted by influential people who could help further his aspirations. Through his Covent Garden connections, he became friendly with an older man, Jack Goodchild, who owned the largest Stand in the Market. He frequently took John to the Savoy Hotel for lunches, introducing him to extravagant living.

He also introduced him to society charities, which entailed John donating enough fresh flowers for decorating the fronts of Royal boxes at theatre Openings. These occasions were attended by various members of the Royal Family with the proceeds of the evening going to a major charity. John was more generous than he could afford, but he was appreciated and soon invited to many of the evenings too. As his social partner, my mantlepiece seldom had less than a dozen gold engraved invitation cards. He often generously purchased a new gown for me while in London so I had something spectacular to wear to our outings. I met many fascinating people, loving the new experience for a time. The excitement eventually wore off and I became bored with the London people who seldom had anything to talk about in which I was interested. My country lifestyle did not appeal to them either — just like Felixstowe.

Meanwhile, John was making an effort to become important in Kevin's life. He was a bright little boy, who did not seem to care for John monopolizing my time and attempting to become a father figure. He took him for high speed rides in his Daimler sports car on the landing strips of local aerodromes, probably scaring the daylights out of him, but certainly horrifying my mother who thought John wild and totally unsuitable. I was nervous, afraid for my son's safety. I tried to recognize the attempts John made to bond with my young son.

In the late spring of 1955 we flew over to Amsterdam for a day to view the tulip and daffodil fields. Three major growers competed for our business, sumptuously entertaining us. We were shown new exotic varieties in the knowledge they would later be sold into the lucrative British markets. Other growers too in England were searching for special bulbs in the highly competitive market. John purchased several million bulbs, mostly through a mortgage type of arrangement, where they would be paid for after their sale. I was honoured by a new variety named after me — Joykins.

John was very excited with both the quality and quantity. They had been sterilized before leaving Holland, and once home, were planted in six inch deep boxes of soil, temporarily dug into rows out in the fields. This was to thoroughly chill the bulbs down through the frosts. After two months they were lifted into the hot greenhouses. John was able to force the flowers ready for specific dates throughout December, specifically the Christmas trade.

You should never count your chickens before they are hatched.

We envisioned a fortune. The bulbs produced very special blooms, being highly sought after in the Mayfair London district.

Jack Goodchild claimed huge quantities for his Covent Garden Market stands, as did others in Bristol and Birmingham.

The flowers were carefully packed in bunches of a dozen, wrapped in tissue paper, laid in strong cardboard boxes for the journey. Tragically, unusually hot weather defeated John. There were no refrigerated trucks, temperatures rising to nearly 70 degrees, causing the flowers to wilt. Arriving at their destinations, they resembled floppy poppies. Some were sold for today's equivalent of 20 cents a dozen, with many being given away, when they ought to have fetched $40.00 wholesale.

John was financially ruined, yet he still had the Dutch growers to pay. Far from producing the finest flowers in the trade that year, he had nothing.

In desperation John made many fruitless errands to banks, also trying through his various charity connections to find private financiers, to no avail. He talked with his father, but he was unwilling to sell one of his farms to meet John's debt. He begged the Dutch growers for more time, but they wanted their money.

As the months passed, pressures to make payments on his debts increased. He kept a few workmen to grow tomatoes, his business just barely limping along. The few pounds he was able to raise was merely a drop in a very large ocean, but enough to keep his creditors quiet, at least for awhile.

My cousin Paul's girlfriend, Margaret Emerson, was an outstanding tennis player, winning many major tournaments including Junior Wimbledon. I also played well, having represented Lincolnshire County several times, along with winning numerous doubles tournaments and playing First Couple for the Bourne Tennis Club. So when Margaret was invited to play in the European Winter Championships at the Imperial Hotel in Torquay in Devonshire, she asked me to be her doubles partner. We planned to drive down, share a room, and devote all our mental energy to preparing for the matches.

"Nonsense," John declared. "I'll drive you there and stay over in case you or Margaret need me."

I found his thoughtfulness endearing. Margaret, though not ecstatic, did not object to the change in plans. Our drive to Torquay was pleasant, and we were delighted by the picturesque Imperial Hotel situated on a cliff overlooking the English Channel, its acres of gardens dominated by blue and pink hydrangeas in the summer, now presenting huge green leaved rhododenrons waiting for the spring warmth to flower. The hotel's architecture and elegant furnishings reflected a soothing combination of the Victorian and Edwardian eras, with tables in the spacious dining room adorned in white linen, heavy silver, and fragile crystal.

Autumn is unpredictable in England, and 1955 was no exception. Tumultuous thunderstorms struck and whirled incessantly, rain whipping through leaks in the arena roof, soaking the three indoor courts. Between rains we practiced on the hard outdoor courts.

Despite the espri de corps of the maintenance crew, only two courts could be transformed into suitable playing areas, forcing tournament management to revise the schedule and extend playing through the night.

Margaret and I were informed our first doubles match would be played around 2 a.m. In anticipation we went to bed early. Our wake-up call came at one when we were told to appear on court in forty minutes.

The rain continued. We were buffeted about by the strong sea winds, but we were swift runners and knew we could make the dash from hotel to courts pavilion without too much harm from the cold and wet.

When we arrived in the lobby, John was waiting for me looking distraught. Saying he had to speak with me immediately, he grabbed my arm, led me out of the hotel and continued across the sodden lawn toward the cliff edge, with the sting of the hard rain painful on my bare legs. My clothes and hair were quickly soaked along the way. He ignored my entreaties to stop.

Near the cliff edge John shouted at me, telling how much he loved me, how he did not trust my being around other men, and how he felt he had to protect me from them.

"You're making no sense!" I shouted.

"If you leave me I'll jump off the cliff!" he shouted back.

"Then do it!" I shouted, knowing he did not have the guts.

I broke away and ran to the courts to join a desperate Margaret. We were due to play in two minutes, there being no time even for a towel rubdown. I tossed back my hair, claimed my racquet and sprinted onto the court. Glancing toward the bleachers, I was not surprised to see John among the spectators.

We were allowed a few minutes for warming up, and after winning the toss I went down to the net whilst Margaret served. Her first ball was an ace. I trotted to the other side of the court, and after another serve from Margaret, our opponents drove the ball above my head. I leaped to return it at a sharp cross court angle, but upon landing my leg gave way, and I fell.

I tore a ligament in my thigh due to exposure on the cold clifftop during those anguished moments with John. We finished the match but were soundly beaten, as of course, the opposition played the majority of their balls at me. I was so terribly sorry for letting Margaret down and furious at John for having caused the ruckus.

John was not in the viewing bleachers at the end of the game and did not contact me during the remainder of the night nor the next morning. The clerk on duty said his door was locked, and he was presumed to be sleeping.

Margaret fared well in singles, and I remained close by to cheer her on. At the end of the afternoon we had a lull and several of us settled in the comfortable lounge for tea and cakes. We had not been there long when a tall, refined man stopped beside our table and asked if he could speak privately with me.

We walked away from the others, and the man said, "My dear, I have been watching you with that young man of yours and feel something is dreadfully wrong. I head a psychiatric clinic here in Torquay and wonder if I may be of help?"

He asked where John was and suggested we call his room. We did, receiving no answer and he asked the manager to let us in.

We found him lying in bed in the fetal position, facing the wall. John would not acknowledge our presence. The psychiatrist said he was in a catatonic coma and suggested the manager and I leave. After only a short while, the doctor came out and told me John should be committed to a clinic at once. Giving permission was clearly John's father's prerogative, not mine. We called Tom Richardson in Lincolnshire, he gave his immediate consent, and I signed the necessary papers.

John was taken by ambulance to the clinic. During the rest of the tournament I divided my time between sessions with a physiotherapist and encouraging Margaret during her advance in the singles competition. She played well, but the stress resulting from John's histrionics denied her advancement to the finals.

While we were watching a final I was called to the phone and heard John's wild, hysterical voice.

"They're sticking needles into me all the time, they're killing me! All I need is you! Forgive me, I love you, I need you desperately, come and get me out of here!"

I spoke with the psychiatrist.

"If you want to take John away, I can't stop you," he said. "But he is a greatly disturbed paranoid schizophrenic and will become far worse without treatment. Do not marry him whatever you do."

"All I need is you," John said calmly. "Don't desert me now."

I took John out of the clinic, and we drove back to Lincolnshire disconsolantly. His father said he was not equipped to care for him at home and asked me to keep him at The Mullions. I took him home, not knowing what else to do. John slept solidly for nearly a week, while I ensured he took the medication my physician had prescribed, after consulting with the psychiatrist in Torquay.

Upon awakening, he was greatly improved, apologizing for the trouble he had caused. He returned to his father's home and to his business, giving no hint of further mental instability. We continued to date, I lulled into safety, believing this was a singular occurrence caused by his business troubles.

My lawyers had advised divorce proceedings between Bobbie and I would be heard in the Gloucester Courts in early November. The five long years were nearly over. thankfully Bobbie had found a new love, a Women's Voluntary Service officer also stationed with the army in Korea, and whom he wanted to marry.

Oh, how I longed for Brian! What a cruel trick of fate was befalling us. Just as I was becoming free, Brian was coming home to England with his new wife, to aid his ailing father in the management of the home farms. I kept very much out of the way.

John was still determined to marry me. He took out a marriage license in Spalding, the town nearest his home, one in Bourne and another at Caxton Hall in London, making sure all bases were covered when my Decree Absolute came through.

My decision to marry John greatly disturbed my family. Andrew and Paul begged me to abandon him. My mother said my life was already ruined because I was a divorced woman, but marrying into the unstable Richardson family was totally unacceptable. My father was concerned, not only because of John's mental state, but also because he was six years younger than I. Daddy would have preferred my marrying one of the older men who had squired me around, but the last thing I wanted, I thought, was to be "an old man's darling." I was wrong. I did not know I was to become a "young man's slave."

John's brother tried to convince John I did not really love him and would leave if bad times came along. Wherever I looked, people were concerned and saying so, but I listened to no one. I had made mistakes with Bobbie, and lost Brian, and it was time to prove my worth. Standing by John, who loved me so much, and making our marriage work, seemed the only way.

My parents spent the Christmas Holidays in a luxury hotel in Bournemouth taking Kevin with them. They wanted nothing to do with my involvement with John. The Decree Absolute was held up in the Christmas mail, John rang several times a day to see if it had arrived. I could not help but be flattered by his persistence, but was unable to show any enthusiasm or excitement. John was in love with me, but once again, I was not in love with the man I was going to marry.

On the morning of December 28th, 1956, a Monday, I was hanging out my weekly wash on an icy clothes line, when the mailman arrived with the awaited document. John phoned shortly after, insisting he wanted the wedding performed immediately. My friend, Ann Measures, agreed to be our witness, arriving at my house within the hour. John called the Registrar at the Council Offices in Bourne and made arrangements for an immediate ceremony.

I dressed in a lovely brown wool suit, while Ann and John arrived almost at the same time, and we squeezed into his red Daimler sports car, and drove to the Bourne Kesteven Council Offices. The ceremony was quick, and afterward we drove to Ann's farm three miles away where her mother had spruced up their white show cob, Joseph, for the official wedding photograph.

I found I could not stop laughing, whether from happiness or hysteria, I'm not sure.

"Hey," John murmured, smiling softly, "It's a sin to be so happy."

"I want so much to be happy" I laughed, "and I'm so glad you chose Ireland for our honeymoon, I have so many friends there."

"We do not need friends," he said "all we need is each other." Already his insecurity was showing had I but recognized it.

I told the McNamees we would be staying at the Royal Cruises Hotel in Limerick and knew they would have a party going by the time we flew in. I also hoped John would change his mind about needing no one but each other, once he met my lively, funloving Irish friends.

The Royal Cruises had been used during the war by airlines to house pilots and their crews, when they put into nearby Shannon Airport after flights from Canada and the United States, with insufficient fuel to carry on to England. It was customary to put the

Wedding photograph with John Richardson
on Kathleen Measures' show cob Joseph, December 28th, 1956.

crew in one huge room in which there were three double beds and two single, with an adjoining bathroom.

We were given one of those large rooms still equipped with all of the beds, so of course my Irish friends were ready with quips about them when we arrived. They had arranged a champagne buffet and the party was in full swing.

John was rude to my friends and within an hour suggested they leave. I was mortified. He looked drawn and haggard and had lost so much weight his clothes hung from his frame. I accepted his excuse when he said he had worked extremely hard, and was overexcited about our sharing a life together.

"Sorry," he said after they had gone, " but all I want is you."

I believed him, but when I cuddled up to him once we were in bed, he rolled away and moved to another bed. Thinking it a game, I followed. The same thing happened.

Hurt by his rejection, I moved to still another bed, huddled under the covers turning away from my new husband.

"I am sorry," he said, but you must know my business isn't in the best shape these days. I have a great deal on my mind."

During the rest of the honeymoon we did not make love at all. It did not bother me too much as I knew many men were impotent when under stress. Our marriage would begin when John's finances were in order. In the meantime, I would be patient and understanding.

The only bright note of the whole honeymoon spent alone with my husband, came on the day we visited Blarney Castle. We climbed the ancient walls, then fell prey to peals of laughter when our guide lowered me down over the high doorway by my ankles, to kiss the venerable Blarney Stone, giving me the gift of the gab. The stone was cold.

We cut the honeymoon short, and on arriving home found John's financial situation was indeed dreadful. The problems which had been building for a year, resurfaced worse than ever.

"I've been threatened with physical injury if I don't pay," he told me, "I could get out of this if you showed your wifely support and mortgaged The Mullions."

I arranged the mortgage for a considerable sum of cash through my bank, not daring to tell my parents. It staved off the growers for a little while, but I eventually learned John was in serious debt far beyond just this one venture. When he was almost bankrupt, the situation could no longer be kept secret from my family and friends.

John's nerves were gone, and he was demanding of little Kevin, expecting him to sit motionless in the living room with us, making no noise even in his playroom, and never questioning any of John's orders. My parents knew of our troubles, and one night after I had caught John spanking Kevin, we were invited to dinner at the George Hotel in Stamford. I was miserably unhappy, and during the evening, Daddy and I had an opportunity for a few private words. He recognized my unhappiness, reminding me about my disastrous ability to choose the wrong husbands, but the right horses.

The dinner with my parents that night changed our lives, for during the evening I picked up a copy of the Stamford Mercury weekly newspaper, though I did not read it until the following afternoon when John and I were having tea. An advertisement immediately caught my eye: "Emigrate to Canada".

Canada! I thought. Begin a new life in Canada!

"Don't be ridiculous," John said, when I mentioned the idea, "If we went anywhere it would be to Africa."

"Wonderful," I said. "Directly into the midst of all the Kiu Kiu tribe hostilities!"

John stared at the fire saying nothing.

The next afternoon he begrudgingly drove with me the ten miles to Stamford for an appointment with a Mr. McPherson, who had placed the ad. It was a most exciting visit. We learned the Canadian Government was subsidizing emigrants. We could fly to the west coast for only 90 pounds each where opportunities abounded. John could get a job managing personnel in a lumber company. I could handle any available secretarial job. Mr. McPherson suggested we go to Edmonton in Alberta, but we decided on Vancouver, British Columbia. It was not too developed, yet had great potential as a seaport. The selling points for me were mild winters and year round weather much warmer than in England.

I wanted sunshine! I needed sunshine!

"We'll think about it," John said.

"We're going," I said. John glanced at me sharply, hesitated, then quite calmly agreed. "All right."

We made arrangements to fly to Vancouver within three weeks, first going to London for the emigration process at the Canadian Consulate in Green Park. We lined up at 3 a.m. with thousands of others leaving England, six deep around three blocks adjoining Grosvenor Square.

Such would be our future then. A new start in a young, invigorating country! Even John was cheered by the thought.

When I told my parents we were going to Canada they assumed we were off for a holiday. The look on Daddy's face was tragic when he learned we were emigrating. His wayward daughter, so impetuous and prone to mistakes, was going to the other side of the world. Even Mother was saddened at the thought of the distance involved, but after a short time, they put on a brave face and concluded the decision was very practical.

I spoke with a local auctioneer and made arrangements to sell my house, all of my antiques, Georgian silver, glassware, paintings and jewelry. I was heartbroken to sell my things, but when it was over, I had enough money to pay off the mortgage I had arranged for John, and to keep Kevin in good schools until he was ready for university. I agreed for him to stay with my parents until John and I were settled, hopefully within a few months.

All my possessions, except a few family treasures and personal belongings, were sold within two days at the private auction. My father's carpenter made a wooden crate, three feet square. Everything we intended taking with us to Canada was packed in that small space. It was shipped to Vancouver in care of the Canadian Imperial Bank of Commerce, the institution our bank in England had suggested we use.

John had not gone bankrupt, but barely escaped. After selling his nursery he was able to pay off the Dutch growers, but there was less than 300 pounds left in his name.

John's doubtful and despondent mood changed remarkably once the crate had gone. Only then did he realize we were indeed embarking on a new life and new opportunities. The brightness that had been in his eyes when we first met returned, along with the debonair bravado and confidence I had found so intriguing.

Facing a monumental pilgrimage together brought us closer than we had ever been, a closeness more akin to comradeship than conjugal love. We had made love only a few times during our marriage.

The excitement of adventure took over, but leaving my young son behind, however, saddened me. Just before our final goodbyes to the family, my father gave me a cheque for 240 pounds. "For your one way return to us without John, should you ever need it," was all he said.

Chapter Five

Philippians 3 verse 13:
"This one thing I do, forgetting those things which are behind,
and reaching forth unto those things which are before."

We left England May 12, 1957, I chose to wear my designer grey corded silk coat with a flowered hat, and John wore a tailor made suit. We were going to go off into the unknown looking confident if nothing else. Not even the sadness involved in saying goodbye to Kevin and my parents could dispel our anticipation. I felt strangely excited as we boarded the Flying Tigers aircraft, a propeller plane scheduled to deposit us in Vancouver twenty-nine hours later.

Most of the other passengers were Hungarians, carrying brown paper bags with meagre personal belongings acquired through English charities. They had fled the horrific uprisings in their country and were still dazed by their escapes. They knew not what awaited them in Canada and did not care. Any fate was better than what they had left behind. I felt the same way until we stopped in Labrador, a barren wasteland, hundreds of miles from civilization. What have I done! Where are we going! shall we find bears and moose walking down Vancouver's streets?

Nor was I heartened by a stopover in Winnipeg, Manitoba, May 13th. We landed in the midst of a heat wave. I had wanted warmth and sunshine but not the kind powerful enough to sear one's eyes and cheeks. We lined up for the Immigration process, having our papers stamped, receiving a few welcoming words. We knew then how the others had felt fleeing their country.

Most of the Hungarians left the plane in Winnipeg. Passengers were down by two thirds when we resumed the flight, allowing us to stretch out. Flying over the Canadian Prairies, seeing the lonely homesteads below, with vast sections of growing grain on an eternal vast plain, was somewhat daunting.

Soon we were over the Province of Alberta and into the foothills of the Rocky Mountains, majestic portals to the Pacific Ocean that lay beyond the desert, orchards and farmlands of British Columbia. This huge country now below seemed to welcome us with open arms through the sunshine. We were tired, needing encouragement, and the pilot supplied it by pointing out especially high mountains, giving their names and altitudes suggesting we look out to the right or left windows. I remember wondering if the plane would topple over if we all went to one side, a ridiculous notion, but we were very tired.

As we flew beyond the Rockies we were greeted by the brilliant glint of the blue Pacific and could see long flatlands fed by the Fraser River winding its way through a fertile delta at the end of which nestled the airport. The backdrop of snow capped coastal mountains, we were eventually to know so well, was calm and reassuring.

Upon leaving the plane we were met by a kindly group waiting to lend support for the immigrants, most of whom were shabbily dressed, still carrying their life's possessions in paper parcels. Interpreters greeted the Hungarians with buses to take them to overnight hostels.

We were strangely unafraid. We had hit bottom, this was our chance to prove to the world we would survive. The raw deals dealt out were behind us. A new beginning lay ahead in a noble country where so many before us had undergone great privations, if necessary, so would we. The thought never occurred for failure, we now had to take on the future with both arms wide open, to tackle the unknown. This round had to be won on our own, there was no other way. The adventure had begun.

Our money, was so limited, and we knew no one for help or advice. Welfare was not established, but even had it been we would never draw from it. Come what may we intended to find jobs the following day, and become a part of this great country.

John and I had not told our parents how really destitute we were. We arrived in Vancouver with only $170.00 between us and the world. John was exhausted, so we splurged on a $12.00 taxi ride into Vancouver, asking the driver to take us to a comfortable, but inexpensive downtown hotel.

We drove along Granville Street, which was just what John and I needed to bolster our confidence. The sun was shining in a brilliantly blue and cloudless sky. The gardens we passed were abloom with varicoloured azaleas and flowering rhododendrons. Handsome homes, brightly painted and well kept, distantly backdropped by the majestic snow capped Seymour and Grouse Mountains. "We may have come home forever," John said.

"I know we have, this is for us," I agreed.

We signed into the Abbotsford Hotel, unpacked our few night

things whilst John put our shoes out in the hallway for polishing. Exhausted, we fell into bed for a long sleep. Upon awakening the next morning and checking our monies, left after the taxi ride and hotel room, we knew we had to take instant steps finding jobs, but found we would have to make them without polished shoes. No one had touched them during the night. Neither of us said anything but we were surprised. We later found shoes were not cleaned without request in Canada, and we were indeed lucky, as they could have been stolen by anyone passing by; we would have been a bright pair job seeking without shoes.

Walking down nearby Hastings Street we found a coffee shop, ordering just toast and coffee for our breakfast, then purchased The Province newspaper to study the want ads. We circled the positions we felt capable of filling, asked our waitress for directions, then separated and set out to conquer Canada in our own ways.

The first two secretarial jobs I went after were to prove a rude awakening. At least a dozen women were interviewed before me, with the positions taken before my turn came. There had to be a better way. At the next office, and final chance, I took time in the entry hall checking the directory on the wall, noting the manager of the firm to which I was applying, Trader's Finance, was Mr. Norman Rubenstein.

This time I had another plan! Walking smartly into the offices I told the receptionist I had an appointment with Mr. Rubenstein at eleven forty-five, three minutes away.

"I don't seem to have you listed," she said, after checking a full appointment book.

"Slip-ups can happen," I smiled. "Nevertheless I should like to see him as arranged."

At that moment a girl being interviewed for the job walked out of the office, I slipped in smiling confidently.

I claimed the position as Mr. Rubenstein's personal secretary. He later told me he was aware of my bluff regarding the appointment, but forgave it because of my confidence, and superior qualifications. He could tell I intended to stay in Vancouver. The British, I was to learn, were bad news in Canada in those days. Most were transitory, en route to Australia, stopping in Vancouver only long enough to earn money for purchase of a plane ticket to Down Under.

Although I possessed secretarial skills to the level of a Cabinet Minister's Private Secretary, they were quite outdated. I had never used an electric typewriter and was not familiar with transcribing dictation from dictabelts instead of using shorthand or speed typing. Luckily one of the other secretaries was a kind soul who put me through a crash course on fundamentals, tactfully interrupting the lessons each time Mr. Rubenstein appeared.

I was proud of myself when I returned to the hotel that evening, but John's explorations had been fruitless. I shelved my own pride and happiness lest they add to his misery. The agencies he had visited were not at all impressed by another well dressed ex-Englishman. He had tried explaining he was eminently qualified to control a personnel staff of over a hundred if necessary, that he was an expert in horticulture and farming and was therefore worthy of a top paying job. They laughed at him, what knowledge had he to give to Canadian employers?

"Maybe you should try it my way," I suggested. "Don't attempt to start at the top of the ladder, go to the bottom rung if you have to. It would only be temporary. We have such a great deal to learn here."

He groaned but admitted I might be right.

Our financial situation was certainly grim. We had only a few dollars left and would have no more until I received my first paycheck. We had been told cheap but clean motels were available on Vancouver's north shore. We found one, The Capilano, and moved in that evening riding over the magnificent Lion's Gate Bridge by bus.

One of John's interviews had been with a major lumber firm, MacMillan, and Bloedel. He returned the next day saying he would be interested in any job of any kind. The personnel manager said none were available, but as John was leaving, he was stopped by a man who gave him a business card.

"I saw you in here yesterday," he said, "so I know you really want a job. I'm the manager of the Plywood Section; we're over on East Marine Drive. The address in on the card. Get over there as quickly as you can. I'm sure something can be found."

Elated, John set out, not daring to spend even bus fare, considering our finances. Five hours later, with the soles of his good shoes worn through, he limped into the MacBlo offices on Vancouver's East Marine Drive, eighteen miles away.

The manager he had met in the morning, barely acknowledged him.

"If it took you this long to get here, we're not interested," he said.

"You did not tell me it was so far to walk," John said.

"Walked!" The man looked sharply at John. "Eighteen miles...?"

John nodded, and was immediately hired. On learning the name of our motel in North Vancouver, the new friend said he passed by there on his way to work and would give John a lift until he had transportation of his own.

So we were off.

My once elegant husband was issued a yellow hard hat and reinforced boots with strong steel toes, which soon produced evil blisters, but John persevered. His job was to machine-cut knots out of plywood sheets and glue other pieces in. Within three weeks he had received three small raises.

My own job proved depressing. Trader's Finance was a collection agency, and a major portion of my work was sending out threatening letters and making phone calls to people all over British Columbia who were not keeping up with their car payments.

I suppose remembering the way John had been hounded for money made me particularly sympathetic to the imploring explanations I received by phone and by letter. The excuses always seemed real. I hated ignoring them and continuing to press for payment, but that was my job.

On the brighter side, I enjoyed learning the Indian names of the towns in the province with their strange spellings, such as Chilliwack, Nanaimo, Tswwassen, and Saanich.

Also residing at the Capilano Motel were six other English couples, all professionals with impressive degrees. None had a job, all were holding out for prestigious positions. John and I were somewhat scorned for having gone the menial route. I recall getting off the bus on hot afternoons to see the couples, in lounge chairs on the dusty lawn, eating cucumber sandwiches and strawberries. They simply could not give up their old English ways.

I would say "hello", receive a few cool nods in return, and scurry into our little home to prepare an evening meal. For a long while we lived on tea, cornflakes, brown bread, lettuce and for an occasional treat, a tin of sardines. John and I were determined to save every possible cent toward making a down payment on a home, for we soon realized renting did nothing for our hoped for Canadian equity.

Our first paycheques were cause for celebration. Those little pieces of paper in our hands proved we had weathered the first steps toward a new start in life. Certainly we had touched bottom. We had learned that bottom is where one must go before truly appreciating and understanding what life is all about.

We were invigorated by the newness and energy surrounding us everywhere, skyscrapers on the way to completion, new highways, hard workers, the sparkle in people's eyes, cheery faces everywhere, always very polite. Conservative Prime Minister John Diefenbaker, with his "follow John" campaign footsteps all over the pavements in white paint, intrigued us. My first paycheque was $100 for two weeks work. John was working for $1.68 per hour and brought home about the same amount. In our eyes our combined wages added up to a fortune. We paid only $29 a week to the motel, but we disliked its atmosphere and found furnished accommodation in a beautiful old home on south Granville Street in Vancouver, for $90 per month. When John and I moved in, it had been divided into ten efficiency apartments. Ours was once an oaklined study with a fold-up bed in the wall. I used to smile pulling it down each night. What if it sprang back, trapping us inside, with no one to know to come looking for us?

Unfortunately we had to share a tiny kitchen and bath with other tenants, but at least we were in a fine old house, away from the boom-town atmosphere of the more unseasoned but highly populated motels on the north side. Sharing those rooms with strangers is nearly at the bottom too!

We were three miles from my office, so I walked down Granville Street, across the wondrous eight lane bridge, down into Seymour, there and back saving bus fare. Because I wanted to look smart each day I wore high heels, soon developing sore feet and the beginning of a bunion. It never dawned on me to wear flats and carry my fancy shoes.

After my work day was over I trudged back up the hill slowly, frequently stopping to rest on a wide sill on one of the shop windows convinced me people of good taste lived in Vancouver, many of them having to be rich, because only the wealthy could afford the lovely fabrics and furniture I saw.

One day as I paused beside one of those opulent furniture show windows, I wondered why I could not have a job selling beauty to people who could afford it, rather than harassing those who were unable to afford basic necessities. Remembering my approach to the secretarial position at Trader's Finance, and forgetting the pain in my feet, I walked confidently into the store named The Chelsea Shop, asking to speak with the manager.

He was Jim Elliot, a Welshman, who quickly recognized my British accent. I fibbed a little in saying I had heard of his store's excellent reputation, though I was new to Vancouver.

"I worked as an interior designer at Harrods in Knightsbridge,

London, and also in a French studio run by Mrs. Shields, who did beautiful work for the aristocracy."

This was no mere fib, it was an outright lie, but I intuitively felt snob appeal would work best. It did. My mother had regularly purchased from them both.

The store owner, Hugh Russell, was brought out to speak with me. He had muscular dystrophy and sat in a wheelchair. A most refined and charming man who discussed the possibility of my coming to work for him, asking me to call back the following afternoon.

After talking things over with John, we both decided before switching from a steady job to a new one, I should know what would be required of me. We squandered bus fare to the main library, and after looking through a number of books, I realized I was totally out of my depth. I recognized good interior design, for I had been brought up among beautiful antiques and exquisite fabrics, but many of the descriptive words in the books were alien to me. Although I recognized quality in fabrics and furniture in many cases I did not know their names or the periods in which some of the antiques were built.

We checked out ten books, and I studied all night long. The next day Chelsea agreed to take me on for a month's trial at $35 per week plus sales commission.

It seemed each time Lady Luck smiled my way, she abandoned John. The lumber industry was in turmoil. An anticipated major strike was expected to last many months. John had not been employed long enough to receive union recompense during a strike.

Back to want ads.

John's confidence had been somewhat restored by doing physical work well, but his clever mind had stagnated. He knew a little more about Canadian ways, however, and felt his best chance was to move into sales.

"I can sell anything if I try hard," he said. "Our need is critical."

I could not argue that point.

He obtained a position with the British Pacific Health and Accident Insurance Company, enjoying the new challenge and quickly became proficient. We purchased an old car for him to use in making house calls. Continual repair services tapped our meager financial resources, but he did become top salesman within a short period of time, receiving a new shirt as the prize, and we continued by frugal living to put a small sum aside each month.

My employer and his all male staff at The Chelsea Shop were aware of my bluff soon enough, but decided to keep me on for two months while their six decorators took holidays. My daily responsibilities were to dust the furniture, rearrange the windows and catalogue the thousands of fabric samples, weeding out discontinued lines, repricing those still available. No one had attempted the task during the past ten years, as it was a demeaning job decorators, on commission, could not afford to spend time on.

I enjoyed creating order out of confusion and warmly greeting clients, always hoping someone who came in would not already be working with one of our designers. I did sell a few small things such as pillows and lamps and wrote many letters to building firms, possible clients, whose names appeared in the Journal of Commerce listing of companies applying for licenses to build new homes.

The shop had given me the use of an old Morris Minor convertible whose taxes and license were paid up to the end of the year. All I had to do was pay for gas. I followed up my letters, visiting some of the families building new homes, and made a few sales by and by.

When in the shop I hovered around our successful decorators watching how they estimated, and how they created lovely rooms. I learned how to measure furniture, drapes and what styles were suitable for timber homes on the west coast.

I was dismayed by the preponderance of Victorian mahogany furniture. Such furnishings were used only in the kitchens of my background in England. Sometimes I spoke of oak antiques, of Italian Bergere chairs, of Sheraton and Chippendale. I was rather an enigma to the staff. I did not know much of what they knew then, but what I did know was accepted good taste. At the end of the decorator's holidays. Chelsea management decided I had served my usefulness and, as of the end of the week, would no longer be needed. As was usual, the staff retired to a nearby coffee shop whilst I was left to guard the shop. A lady, Mrs. Lillian McGregor, came in saying her daughter and son-in-law were to be away for three months. During that time she wanted to surprise them by redoing the master bedroom, dressing room, bath and adjoining study.

By the time our staff returned from coffee I had fabric books, designs, sketches and swatches of coral velvet, cream silks and French flowered wall paper samples, spread everywhere. Every one of the Chelsea decorators came forward to take over, but Mrs. McGregor firmly said she wanted to work with me because of my fresh European ideas. My work with her was one of the largest orders of the year for Chelsea. Instead of letting me go, Hugh

Russell added me to his permanent staff.

Mrs. McGregor's daughter was delighted with her surprise, and as a consequence I was asked to redo the rest of her home. From this point on I became sought after, and during the next seven years was recognized as one of Vancouver's leading designer decorators. My family's artistic inheritance served me well.

Once John and I were in permanent jobs we agreed renting was a waste of money. We did not quite know how we could manage to purchase a home but decided to try, beginning by going house hunting and dreaming.

One afternoon we drove around the newly sculpted area of North Vancouver, Forest Hills and the Highlands, on the banks of the Capilano River overlooking Vancouver and the Gulf Islands beyond. During the drive we saw a house very different from the rest. Obviously it had not been accepted in the marketplace, as tall weeds dominated the rock-strewn front yard.

The house was contemporary, with cedar siding, and in trouble in the market perhaps because of an enormous peaked window facing south, exposing two-thirds of the interior. It was priced at $19,000, a good price, but $18,000 more than we had. Our $1,000 was the remainder from the sale of my house in England, which was still in the hands of the auctioneers.

We arranged for a transfer of my money, negotiated with the builders and came up with a deal wherein the $1,000 was to be paid immediately. $7,000 within the year as An Agreement for Sale, with the rest on mortgage. The builders wee delighted, quite certain a pair of British immigrants would never be able to secure the balance in the allotted time, meaning the improved house would revert to them, with no monies returned to us.

They did not know us.

Back to cornflakes, lettuce, brown bread and the occasional tin of sardines. Never had John and I worked as hard as we did that year, perhaps because we were competing against each other to see who could provide the most security for our new life. We were both working on commission, had no dependents other than ourselves, no friends to distract us. I missed Kevin so much but had to agree my parents had been right in keeping him with them whilst we became somewhat established. How could we look after him properly both working long hours daily.

We had never spent too much time alone together and spent even less during that period. We painted the interior of the house; I bought carpets from Chelsea at cost, and some second hand chairs. Outside was tougher to get the landscaping under control. John created several curved banks in front of the house, which we built incorporating small stone walls. Each night after work we drove the cars along the newly built Upper Levels Highway towards Horseshoe Bay. From the blasting through the mountain sides; massive piles of rock lay strewn about. It did not take us long to fill the trunks and get it all home and cemented in place, after which we ate our meagre suppers, fell into bed, to rise again before 6 a.m in order to cross the Lions Gate Bridge through Stanley Park, before rush hour traffic turned the route into bumper to bumper bedlam.

Every term within the Agreement for Sale was met on time. Only then did we dare relax a bit. I joined the Jericho Tennis club, soon becoming a member of the Ladies "B" Team, enjoying matches against other clubs in the area and meeting new people.

Even after we had met the requisites for securing the house, John devoted fierce concentration to his sales and was regularly named top salesman, until his paranoia resurfaced. He always had to have an enemy, it seemed. He was overly suspicious of other salesmen and developed a keen hatred for one. They had tremendous verbal fights. John tried every way imaginable to get the other man fired, the beginning of a tragic pattern.

As each day passed I recalled the warning of the Torquay psychiatrist, but I had seen John through his malady during that period, and if need be, I would see him through another. He became increasingly violent towards me, fueled by his own inadequacies. John would not seek help, not believing the problem was his and blaming everyone around him for his troubles. He was jealous of my success, hurling verbal abuse at me and calling me a f...ing bitch to put me in my place when he did not get what he wanted. Gradually, the name calling became more physical, John throwing my beautiful china and collectibles at me, crashing them against the wall. When that did not suffice he beat me, pulling my hair and calling me the foulest names he could think of. My own unhappiness in our marriage was unimportant, could not compare with the dread I suffered each time I thought of divorce. One divorce was bad enough. Divorce twice? Never. No, not me. I had a new life and would make it worthwhile.

My father sent me an airline ticket for a visit home during the Christmas Holidays of 1958, saying Kevin would be on holiday from Neville Holt, his preparatory boarding school, and we could all have

104

a happy time together.

My reunion with Kevin was teary on my part, but he seemed unimpaired by our separation and only wanted to know when he could join me in Canada.

"When summer comes," I told him.

Throughout my visit I regaled my parents and Kevin with lively stories of Canada and our life there, never coming close to mentioning any hardships we had suffered.

When I left England I was certain only a few months would pass before Kevin was with me, but I had not reckoned on my mother.

She despised John and was determined to keep Kevin with her in Bourne. She effected that by writing to Bobbie, suggesting they make Kevin a Ward of the Court, appointing my mother as guardian. Bobbie agreed.

In having complied with my mother's wishes, Bobbie had no say so over Kevin, either, but with my mother's endorsement Kevin did visit several times with Bobbie in Cyprus and later in Saudi Arabia. When staying with her at the Manor House he was constantly told "to go and watch television" to keep him occupied, seldom encouraged to read a good book.

Along with the tragedy over having my son taken from me through the Courts instigated by my mother, I had to face the problem of John. He was fired from British Pacific Insurance Company because of his feuds with the other sales people, a monumental blow to his esteem and to our budget. He could not hope to move immediately into a sales area as lucrative, but continued to search and survived by several small-time projects. One was selling Elna sewing machines in the British Columbia interior where Russian Doukabor emigres lived.

The Russians existed simply, without electricity, but even though the Elnas were electric, John sold some to the wives, suggesting they put a stick in the flywheel to make it turn. He must have been desperate to do that, as I had always thought him basically honest.

On one of his trips to the interior John ran out of his slim resources for a meal. He fished in a trout lake, using string and a hook formed from a paper clip, baited with salmon berries, wild raspberries. He did catch a fish and cooked it over a small fire. That was the only meal he ate for three days.

Selling throughout the province was disastrous on our vintage car, and it ultimately collapsed a mile or so out of Clinton, a small village in the Chilcotin. John talked a lonely garage owner into accepting the old car as down payment on an equally old Studebaker which at least brought him home. Subsequent payments on the new acquisition were difficult to meet. John was spending more than he was earning by going on the road to sell the sewing machines. He took a job with the Hudson Bay company — selling their different makes of machines on the drapery floor. During his first month he earned the grand commission total of fifty cents. He hated it.

Within a few weeks, however, John moved into selling mutual investment funds, after which his eagerness and confidence returned, whilst my luck also changed for the better. I was able to bring Kevin for a visit during August by putting up a bond of $10,000 through the British Courts to ensure he would be duly returned to England at the end of the month. I met the bond by taking out a temporary loan on our house.

We had a lovely visit with Kevin, who travelled alone, watched over by a kindly airlines steward. We took Kevin to the Vancouver Zoo and Aquarium. Our house was at the base of Grouse Mountain, so we made several trips by cable chairs to the ski lodge where he enjoyed exploring the mountaintop.

I was so complete having Kevin with me and felt he could easily adapt to Canada. The month's visit came to an end all too soon, and with it the abject heartbreak of having to send him back.

"I'd so much rather live with you," he had told me.

He was only nine. I could not make him understand that by Court order he was bound to his grandmother and England until he was eighteen, and I suffered a tremendous amount of guilt, for the situation was a direct result of my own action, marrying John.

Regardless of setbacks I was determined to find a way to bring Kevin to Canada for another visit, no matter what it cost, but in early June of 1959 I discovered I was pregnant!

John and I had made love once in 1957, my birthday in October, and once the following April. I shall not lie and say I was happy on learning the news. John was of course ecstatic.

I was soon prey to terrible morning sickness at all hours. Carting heavy carpet and sample books around became tedious. usually I enjoyed driving to all parts of the city, but it too became depressing. Tiredness never left me. Eventually I asked my general practitioner, Dr. Gordon Stranks, if he could give me some medicine to at least curb some of the nausea.

Dr. Stranks gave me a new drug on the market, I enjoyed

immediate relief, and only a few days later was heartened by a note from my childhood friend, Audrey Lyall. She was in Los Angeles, working for Time as a senior secretary, and wanted to bring along a friend, Caroline, for a visit in August.

"It's hardly a time for visitors," John said, "but I suppose we can cope."

"Audrey is one of my closest, lifelong friends!" I said, immediately angry. "'Cope' is hardly a word to be applied to her!"

Sensing my anger, John said no more and was exceptionally cordial when Audrey and Caroline arrived. I never knew where I stood with him.

One of the treats I planned was a "girl's day" on top of Grouse Mountain. Audrey and Caroline would enjoy the chair ride and, especially, leisurely walks along the trails while I, now being five months pregnant, could sit on the ski lodge veranda and doze in the sunshine. Bliss!

Came the day, and John insisted on joining us. He was afraid I would talk about him. On arriving at the lodge, where I settled comfortably into a veranda chair, he vehemently insisted I accompany the group on the hike to Devil's Leap, a spot of particular beauty with a spectacular view over the Capilano Dam and Canyon.

Rather than argue, I gave in. Soon after we began the walk John moved behind me, and if I lagged even a little, he pushed me ahead. Somehow we lost the path and had to pick our way through a large growth of blueberry bushes on a sharply descending slope. When I lost my balance and fell, John did the unbelievable. He kicked me, swearing at my clumsiness, as I rolled farther down the steep mountain side.

Audrey and Caroline were horrified. Not knowing what else to do, they pretended to ignore the situation as John helped me up, pushing me further ahead. When I fell yet again, I was unable to get up.

"Go ahead," I told Audrey. The glances we exchanged were eloquent. Do you really want me to? she asked with her eyes, and I nodded.

They left. I stumbled back to the lodge exhausted, with John following, swearing at my clumsiness.

We had made many plans for Audrey's visit, but she and Caroline left that very day.

"Whatever is between you and John," Audrey said, "isn't being helped by our presence. But if you want us to stay, we will."

"It's best if you leave" I sighed. "He just doesn't like to share me with friends too long at a time. I am afraid he is still very insecure."

I retired to bed as soon as the girls left, not speaking to John until the next morning. Overcome with fatigue, pain and nausea I wanted only oblivion and remained in bed for two days.

"What a lot of fuss you're making," John said when he left for work on the morning of the third day. "Other women have babies and don't make half the commotion. If you're really ill, phone the doctor."

I did just that. Dr. Stranks was on holiday, and I spoke with his partner, telling him what had happened.

"Come in and let me examine you immediately," he said.

"There's no way I can do that, doctor. I'm in no shape to drive. You have no elevator, I can't possibly make it to the second floor, I am very weak."

"If you can't come to me there's no way I can help you," he said curtly, ringing off.

Stunned, I called a friend, Angelika Phillips, who came over immediately taking charge. We were in the midst of an extraordinary heat wave, and she borrowed a heavy duty fan from a neighbor, placed it near my bed, and then called Gynecologist, Dr. Reginald Glass.

I tried explaining what had happened, whilst Angelika bathed my hot face, telling me not to talk. I was happy not to. Pain had joined the fatigue and cramps ruling me, as I tossed in unusual 110-degree heat.

Dr. Glass sensing the urgency, did not call me to his office, but made an immediate house call. He knew upon examining me, I was likely to miscarry, and arranged for an ambulance to take me to the Lions Gate Hospital in North Vancouver immediately. He instructed me to stay in bed, assuring us he would be at the hospital when I arrived.

Angelika relayed the news to John, but he was not interested, and hung up on her. She had just turned away from the phone when a sharp pain ripped through my abdomen, accompanied by a tearing sensation in my pelvic area.

With Angelika's help, I struggled to the toilet and there passed a rotting lump of tissue. To our horror, we saw it was part baby but was greenish in color and hideously deformed, like a lumpy mermaid with a tail instead of legs. I was five and a half months into my pregnancy, the babies ought to have been complete, although tiny.

Angelika called Dr. Glass, who was deeply concerned, asking

that we wrap what I had passed and bring it with us. The ambulance arrived within minutes, and at the hospital I was swiftly given a curettage which revealed a dead twin more horribly deformed than its mate!

John, quite conciliatory, was at my bedside when I came around from the anesthetic. He said he had twin aunts and told me, God in his wisdom, had spared us from further troubles by taking our hereditary babies before they were fully developed. I felt the loss was due more to the kick on the mountaintop than to God's wisdom, but considering the horrible deformities of the twins, I was admittedly relieved they had not survived.

Later I learned the new drug Dr. Stranks gave me was thalidomide! Thus I became one of the first women involved in the appalling thalidomide heartbreak affecting so many infants worldwide. The small tablet that sold for a few cents had precipitated the medical tragedy of this age. Expectant mothers using the new drug to relieve morning sickness in early pregnancy delivered babies without arms and legs, some babies had crude hands joined to the shoulders and foot appendages at the hip.

I was lucky to be alive. The babies had most probably been killed in the mountain fall three days earlier. I had presented a most interesting tragedy for the medical profession resulting from the drug.

Yes, the miscarriage had spared me infinite heartbreak later, but I still could not forgive John for his unreasonable and cruel behavior on Grouse Mountain. Thalidomide drugs and his schizophrenia would have resulted in children I could not have coped with.

Why did I not leave him then and there?

The thought of a second divorce was worse than remaining in a situation I had created by entering into a marriage, all who cared for me, had attempted to discourage. Also, I knew John had always been jealous of my longstanding English friends, because he had never been accepted by our families, until I became a pass key of sorts. His constant apologies and promises never to hurt me ever again always convinced me I must retry. What an incredible fool I was. Why did I think I could conquer his cruelties by 'trying again' when so many others failed too?

John and I were paying off the mortgage on our house through hard work, and we concluded a better solution might be using the equity to buy either a duplex or small apartment building, so that renters could then assist in paying the mortgage, increasing the property ownership in our new country.

We soon traded the house equity on a nine-suite apartment building on 4th Avenue in North Vancouver, moving into a top-floor suite facing beautiful Burrard Inlet Harbour. I vacuumed hallways every day, after work, whilst John took care of the garbage thrown down the chute from the hallways.

When we purchased the building, John had made a deal with the vendor, Mr. George Cunningham, to take our house on Highland Boulevard in lieu of a downpayment. John had been quite smart about it. In the contract he stipulated we were depending on Cunningham's contracted estimate of oil and electricity consumption, in order for us to come out ahead.

The rental market was down in late 1960, so to encourage renters we offered the first month free. We did catch one family trying to move their belongings in the middle of the night at the end of their first month. The husband years later became sales manager for a major realtor!

Our new home was certainly different, but we made it attractive with the handsome furniture I was gradually acquiring through Chelsea, plus a few antiques my parents had shipped over.

Leaving daily before 6 a.m. driving around the city for my clients during work hours, returning home to vacuum and prepare supper for John, all of it was tiring, but we thought we were building equity. After a few months, however, we knew the oil and electricity consumption were far more than estimated. We struggled on, hoping the new renter's monies would pay for the difference, but it was not to be.

We worried lest we would be unable to keep up the mortgage payments until John met with George Cunningham again to discuss the original terms. Being an honorable man, he agreed to reverse the contract. We returned to our original home, somewhat the wiser where real estate deals were concerned, licking our wounds.

I was well respected by my clients through the Chelsea Shop, and they in turn recognizing my talent, suggested I become a member of the Women's Auxiliary to the prestigious Vancouver Art Gallery. I met interesting people, many of whom I became involved with in business. Most important, I was mixing more with successful young Vancouver women, some who were to become my future lifelong friends.

We were moving up in Vancouver's social scene rather swiftly.

Many new restaurants were opening, and it became fashionable to eat dinner out with friends rather than eating in one another's homes. The steak and seafood restaurants, with their appealing salads, had become a way of western lifestyle. One night we visited the popular Sands on Davie Street in Vancouver. At an adjoining table were two well dressed couples; one of the women was particularly attractive, dark and Jewish. Our eyes met, we smiled, and before many moments passed began a conversation.

Noni Frank's husband, David, owned the leading electrical store, Y. Franks. As it happened, Noni was also a designer decorator, and an artist. The Franks were intrigued by our British accents, and the beginning of a long friendship was established within those few moments.

The following day Noni invited me to their beautiful rustic home situated on the banks of the Seymour River, in North Vancouver, on two acres perched above a mighty rock canyon where, in the spring runoffs, vast floods of water teemed noisily past the property. The hundreds of years old cedar trees had never been logged. They were massive and magnificent, over a hundred and fifty feet high growing on the banks above the river. The canyon opened into the lower reaches of a deep pool, reflecting the green of the surrounding trees, before the water broke into twinkling rapids flowing down to Burrard Inlet two miles below. This was why I named this idyllic spot Greenwaters.

It was an enchanting place where the movie, Rose Marie, starring Jeanette MacDonald and Nelson Eddy, was filmed. The high outcrop rock overhung the river, on which MacDonald had sung the Indian Love Call as Eddy, a Canadian Mountie, paddled downstream in a canoe.

Cedar wooden steps had been carved into the hillside amongst huckleberry and wild grapevines, down to the beach. An old cave had once been a small goldmine, from which two families survived during the Great Depression of 1929.

I was fascinated with the distinctive charm of the house, and its surroundings. I was surprised to find the Franks wanted to sell and move back into Vancouver providing they could find the right buyers, who would understand the intrinsic potential. The house had once been a fisherman's cabin. Noni had started from there, building it into the showplace cottage it had become. She would never part with it other than to someone who would love it equally and carry on where she had left off.

Noni and I were strangely kindred spirits, and I believe we

knew, that first day, John and I would purchase the property. At any rate not much time passed before we discussed the idea and agreed it was what we both wanted. All we had left to do was convince our husbands!

Both were receptive. Our own financial resources had been sapped by the apartment fiasco, but we were both earning attractive commissions now and felt we could manage the purchase. Considering the congeniality we four shared, we saw no reason to bring in a realtor, thus saving those commissions.

John and I took possession of the Riverside Drive home in the summertime of 1960.

The property was beautiful in its natural state but we decided it should become a showplace, a challenge for John from his horticulture background. We drove down to the main garden supply nursery, looking around at the many kinds of shrubs and flowers, not really knowing where to start. A most handsome young man came up to talk with us who seemed knowledgeable. We arranged for him to come up to Greenwaters the following two days to work with John and plan many natural beds in the terrain with colourful shrubs, set in groups of no less than 20 for maximum effect. We became very fond of the young man, establishing a strong bond which was to last through many years. He was Dutch, an immigrant like ourselves, and was eventually to become Mayor of Surrey and Social Credit Premier of the Province, Bill Vander Zalm.

It appeared the big pool at the foot of the canyon was an outstanding fishing hole from which fishermen had been accustomed to take their catches for many years. There were always two or three men staking their claim, passing through our private garden. As we created the new garden, close to the house at the top of the cliffside, we were constantly dismayed with people walking past our windows, leaving their trash behind up the hillside and on the beach. Speaking to each group proved useless, they all stated it was a natural fishing hole owned by the Province, and that we could not keep them out.

We suffered the expense of erecting an eight-foot high wire fence along the beach and on one side of our property. We leased a 150 pound professionally trained German Shepherd guard dog. Following the advice of his trainer, we leashed him to an overhead 100-foot long wire strung about ten feet high, giving him restricted, but ample freedom. We made him a shelter and took down his food twice daily.

One afternoon I was working around the house and saw five youths dodging through the bushes. John was on the beach, clearing logs brought down in a recent runoff through the canyon. King was beside him. I felt very uneasy, immediately calling the police.

As the youths stormed noisily down the wooden steps leading to our private beach King became aware of them, straining strongly against the wire, breaking it. He had been trained to fight the Russian Doukabors, who dynamited trains passing through the quiet areas of the Kootneys in B.C. Once on the attack the dog could not be stopped.

The invaders did a swift about face, yelling in fear, running back up the steps. King, barking fiercely, was not to be outpaced, soon herding them into a tight group. John, out of breath, arrived moments later deftly managing to prevent King from inflicting serious bites before the police arrived to remove the trespassers.

Word of the incident spread quickly in the fishermen's community. Never again did they make attempts to invade our property.

John consulted with an industrial Psychologist, Dr. Conrad Lamond, who gave him a series of tests, determining his forte should be in stocks and bonds rather than mutual funds. An appointment was soon made with Dick Malkin, managing director of Gairdners, a major investment house in Vancouver's financial district. He was hired as a bond salesman becoming enthralled with the new challenge, just down his street, working with many New York investment firms.

With his new career John became friendly with Deputy Minister of Finance, Gerald Bryson, who had made major contributions to the financial success of the Social Credit Government of British Columbia with the venerable Premier W.A.C. Bennett. That association led to John's investing millions of dollars daily for the government in the bond market throughout the world.

I became devoted to Gerry's wife, Grace, who often weekended at Greenwaters or we stayed at the Bryson's lovely home in Victoria, where she regaled us with stories of her socialite life.

In 1961 I was elected chairman of the Vancouver Art Gallery Women's Auxiliary Social Committee. During the first year my volunteers catered to more than 60,000 guests for special opening and fund raising events. I organized an elegant Winter Ball on a Spanish theme, with decorations, food and wine procured through the Spanish Consul, characterizing the country. The Ball was recognized as the Vancouver social occasion of the year.

The peaceful and inspiring interlude was not to last. A hurricane from the Caribbean left its final dying twist in Vancouver! Most unusual. Beautiful Stanley Park, across the Burrard Inlet from our home, received the vicious final throes, resulting in hundreds of trees being blown down, almost obliterating the causeway. Fallen trees along our Riverside Drive knocked out the electricity for four days which, as it was winter, meant the house was practically unlivable. I carried my two Siamese cats, Pukey and Top Cat, down the two miles of road, begging a lift with a friend over to the Chelsea Shop. I do not think my co-designers were too enthused having cats in the store.

Our house withstood the powerful winds, perhaps protected by our huge trees. Since it had survived the powerful storm we were encouraged to add on another wing, a bedroom suite above a new dining room and den. All the windows overlooked the towering cedar trees descending to the river twinkling below.

Perhaps at last the beauty and solitude reaching out to us from Greenwaters would grace our lives in this wonderful country, away from reminders of past follies in England.

"Everyone is enthusiastic at times.
Some have enthusiasm for thirty minutes,
Others have it for thirty days, but it is the person
That has it for thirty years who makes a success of life."

Chapter Six

Hugh Kingsmill
"Friends are God's apology for our relations".

On the morning of Kevin's birthday, January 3rd, 1962, I received a telephone call from my brother. I was utterly devastated to hear my father had just died at the wheel of his car. Andrew, in his usual brief fashion, said he was making the funeral arrangements for two days later, could I be there?

"I'll be there" I told him, and then an unexpected and bittersweet memory of my father's favourite flowers overshadowed all other thoughts: "When you order the flowers, Andrew, tell them we want only roses and carnations... I'll phone you as soon as I know my arrival time at Heathrow. I will probably have quite a time getting a plane at this short notice."

It was an early Monday morning and I had only just arrived at The Chelsea Shop. Quickly collecting my thoughts, I phoned John. He was most considerate, telling me to phone a friend, Julie Lamond, who lived on Riverside Drive, asking her to pack a few of my necessities and bring them, and my passport from the oak desk, down to the shop for me. In the meantime he would somehow arrange an emergency plane reservation through a mutual friend, Hugh, then a Vice President of Canadian Airlines. John picked me up in his car within the hour, and driving to the airport, neither of us gave a thought about my passport or money. How did we think I was going to fly the other side of the world without either? Fortunately John had arranged for the ticket payment to be looked after later, which was one thing. However, my passport had expired. In an emergency it is amazing how senior officials bend the rules to move mountains of red tape. I was wafted through terminals with no delays having signed a waiver stating a new passport would be procured. I had less than $5.00 with me, all there was between John and I in our pockets at the time, which somehow did not seem of great importance. Looking back I cannot recall how I carried on, but fearlessly my demands were met along the way. Two hours after Andrew's telephone call I was en route.

One other major hitch. An engine of the plane failed over The Rockies forcing an unscheduled stop in Edmonton, Alberta, where we passengers spent ten frustrating hours in a motel whilst the engine was repaired. I rang Andrew asking him to postpone the funeral for twenty-four hours. He was somewhat frosty and I felt he thought it had all been my fault. There could have been two family funerals.

Sitting quietly in the plane, as we flew the nearly seven thousand miles, I had time to reflect upon my life and how I must have disappointed my father.

I have felt sorry for my parents in many ways. Their handsome, well educated children let them down in so many crunches. Andrew, educated at Oundle, a leading boys public school specializing in engineering and agriculture, was unable to even pass two attempts for the School Certificate, basically a twelfth graduation level by Canadian standards. Not an impressive beginning for someone destined to take over the Cooke farming empire. In my parent's estimation he did not marry well, they did not care for Rosemary's parents extravagant lifestyle, showing off their wealth. Her financial demands on my brother were greedy, thoughtless and pretentious. She wanted the best of everything immediately. He was on a limited income from my father, until he had earned enough farm shares he had been given on his wedding day.

My first marriage had ended in pieces, as my father had known it would. His dreams for my outstanding success with horses, on the stage, or to join him in his farming ventures did not materialize. Although he liked Brian Franks, the eventful collapse of our romance through the improbability of a divorce from Bobbie, was something he had no control over. His greatest sadness was when I left with another impossible husband to live in Canada. His sayings within the family, "Joy knows how to pick horses, but is a disaster with husbands" was so true. The pain he felt seeing the mistakes I repeatedly made, as he had been unable to guide me, must have eaten away at his heart. What a disappointment I must have been.

And then of course ... horses. My father's passion, and mine. Daddy and I were kindred spirits in so many ways, but our strongest link was our abiding love of horses, of bringing them along to their fullest potential, never failing to be considerate of them along the way, never failing to look upon the best of them as close friends that might pull a silly trick or two, but never forsake or betray us.

Most people who watched my affair with Brian unfold blamed the failure of my marriage on that. But another force, just as strong, stood between a handsome soldier husband and adventures in that Far East. I know quite well that although Brian was in the background, and the Government would not allow military dependents to follow because of continued fighting in Palestine, Germany, Cyprus, Malaya, and Korea in the late 1950s, I could at some point have followed Bobbie to them all, and we just might have saved our marriage. But I did not want to leave my horses.

My father was no less devoted to his horses, with the supreme one of his life always his foundation mare, the beautiful grey thoroughbred, Valsand, a 2 mile stayer who had won him many races. She was by the the fine racehorse stallion Valarian out of the mare Sandstorm.

Although Andrew did not care about horses to the extent my father and I did, he was an avid fox hunting man. After he assumed some management of our farms he often neglected his duties in favor of a day following hounds in Leicestershire several times a week. On one tragic occasion Andrew delayed leaving for a day with the Belvoir hounds just long enough to watch Valsand give birth. As soon as the foal was on the ground, Andrew left for the hunt, not staying to ensure the mare had parturated. Valsand then produced a twin and bled to death.

Daddy grieved for Valsand. She had given so much to him winning The Ascot Gold Vase and other impressive long distance races, and he was so proud of her. From that day on he was through with Andrew, so to speak. Their relationship was never the same. Not long after Valsand's, death, Daddy's own health deteriorated. He was never again to show the brilliance of past years.

After Andrew married Rosemary, the ideal situation would have been for them to move into the Manor, allowing my parents, who were growing older, to move into a smaller home and lead more peaceful lives. Rosemary wanted nothing to do with the hard work of a farm house, so the newlyweds moved into a nearby modern home, spending a fortune renovating. Not satisfied, a few years later they moved into a larger setting on three acres, The Croft. This lovely home was tucked away in Bourne's most prestigious district.

Andrew took to raising chickens on some of the farms, going into a partnership with the foreman to do the actual work, selling the eggs, pocketing the undeclared money to supplement his income in order to help pay for the new home and servants its proper upkeep demanded.

Andrew and Rosemary had three children, all expensively

educated in boarding schools. They took annual holidays abroad and entertained lavishly between trips. They hobnobbed with the most socially accepted landowners, the fox hunting set in Leicestershire, the game shooting farmers from Lincolnshire and the horse racing owners from virtually everywhere. My father was heartbroken to see the money he had worked so hard for being thrown away, but he could get nowhere with Andrew, who was completely dominated by his strong wife.

Upon their marriage E.D. had given his only son, according to land owning and farming tradition, 49% of the joint ventures. Aware of Andrew's extravagant lifestyle, my father worried about what would happen to his holdings, more than five thousand acres, after his death.

My mother kept pestering my father, urging him to change his will. She wanted to ensure her own life would be secure and was convinced I could not be trusted with money after mortgaging The Mullions for John. She seemed to overlook Andrew's haphazard management of money, but continually declared I would squander away anything that might come to me. However, she did feel E.D. had given Andrew far too much and that he must make my inheritance more equal.

By dint of heavy pressure, Daddy asked his card-playing lawyer friend, Dr. Jack Hunt of Peterborough, to draw up a new Will. Dr. Hunt never did understand how the farms shares had been divided, for bank borrowing, to erect new buildings in keeping with the size of the operations, during the difficult post war years. My father instructed Dr. Hunt to ensure I was to inherit the largest, most profitable farm, Chatterton and Cooke, come what may. It consisted of 1,000 acres with a modern pig breeding operation complex, from which 10,000 pigs were annually sold on contract to Sainsburys grocery chain. They overlooked the fact the shares only existed then in my father's imagination, for during the bank borrowings, the whole system had been changed, and he had never understood what the accountants and lawyers re-arranged. He had hated sitting around a table discussing money, wanting to be out on the farms. He had felt Jack Hunt would be able to put all the shares back where he felt they belonged, under his control.

During the post war years when money was very tight in England, the banks demanded high security, even from their best customers, due to the Governments high interest rates. My father had borrowed huge sums to cover farm improvements, and to purchase giant grain dryers and massive new equipment. All but 950 shares of the 17,500 which should have come to me from the farm companies, were put up as collateral and transferred from my father's personal holdings into the company names of E.D. and A.D. Cooke Ltd., and Bourne Farms, and three other companies I had been unaware of.

Christmas 1961, my parents spent at the Palacio Hotel in Estoril, Portugal, but prior to leaving, my father had contacted his original Bourne family lawyers, Andrew, Stanton and Ringrose. He realized Dr. Hunt had no idea how to ensure I received what he, my father, intended, with the horrendous share mix-up which had only been intended for a short while in any case. Mr. Ringrose was asked to draw another will, transfer the shares back into Daddy's own holdings, to ensure I would be the real inheritor of Chatterton and Cooke, with the rest to be divided between Andrew and I after Mother's death, presumably far in the distant future.

Before giving the lawyer his final instructions, Daddy showed a provisional will to Mother and Andrew, sending me a copy. The new papers were to be signed January 3rd, the day after my parents returned from Portugal. At two pm that day, Daddy climbed into his Rolls Bentley intending to visit Mr. Ringrose. He started the car, backed out of the garage, dying at the wheel from a massive heart attack. The car continued through the shrubbery into a flowering cherry tree. A blood clot had restricted the blood flow to his heart.

The new will was of course never signed. All concerned knew of its existence, and I assumed it would be the effective one.

We reached the skies over England before dawn, dense fog precluded landing at Heathrow. We were diverted to Manchester in the North of England. It seemed ridiculous busing back down to London with the other passengers in the slow driving fog, and then to travel back half the distance by car again. Time was already of the essence. It was past midnight.

The five dollars I had left Vancouver with was obviously useless, I was basically penniless, in a cheerless country, knowing no one to ask for help. Also I was very tired, living on the edge of my nerves, but finding my own brand of determination to 'get on with the immediate matters'.

Claiming my luggage, I went to the Information desk, explaining my predicament to the woman behind the barrier. She was not amused or inclined to be helpful. I stood tip-toe, demanding to speak with her superior, a matter seldom encountered in

England, apart from the fact whoever it was had left for the night. I think to get rid of me quickly, as there was quite a queue standing behind, she suggested I take the milk train to Newark, about half way to Bourne, slyly saying it did not go any further, and stopped very frequently, taking about four hours for a journey normally accomplished in an hour. I would be stranded there so should make arrangements to be collected.

She gave me a requisition form for the railway ensuring I be assured of a free ticket. I thanked her gratefully, but before turning away, asked for another to enable me to pay for a taxi to deliver me to the railway station. She quietly reached into another cubby hole and then proffered a second form. I was off again.

Before climbing into the taxi I rang Andrew with the change of plans, fortunately just in time, as he was able to contact the gardener who had driven to Heathrow to collect me, and was still waiting for the bus to come in from Manchester with the other plane passengers.

Andrew was not amused having to turn out from a warm bed to fetch me.

As I walked to the frigid train standing in the station, it hit me I really was alone. The only member of my family other than my dear son Kevin, who really loved me, would be lying cold in his coffin back at the Manor.

Once collected, Andrew and I said very little to each other driving through thick fog on the way back to my old home. There my mother and I embraced, spoke a few words of comfort to one another, and I went immediately to the guest room where my father lay, so still, in his coffin.

Beside him at last, memories flooded vividly before me of the special times we had shared. Most of all I acknowledged, not for the first time, but perhaps more intensely than before, all he had taught me, or tried to.

I knew I would be taking his old friends to that room to pay their final respects, as was the custom, so made my private farewell, along with a promise to let nothing happen, between then and the time he was put to final rest, which would have disappointed or displeased him.

I found most of the funeral arrangements Andrew and Mother had made quite contrary to anything Daddy would have wanted. Andrew had ignored my request on the phone. They had ordered the wrong flowers, chrysanthemums. I intervened quickly, being able to substitute his favourite roses and carnations into wreaths created by our gardener, Fowler.

My father had led a Christian life, unselfishly donating to charities, especially the Salvation Army, for he never forgot the comfort they gave to the many soldiers in the muddy trenches in France during WW1. He had spread good will wherever he travelled, but he had never been a regular church man. He had, many times, expressed a wish for cremation with instructions given accordingly, but Mother wanted him carried in state into the Abbey Church of St. Peter and St. Paul in Bourne where I had been married.

"It is the proper way to see him go," she said.

"No," I told her, "he never wanted that. He wanted a special service at the Marholm Crematorium with his friends around him there. We'll have his favourite hymns."

He had loved "Abide with me" sung by the Westminster Abbey choir. Securing a recording involved a series of frustrating phone calls for the Funeral Director, Reid Carlton, but it was arranged. The next step was to speak with the undertakers to ensure there would be enough seating for the anticipated 400 mourners. Mother and Andrew protested, saying we were planning only a small service.

"Pockets of his friends are scattered all over England, they will want to say their final goodbyes." I told them.

Nineteen carloads of mourners, who had gathered at the Manor, made up the sad cortege for the journey to Marholm 16 miles away. Andrew and Mother looked at the crowd saying nothing. I said nothing either, my eyes burned, my heart ached. I rode in the first car with Reid Carlton whilst my mother, Andrew, and Rosemary followed behind.

My first husband, now a Lt. Colonel, and his wife, arrived along with Kevin, who was studying for a year in Hereford under the counselling of his paternal grandfather. Our meeting was emotional, and we stood together whilst the wreaths were placed out for Everett Delanoix Cooke.

I noticed one long-stemmed red rose amongst the many tributes, and have often wondered who the special friend was who sent the lonely, lovely flower. The attached card merely said "with love." I insisted it remain, inspite of Reid saying we should remove is so that my mother did not see it.

The day after the funeral, the family met with the lawyers and Executors, Harry Lyall and Paul Tointon, who had been asked in the new will "to look after Joy". We were sitting around the dining room table when the lawyers stated, as the new will was unsigned, it was worthless unless my mother and Andrew were prepared to honour Daddy's last wishes. They vehemently refused. Paul stated, as he had not been left any money from my father, he would not look after me, and Harry, an auctioneer who did a lot of business with Andrew, refused to help me too.

The room was silent. I was in total shock. Andrew had inherited everything, the near five thousand acres of farmland and all of its equipment, buildings and holdings, while I received virtually nothing. I never received a penny from Chatterton Cooke and Andrew eventually sold it to Prince Charles, pocketing the money for himself, and never, ever, once offering any of the money to me, his only sister. All I received was nine hundred and fifty pounds for a few shares and a five thousand pound insurance, which both my mother and Andrew had too. I remembered my father saying once, he was leaving the policy for each of us to help fight the chaos he knew would come after his death.

In retrospect, I have to admit, knowing his wife and son, my father had been incredibly naive. He had surely been aware of the rancor between Andrew and I. He underestimated Andrew's jealousy, not finding it in his own heart in the end, to believe his only son would not look after me. So often had I seen Andrew wince when Daddy said he "wished Joy had been the boy, for she had more guts and knew how to work".

Maybe I was conceived on whisky and Andrew on lemonade, as our father said so often.

I returned heartbroken to Canada, taking with me the family horse portraits, including the oil painting of Valsand by Nicholas Vergette, along with some silver trophies won by my father with his livestock and horses. None of the family were interested in keeping those.

Understanding my sorrow, John was most considerate on my return from the funeral. The serene beauty of Greenwaters eased the vision of my grief, making it a little easier somehow. No matter what happens to John and me, or to the rest of the world, I thought, I shall never leave the tranquility here.

We hung Valsand's portrait, which I had brought on the plane with me, above the chesterfield in the living room, where the reflected lights from the fireplace danced on her silver coat, and I spent long periods gazing at her, memories flooding my thoughts of the love my father had held for his favourite racehorse.

A week after my return I was awakened by John's painful grip on my arm. "Hurry, Joy!" he shouted.

The heaviness of sleep parted like two rolling logs, as I saw flames flaring down from the ceiling directly above us. More were scudding along outside the windows from the lower roof of the older part of the house. With the constant roar of the Seymour River below we had been unaware of the roaring of the flames around us.

John pushed me towards the windows. I broke away, ran to the bedroom door flinging it open, calling for my cats. Black smoke billowed in, carrying forked tips of scarlet flame. John pushed me aside, slammed the door, then ran to the window and swung a leg over the sill.

"Come on!" he shouted. "I'll catch you!"

He leapt from the window into several feet of snow sixteen feet below. Wanting to have something- anything- I grabbed a new red evening dress and our green velvet bedspread, threw both items out of the window, then crawled over the sill, hung there, letting my legs dangle, searching for a glimpse of John. He was nowhere in sight! I hung on, afraid to let go, until I was frightened by a loud, ripping noise. I discovered it was made by muscles tearing in my back and right arm.

I let go on reflex, with my fall cushioned by the snow. At the same time I landed a loud explosion came from within the house.

Oh, God... my cats!

I wrapped the bedspread around me, clutched the dress in my arms, striking out barefoot in the icy footing, then fell over as my toes caught in the hem of my long nightgown. Rolling in the deep snow, I managed to get up and stumble around the burning house, calling for Top Cat and Pukey.

As I rounded a corner I saw little blue Pukey crouched on a tiny section of the shingle roof not yet ablaze. "Come to me, Pukey!" I shouted, but he was too terrified to move.

I continued on pleading with the little cat, throwing snowballs trying to dislodge him, until a neighbour, Jim Kirk, appeared. He ran home, returned with a ladder and bravely rescued my cat.

Meantime John had rushed off to another neighbours to call the fire department. But our Riverside Drive was only a narrow lane at the best of times, now made narrower with deep snowbanks, and consequently the fire engines were unable to pass.

I sat in the snow on my bedspread holding Pukey. His brother did not survive the fire, nor did any of our possessions, or Valsand's portrait. Everything we owned was reduced to ashes, including my false teeth, legacy from the horrendous car crash in England and a later cancer operation. Normally I had placed them in a glass of water beside the bed but had not remembered them when I jumped.

The radio and daily newspapers carried the news of the disaster for days, with friends able to keep track of us through the Province Newspaper Social column written by Pat Wallace.

Noni Franks appeared a scant two hours later, bringing warm underwear and clothes. She was far smaller than me, and my struggles to fit into the welcome apparel amused us both. I looked a sight, especially with a gap where my front teeth should be. My reaction was to laugh, with amusement rather than hysteria, and took pride in knowing I could do that when surrounded by tragedy. The Franks kindly asked us to stay in their home in Vancouver, helping to ease the shock and torment from our situation.

Insurance adjusters arrived the following morning, and during their prowl discovered our new refrigerator had jumped clear across the kitchen. Had the gases inside the freezing compartment somehow malfunctioned? Was that the cause of the fire? The true cause was never determined.

When taking out the house insurance John had inserted a clause to the effect, if we should be burned out, an unlikely possibility, the company would house us in a place of equal size and comfort. Thus we moved into the elegant Vancouver Bayshore Hotel. I was finding it very difficult living in the Frank's home in so much pain, unable to contribute with simple chores.

My back and arm were hurting, I needed to see a doctor but had nothing to wear. It was an unsurmountable problem in my shocked state. Eventually common sense returned, and I made arrangements for The Hudson Bay department store to send over items to try on. Once clad, I visited my doctor, who helped, but was unable to relieve the pain in my torn muscles. He advised infinite rest, and I followed through by spending most of the time in the hotel room, working on listing our possessions for the insurance claim. It was a gigantic task, but with John's help, taking one room at a time and going from the floor covering, furniture and contents of each drawer, we listed all we had lost.

Insurance agents were not pleased with our figures. We were insured to the maximum but were not covered sufficiently for the antiques, fine silver, paintings and other treasures we had accumulated. We claimed everything anyway. My special heartbreak was loosing my father's portrait of Valsand so recently brought over from England.

124

Our insurance company wanted to pay out for us to rebuild on the same property. We knew the original design could be improved by minor alterations to the size and shape, but they insisted every inch would have to be the same. Their adjustors had even measured every centimeter of quarter round above the new carpeting, and all had been devalued from the initial costs by more than 70%, yet was less than three months old.

We might have finally arranged a settlement and rebuilt, but I had lost courage and did not want to live there again.

For three weeks the agents fought to reduce the claim, which was to be our foundation for beginning again. But John, a master of persistence, wore them down, and they agreed to pay us in full after another huge fire in a lumber yard at False Creek consumed their time, and we threatened them with a Writ unless we were paid immediately.

We put the two acres on the market. They sold quickly and another home was subsequently built, one of Vancouver's most beautiful, by David and Joan Tupper.

Good friends, Jean and Fred Long, owned a magnificent West Coast contemporary cedar home, designed by leading architect Ron Thom, in Glen Eagles, West Vancouver. It was a perfect location overlooking Howe Sound and Vancouver Island. They generously invited us to live with them whilst we looked for another home. John and I were given the downstairs level and shared the dining room and kitchen with our hosts. John pitched in and helped with the cooking, but I was useless because of my injuries, but we supplied the daily wines and some of the food.

The Longs never ceased being hospitable and incredibly good natured, but we must have been horrendous guests, considering the trauma of it all. The tranquillity of Greenwaters was lost, we no longer had firm roots. John's manner became more erratic, as always in uncertain times. His temper flared faster than usual, then suddenly quieting down when he realized where we were, acting as charming as only he knew how. Once on our own again, he could no longer control himself, constantly berating me.

A bright note came when we were invited to the Vancouver Yacht Club Sail Past, with the Commodore, Andy Robertson, past through the glorious water of English Bay. We forgot our problems, invigorated by the salt air and the peaceful silhouettes of snow capped mountains in the background. Unfortunately my pains increased throughout the day, and our hostess, Helen Robertson, a past nursing sister, insisted on arranging an appointment for me with an old Chinese acupuncturist, Dr. Harold Saita.

I was frightened by the thought of the needles, but the old man was considerate and gentle. After only three sessions, days apart, my pains left, and I was ready to begin putting my life together again. Not an easy task, as John was becoming increasingly more difficult. He vent his emotions on me but did not spare the Longs either, going into difficult silences, refusing to talk to me or them. Fred, a lawyer, said he would represent me if I were considering divorce. The Longs heard John's shouts and my weeping at night, and were worried about what might happen to me when we left the security of their home.

Once more the eternal question: Why did I not leave John then and there? Because I thought he still needed me. It would have been so easy, in hindsight, with the Longs to help me. I had many friends, and he had so few. Eric Husband, an older stockbroker from the offices of Burns Bros., would have listened to John and advised him, but I doubt John wanted Eric to know of his mental problems. I could not walk out on John. I had to be his strength. When was I to learn?

We knew it would not be easy finding a home to equal Greenwaters, but we were anxious to get started on a new life. John was happiest when using his horticultural knowledge to create a garden whilst I took pleasure in transforming a house. Together, we thought, we could make a home out of anything. Many years were to pass before we understood we could improve on any house and grounds but could never, together, make a home.

We fell in love with West Vancouver. It has some of the most sought after real estate in the world, overlooking majestic English Bay, the University of British Columbia, the Gulf Islands and soaring mountains beyond. West Vancouver is perched on the North Shore mountains, a magical playground where you can snow ski in a bikini in June and water ski in the sea below, within a half hour's drive.

Searching around we found mostly young homes, built in the West Coast tradition of timber, sited on rocks with arbutus and cedar tress for green relief. We wanted an older home with past style, situated where, even if on rocks, a large garden could be created by bringing in soil.

One day when Jean and I were house hunting, we came across an older home built on a huge rock outcrop, painted a hideous pink with purple steps, surrounded by two acres of unkempt trees and brambles. Its long terrace overlooked English Bay, with a 280 degree view of the ocean and Mount Baker. An old For Sale sign, covered with green mold, hung awry in an overgrowth of dreary bushes.

"Spooky," Jean exclaimed.

We sat looking at it all from the quietness of her car. "It's the one John and I will buy," I said, "but I think we had better talk to the realtor and not go in there alone!"

"Good." Jean said with relief. "I wouldn't want to go in there, just you and I ... I hope you know what you're doing."

I did. I saw the house, not as it was, but as it could be.

With the aid of a friendly realtor, Audrey Sayle, we purchased the house from the skinny, unkempt old woman who lived there with a meek daughter. Odors of stale cooking emanated from her lank hair and soiled, faded dress. The same odors were ingrained in the walls and in dingy curtains shrouding all windows. Once they were stripped, the fabulous view was revealed, and with proper airing out and disinfectant scrubbing, the house began to smell fresh gathering itself with glad anticipation for the facelift to come.

The house was forty years old. The oak paneled dining room, crowned with a mirrored ceiling, no doubt had pleased men guests at table by reflecting sexy views of lady's bosoms. The huge living room, partially oak lined, had an Italian fireplace of carved stone. The main window was a solid pane of Belgian glass, eighteen feet long, five feet high.

We moved into our new house in the springtime of 1963, naming it Casa Encantada, House of Enchantment. My first purchase was a set of seven humorous antique hunting prints of Leicestershire hunting scenes by Count Sandor. I could not resist. John was not pleased, as he felt the money should have been directed towards essentials, such as a bed. He might have been right.

"You're lucky I purchased the prints instead of a Sheraton table", I told him. "It was rich mahogany, with eight chairs upholstered in gold velvet. Fabulous. They would have been perfect with our new Oriental rug, but I really was sensible and resisted temptation!"

"Good for you," he smiled.

John's first project at Casa Encantada was to take machete in hand and whack away at the tangled growth making way for sunshine in front of the house. He was swinging away with venom two days after we moved in, when a furniture van arrived. The driver and his assistant carried a Sheraton table and chairs into the diningroom, where they splendidly complimented the gleaming satin-smooth oak walls. They were the same ones I had admired the week before.

John smiled through the window and continued with his gardening.

My heart sang! The total happiness I had wanted for us had perhaps begun! Oh, Enchanted House, Oh, Casa Encantada! Let us start again.

Within three months we had created a beautiful home, painting soft grey over the garrish pink and purple exterior. Since friends were anxious to see what we had accomplished, I arranged a catered formal dinner party for twenty-four guests. Flowers cascaded throughout the house, and sunshine sparkled across our glasses during the cocktail hour on the ninety foot terrace overlooking the majestic view. All our guests were delighted. We were back in the swim of Vancouver again.

John, now a very successful Bond salesman of a National House, was in a better financial position than all the time I had known him. To encourage his image, he no longer wanted me to work. So I quit my job at the Chelsea Shop, maintaining a few private clients, mainly friends, whom I continued to help from time to time.

I was busy with the Vancouver Art Gallery as Chairman of the Social Committee for the Auxiliary. My life had taken a new turn with bridge games and tennis again, eternal rounds of cocktail and dinner parties, evenings at the opera, symphony and theatre. Those were the days when women still wore gloves and flowered hats with pretty dresses, and I enjoyed dressing up.

Kevin paid us a visit; he was a svelte young man of seventeen. The Ward of Court Order, created by my mother, would end in a year. I dreamt of having my son permanently with us and with that consolation in mind, I was able to say goodbye to him after the month's visit without too many tears.

Kevin, age 17,
visiting us at Casa Encantade.
West Vancouver, B.C.

Early in 1964 John moved up in the firm. He was appointed Sales Manager of the Vancouver Branch Office of Burns, Bros. and Denton Investments, the national brokerage house headquartered in Toronto. He was happy in his new surroundings, proud of himself and proud of me. He was now presenting an image of financial success to anyone who cared.

A fund raiser I arranged for the Vancouver Art Gallery went across extremely well, surprisingly for men as well as women.We booked a large ampitheatre in the exclusive Oakridge shopping centre one night a week for two months. Mona Brun, the BCTV demonstrator for Woodward's Department store, agreed to be the feature chef along with Helen Takach, Bob Switzer and John Lindenlaub.

Each night we had a guest speaker. James Barber, the well known Urban Peasant of TV fame, spoke on 'Adventures in Food'. Lorne Sheldrup explained 'Artistry in Sugar'. Different members of my committee presented table decor arrangements complimenting the menus being prepared. We were sold out, often with enthused men eager to learn French, Italian, Scandanavian and English cooking techniques. We compiled and sold a cook book, "Cuisine Sourcery", which became a valued addition to many bookshelves. The Vancouver Art Gallery benefitted financially whilst we had presented an informative and elegant occasion.

We organized Gallery Day at the Exhibition Park Thoroughbred Racetrack, with proceeds coming to the Art Gallery, when my friend Ann Louise Tornroos, the Auxiliary President, helped me present the winning horse coolers during the evening. I enjoyed the glamour, dressing up and helping the Gallery, but after two years felt someone else should add fresh enthusiasm, and resigned my position.

I was experiencing a great deal of pain in my upper jaw, legacy from the car accident after the Hunt Ball. My dentist consulted the head of the College of Dental Surgeons, B.C. in Vancouver, after which they together removed much of the injured bone which had turned cancerous. Fortunately they took it all. Thanks to a cleverly designed upper plate filling in some of the sunken jawline, I was, and remain, nearly as good as new.

All was well with John until a Director from the Toronto office, Ev Choate, was retired and pensioned off to the Vancouver office. He worked closely with John, who became at once resentful, suspicious and unjustifiably fearful, his own position was in jeopardy. This resulted in constant disagreements as to how the office should be managed and he came home in bitter moods.

John was becoming anti-social unless in the presence of people he felt could help his professional status. He was rude to my old friends, or embarrassed them, and me, by telling crude sexual stories we loathed. Most stopped coming to visit us, whilst invitations to their homes dwindled and finally ceased for us as a couple. Special friends continued to invite me to luncheons and teas, where John was never mentioned. We had seemed to have been on the crest of a wave, but his imagined loss of security threw it all away. The lonely days began.

In 1967, a scant two years after purchasing Casa Encantada, whatever 'enchantment' it had held was but an echo that had escaped our grasp.

Chapter Seven

*"Who knows the joys of friendship? The trust, security, and
mutual tenderness. The double joys where each is glad for both."*
— *Nicholas Rowe*

We had come to Canada in 1957 and for nearly ten years I had
not touched a horse. There was a huge hole in my heart from the
longing to be involved with one again. Living the social life in West
Vancouver did not fulfill the yearnings for animals around me. I had
done all I could for John and began to feel it was my turn; I loved our
two Siamese cats, but now it was not enough.

The Pacific National Exhibition, a major agricultural fair in
Vancouver, British Columbia, is held each August for eighteen days.
I was drawn to the Hastings Park location like a magnet, attending
every evening to watch the horse show. Arabians, Quarter Horses,
thoroughbreds, hunters, jumpers, heavy horses paraded before the
packed audience in the Agrodome, and I walked around amongst the
stable area watching the excitement of exhibitors preparing their
horses. I could not keep away, and although it was torture to see, and
not touch, the gleaming animals, I relived some of the victories, I too,
had amassed back in England. John joined me one evening. He was
distressed seeing the silent tears cascading down my cheeks,
sensing the longing and loneliness for my own horses.

I was no further knowing John's makeup than the day we had
met. On the one hand he would beat me with no qualms, but then on
the other, he became concerned seeing my heart was breaking from
the long isolation away from horses. Living close to us was an elderly
stockbroker friend, Eric Husband, who worked in Burns Bros. and
Denton with John. He had not been insensitive to the increasing
unhappiness between us.

He knew something of our backgrounds, of our affinity with land
and farming, and one day drove us out to the Valley through Haney,
along the north banks of the Fraser River, which was lined with
attractive homes whose lawns and grounds dipped gracefully to the
water. Cattle and horses grazed contently in white-fenced pastures.

Horses!

131

We had not talked of leaving Casa Encantada, but before the day ended we knew moving to the countryside was inevitable. The farming background we had both shared was calling. I felt moving to the country would take John away from the sophisticated night life of Vancouver and afford him the opportunity of reverting to his old roots, and be contented, but did not say so. Chances for making the move would be better if he assumed it was all his own idea. I could feel my heart tingling with thoughts of a horse to look after nearby again.

John took the following day off from the office. We contacted a knowledgeable realtor from MacAuley Nichols, who drove us around Langley and Aldergrove in the Fraser Valley about forty miles east of Vancouver. The distance was easily covered on a new major freeway, Highway 1, stretching the width of Canada from coast to coast.

We did not know what we were seeking - forty acres? One hundred, more, maybe a small hobby farm of five acres? The poor realtor showed us many potential sites and we walked miles, testing fence posts, the soil conditions, the trees, the drainage. Nothing really attracted us until, toward the end of the afternoon, we viewed a tract of 32 acres recently carefully cleared with small stands of maple and cedar trees. Once a landfill, it boasted a two acre lake with two small islands. It was well enclosed by a new five strand barbed wire fence.

The sun was setting, casting a delicate pink over the lake. No house existed, but John and I glanced at each other and knew we saw one there.

We sold Casa Encantada quickly, too cheaply, but we were excited and anxious to purchase the Aldergrove acreage. For $28,000, the land was ours. During the interim, between acquiring the property and building a new house, we rented a townhouse in West Vancouver for a year.

I sketched the new house, asking a leading architect to design it properly. Timber, with large windows and a slightly oriental, heavy cedar roof. 2,400 square feet as a bungalow, angled so the front faced over the lake towards a distant view of my old friend, Mount Baker. Every room received sunshine at various times of the day, and all would overlook peaceful areas of the farm. John said I could spend $42,000, and no more, on both the interior and exterior. I managed it, choosing country-styled wallpapers, carpets and oak cupboard fittings, purchased through my old wholesale connections. I designed a large sunken living room with a high-peaked, beamed ceiling with a heavy wrought iron light fitting. The picture window, with a splendid view of Mount Baker, had a twelve foot fitted window seat which was upholstered in a flowered print.

The passage to our bedroom served as an open picture gallery with octagonal pillars overlooking the sunken living room with an old brick fireplace with steps leading up to a den and attached bedroom wing.

Weekends we kept busy collecting timber left behind from the original clearing of the property, building bonfires. We piled loose stones into depressions to help with drainage. We brought in eight loads of chicken manure, helping spread it over the land, then seeding it by hand with orchard grass. We had two wheel barrows as our only equipment, deciding not to spend any money on unnecessary items, although a small tractor would have been so useful. We did arrange for a winding quarter-mile driveway and helped build cross fencing for large paddocks. On Christmas Day we booked a cheap flight to San Francisco where we spent a luxurious night at the old St. Francis Hotel. People were busy with holiday celebrations and most of the famous stores in Jackson Square, recognized for interior design, were closed. However, we were lucky enough to find one open which specialized in hand painted porcelain door knobs, handles and bathroom fixtures imported from Italy. We purchased all we needed for the whole house. A trolley ride to the Giradelli Warehouse district proved another windfall, as in a Korean import outlet we bought heavy brass electric switch plates, sixty-nine in all. After a delicious crab dinner on Fisherman's Wharf we returned to the airport, with complimentary champagne served on our return flight. The light, fresh champagne bubbles matched our own effervescent moods. Once again we were back building a home and the future was ours to claim!

We had named our homes appropriately in the past, so had to make a major decision for our farm, eventually agreeing on "Heritage" as it represented the lives we had left behind in England. There was no other name for me, although due to the abundance of frogs around the lake John's suggestion had been "Conception Lake Stud Farm."

We moved into Heritage in April 1968, with John leaving each morning by six a.m. in order to be at his desk by seven, synchronizing his work with the New York and Toronto financial houses, which were on Eastern Standard Time, three hours ahead of Vancouver.

My friends were keen for me to continue the twice weekly bridge games, enjoying driving out to the farm, but those get togethers quietly dwindled as they faced increasing rush hour traffic on the way home.

I planted a garden on the north side of the house, sheltered by tall evergreens, watered from our drilled well close by. I sowed herbs and borage, pretty blue flowers with silvery stems and leaves. I needed those to complete our Pimms No. 1 fruit cup, soon to become the 'house' summer speciality. We planted vegetables, imported a walnut tree, numerous fruit trees and shrubs.

John sensed our taxes would be quite severe if we did not produce some income from the farm. We decided to raise four month old calves, to be purchased from the Woodward Ranch in Merritt near Kamloops, for eventual butchering as yearlings. I had not considered managing a feed lot, but it soon became our plan. Two men were hired to build a barn with attached loafing sheds and yards, soon creating a business like farmyard. John discussed cattle feeding with the leading feed store, Buckerfields, who planned an elaborate programme for fattening calves to weigh a thousand pounds by twelve months of age. We would graze them in our rich grass for a few months and then bring them into the yards, supplementing their diets with grain and alfalfa. It seemed we would be taking on a very different type of work than ever before. I wondered then, if it would not have saved far more money, had we just agreed to pay the taxes.

The grass we had sown the previous year had grown thick and strong. We asked a neighbour to cut and bale the hay for us, recruiting friends from Vancouver, to give us a hand carting it from the paddocks to the yard for stacking. My job was to drive the tractor slowly beside the hay bales whilst John and our friends loaded the trailer. None of us were experienced and fancied it would be easy, but I was soon in disgrace for having stepped on the accelerator too sharply on an incline, tipping the whole load over. John was furious, remaining at the wheel, whilst the rest of us reloaded the trailer. It did not seem as though I would make a good tractor driver! Ultimately we were proud of the haystack we built behind the barn, it was not neat and square, as my fathers' had been, but at least it did not topple over. Our friends enjoyed the steak barbeque with cold beer we gave them as thanks for their efforts, volunteering to come again. Whilst living with the Longs, prior to moving into Casa Encantada, we regularly visited with their German friends who had arrived in Canada a short while before us. We had arrived penniless, they came with a large fortune. Baron Jesco von Puttkamer had been an Admiral with the German Navy serving on the Chinese coast throughout most of the war. Delia, his young second wife, also carried her own title of Baroness. We were very comfortable with their culture and European background, their love of horses sealed the friendship.

The Puttkamers had purchased a large acreage on the banks of the river, north of Squamish, at the end of the Howe Sound, creating a charming dude ranch of main lodge and a dozen guest cottages from cedar logs, and well insulated horse barn. Their intention was to run a string of 40 dude horses with weekend paying guests from the Vancouver area. Sadly the ranch did not catch as it should. The Whistler Ski Resort had detoured away from the original road plans, making it difficult for people to locate them, and impractical to continue the venture.

Decisions had to be made for the disposal of the forty horses in the riding string. Fearing the animals would not receive the same love, care and attention they had been given, under Jesco and Delia's direction, they decided to put them down on the ranch. (Delia still has nightmares remembering the utter sadness throughout that time, along with the tragic helplessness in the eyes of the horses).

Jesco also loved standardbred trotters and with another friend, Ernest Kehler, masterminded the Patterson Park Standardbred Racetrack racing their successful horses. Jesco imported two outstanding Russian stallions, intending to cross them with Canadian horses. He personally rode with them in their containers across thousands of miles by land and sea on their journey to British Columbia. The most difficult problem had been what to do with their other three horses. American Quarter horse, Star, the Heinz 57 variety, King, and Shafter Spud, a Standardbred, twice Canadian Trotting Champion, a gelding standing 17.2 hands high. In contemplating the future of their beloved trio they remembered the Richardsons on their new farm in the Fraser Valley, presenting all three horses to us as gifts.

I became much happier now. We had three horses of our own! Star had been shown a little after cutting successfully at Cherry Creek, near Kamloops. He was eight years old, a bright bay gelding with a white star. Delia hoped I might enjoy partnering Star in the newly formed Fraser Valley Hunt. King was very quiet, ideal for beginner John. Shafter deserved to be retired for he had won many races. The Drivers, when drawing for race positions, prayed not to draw next to him. His acceleration was so dramatic most horses shot back rather than try to match his explosive start. (He had been named after the potato district Shafter where he was born - Shafter Spud).

The horses arrived complete with New Zealand blankets, saddles and bridles. We built three stalls in the cattle barn, equipped with automatic water bowls. I soon mastered the new chores, using wood shavings rather than straw bedding, and enjoyed the feeding and grooming sessions. Star being nearer my size at just 15.3, received most attention and we became great friends, his dark coat gleaming, and eyes sparkling from all the attention. I rode him daily and found he knew nothing about English ways and I nothing about Western, so we learned together. Sitting in his stock saddle, holding the reins lightly from the easy bit, I soon understood about neck reining, riding quietly amongst our trees.

One day, feeling more secure, thinking to emulate film cowboys, I reined him quickly round on his haunches, with a swift take off. We did this several times, he obviously enjoyed it and I was thrilled with his suppleness and speed. Oh, yes, he was indeed agile, and I understood the value of the fine hocks and strong quarters of the breed. Walking through a pasture we disturbed a swarm of bees whose frantic buzzing terrorized Star. He seemed to go in several directions all at once, dumping me in the process, and running headlong to the other side of the pasture.

Coincidentally John was returning from Vancouver and was more than surprised to find me motionless in the long grass. Ensuring I was merely shaken, he caught Star, brought him back to me, and I remounted. We retraced our steps to ensure my horse would not be scared and that I was in control. The whole scenario was repeated! I could not believe my own ineptitude when I was thrown the second time.

John caught Star once again, whilst I watched the bees buzzing about. Perhaps Star in his earlier years, had been frightened by rattlesnakes, common to the Cherry Creek area where he was raised, it had to have been the only answer.

That was the only misdemeanor Star ever committed. I loved his heart, he had been protecting us both had I but understood.

I purchased a second hand English saddle and bridle, and enjoyed teaching him to collect and shorten his frame. We explored the district, trotting for miles on the wide shoulders of the major roads. I particularly enjoyed riding the three miles south to the United States border and nipping across an unprotected ditch to another country! In those days the woods were not well patrolled and we enjoyed wandering happily in the foreign territory. No one ever caught us, which was lucky, as some riders had their horses confiscated when caught several years later. Star understood my mind, we loved exploring together. Sometimes in the woods I let him choose the way, bending beneath overhanging branches, or slipping gently between close trees. One day he took me to a particularly overgrown area necessitating slow steps with frequent stops to check for a new pathway. I leaned down, holding branches away from his path. I am sure he closed his eyes as he pushed through, waiting for my leg pressure to guide him. Further into a thicket I lifted an especially heavy branch out of his way. He ducked his head, I lost control, letting go of the branch, sweeping me cleanly over Star's tail to the ground. He gazed at me while I sat there laughing. I think he was laughing, too.

In years to come I would read many times of famous Quarter Horse breeders of yester year, and in many accounts the breeders would pay tribute to their first stallion by crediting him as 'having laid the foundation of my breeding programme.' Well, Star laid the foundation of my love and belief in the American Quarter Horse.

I created a good training exercise for Star of five poles laid on the ground, five feet apart, over which we trotted freely, giving him confidence and encouraging longer strides. Then I added a cross pole at the end, about 2'6" high, making an inviting jump, and taught Star to trot smoothly over it, gradually raising it to three feet. He loved the challenge, soon mastering anything I asked of him. I felt we were ready for the Fraser Valley Hunt.

Hunt territory stretched from the U.S. border north to the Fraser River, from Vancouver east to Sumas Mountain, taking in nearly forty square miles. A pseudo-fox scent, called a drag, was laid each morning by a foot runner, then sixteen couples of hounds followed, under control of a Master and Huntsman, with usually two Whips riding alongside to ensure hounds stuck with the drag line. Riders came from all directions to the eleven a.m. Saturday winter meets. The Field consisted of about seventy riders on a wide assortment of horses. Riders were mostly in English attire with black jackets and velvet caps, while the hunt kingpins wore scarlet coats. Occasionally a few western riders joined us, but for sake of safety were asked to wear hard caps instead of their traditional Stetsons.

Those crisp mornings were a special treat for the followers. The hunt generally lasted about two hours through fields, woodlands or gravel pits, for two or three runs, giving horses and hounds chances to catch their breath inbetween for ten minutes or so. If anyone fell, or horses ran in the wrong direction, or refused one of the simple panel jumps, it became a kindly hunt courtesy to hold up briefly until order was restored.

The friendly atmosphere increased at the end of the hunt. The horses were rubbed down by caring riders, wrapped warmly in their blankets, then tied either in or outside of the trailer with sweet hay to contentedly munch. Riders then partook of the hunt breakfast, traditionally an appetizing brunch washed down with Irish coffee, crowned with a layer of cream and generously laced with whiskey.

As yet we had no trailer, so I attended only the hunts within riding distance. Star conducted himself like gentleman, a true Quarter Horse, and was the envy of many for his beautiful manners, quiet way of going, smooth jumping and especially for the burst of speed he could call upon when necessary.

John became quite fond of King, a cuddly, blundering kind of horse of mixed parentage. He had a wide back from which it was impossible to roll off. It was fun watching them together, although John would never persevere to jump correctly or practice simple gymnastic exercises I gave them. He was simply too impatient. (When friends visited with their children John enjoyed letting them ride King).

Generally he attended the hunt breakfasts, enjoying meeting the other horsey folk. Since King was too clumsy for John, he recruited Star from me for the Saturday fun. I missed riding the little horse who had learned so quickly with me, but hoped to encourage John to enjoy the pursuits I loved. It grieved me, however, having to watch him jump with brave Star, who had learned to trust me, but was obviously never sure of John's instructions.

Shafter Spud, the huge Standardbred, had to learn a new game for me. Standing 17.2 he was an impossible problem for me to mount, but he soon learned to stand quietly while I climbed from the top rail of a fence onto his back. Shafter had spent his successful life in the shafts of a trotting buggy and had never learned to bend his neck or body, nor had he been allowed to break into a canter or gallop. Introducing him to those gaits was a slow process encouraged with kindness. I trotted him in circles, narrowing them down, then as he was about to trip over himself, urging him faster forward into a canter. It took me three months. After Shafter came to trust me, he mastered galloping beautifully, although it was rather unwieldy with his lack of bending. Ultimately with his bravery we jumped well together, although he was never as calm and proficient as Star.

I rode him in the Hunter Trials at Livingstone Park, Langley, soaring over all the fences with ease, although in his excitement he ignored my requests to slow down, and I had a near runaway to the finish line with tears streaming from my eyes as we were flying so fast!

In the springtime of 1969 we purchased eighty calves, four and a half month old, and would have been able to unload them properly from the double decked truck, had a neighbour's unruly dog not appeared. The dog frightened the calves, and they took off, stampeding along the road towards the U.S. border. Thanks to our kind hearted neighbours being experienced in such matters, we were able to ride the calves down and drive them home. It was my first experience of herding cattle, other than as a child in England, and I was riding a master at the profession - Star. How proud I was each time he quietly turned back the ones trying to escape! Amid the cattle dust, creaking saddle leather, the high pitched lowing of calves and business-like nickering of the horses, I fancied myself quite the cowgirl, and was once more enchanted by the agility and intelligence of the Quarter Horse. The calves settled after a few days and two of them 477 and 533, or so their eartags read, came into my life. 477 was a dainty heifer who took an especial fancy to me. Never afraid, she would come to me when I appeared, and she loved it when I rubbed her curly hair, following me about. 533 was a strong little steer, who also sought my attention. He was jealous of 477, larger and a deeper red, with many more curls on his handsome, white forehead. When he came near, I rubbed his head, too. If they appeared together 533 would push 477 away with little angry butts of his head. Animals feel as much jealousy as people, and I managed to find ways to visit the pair separately in the end.

We turned the cattle onto our lush grassland, where they grazed a few months fattening, before being brought into the yard where they were built up on 20 lbs of finisher grain daily. That gave the meat buyers what they wanted, little fat, and good marbelling of the flesh.

I glimpsed 477 and 533 frequently when they were in the yard, but tried not to go near them. The day the livestock were shipped to market I stayed away from Heritage. I do realize what the cattle industry has meant to the world, but I could never be a rancher. I become too attached to my animals. Unfortunately my memory of 477 and 533 has never dimmed.

During the summer I had a presentiment of the future. John's schizophrenia seemed impossible to control. He had always found a way to make life miserable for anyone who was a near achiever to himself, invariably forcing them to move elsewhere to another job. He had to be the supreme producer and was incapable of endorsing or encouraging anyone who was competition. I feared he would one day lose his job, and when he did we would once more be strapped financially. Perhaps avoiding another trap of that kind was on my mind, or perhaps subconsciously I wanted to be more deeply involved with horses, or perhaps memory of little 477 and 533 suggested that raising market beef was not my future, and never could be, regardless of the tax advantages it apparently offered. I used a mistreated mare as a steppingstone to a new venture. One of John's clients, whose wife had a thoroughbred mare, Tippy, boarded in North Vancouver, was far from happy with her appearance and behavior. John suggested the mare spend a holiday month with me at Heritage, and her owner swiftly agreed. Tippy's arrival was shocking. She was thin, listless and covered with lice! I applied lice powder several times daily, giving the poor animal frequent baths. I wormed her, put her on a build up diet, and turned her into a white clover and timothy pasture with Star. She was soon round, shiny and happy, so by the end of the month her owner prevailed upon me to keep her permanently.

Tippy's owner's reaction to the change in her appearance convinced me to believe other owners might also want considerate care and treatment for their horses. John and I reasoned if we were to begin such a new life, it should be with finesse. We converted the cattle yards into turnout paddocks, creating twenty-nine comfortable, large stalls in the barn, spruced the farm up, then advertised in the local papers, and The Vancouver Sun, being inundated with calls from potential boarders from 40 miles away in Vancouver and throughout the surrounding district.

So began Heritage Boarding Stables. Creating the facilities and promoting them was easy. Providing care and maintenance was another matter for we had little experience in knowing the demands of horse owners in Canada. I certainly knew how to look after all kinds of horses, but whether it would prove to be economically successful was something we had to find out.

With John working in Vancouver five days a week, the responsibility would be mine. Neither of us wanted to hire help at first, even for stall cleaning, until we had some kind of respectable bank balance. Buying grain and good Washington alfalfa for the horses took a big sum. Regardless of the toil and labour involved, I loved the work, although common sense soon told me twenty-four hours in the day did not afford enough time to complete all the tasks properly.

We had under-drained one of the larger cattle yards, layering it with sand and tree bark chippings - known as hog fuel, making a sound, dry footing which our boarders enjoyed when weather prevented them riding in the fields. As our boarders increased, we added another ring,

200 x 300 foot, at the north end of the barn which proved more stimulating and, with eventual addition of jumps and trail obstacles, kept everyone busy.

My routine was to feed the horses their breakfasts at 6:30 then an hour later turn the geldings into one big field, of eleven acres, and the mares in another of eight acres. This stopped horsey jealousy and infighting, maintaining a happy atmosphere. Next began the stall cleaning but inevitably, some owners arrived to ride their horses, all wanting to chat with me about their various animals, and to hear little anecdotes of their behavior. However, I was growing weary with over thirty horses to look after, along with riding Star and Shafter. I loved having the horses around, loved what I was doing, but knew I had to have some help.

"I'm here on weekends," John said. "That has to be enough for now."

"But I am working seven days a week," I told him. "You don't realize how heavy those wheelbarrows can get, or how important it is to maintain the place well all the time. I am exhausted."

He remained firm in keeping things as they were, but I arranged for a neighbour, Clara Lavinsky, to come in each morning to help with the stall cleaning. John was very angry when he found out, demanding to know where the money came from to pay her wages. I replied I had taken it from one of the boarder's cheques and it was going to continue. For once he did not argue further and we two women kept the barn clean and tidy.

Heritage was becoming successful, John decided to build a small indoor arena with a further fourteen new stalls. When they filled quickly he arranged for two boys to clean stalls each afternoon after leaving school. Things were looking up. We had thirty Hereford calves for fattening again.

It seemed natural to consider offering training as well as boarding. We brought in trainers specializing in different disciplines, Penny Martin for hunter, Heather Innes for western, Klaus Albin for dressage and Janis Jarvis to prepare Quarter Horse yearlings for Futurities, for me to show. All, in turn, brought in more boarders. Thus we became the Heritage Boarding and Training Stables, receiving board money and a small percentage from trainers each time they worked a horse in the ring or indoor arena. It was a good arrangement. Horses from Heritage were soon earning reputations as serious contenders in the local shows.

Within a ten mile radius were four enterprising boarding

141

stables, including ourselves. San Pedro, owned by Inez Fischer-Credo, concentrated on dressage. Inez had ridden in two Olympic Games for Canada and was an inspiration to all of us.

Livingstone Park owned by Errol Fisher, was operated by Pamela Arthur, who had a sound British Pony Club background, and was involved in jumping and eventing. Thunderbird Equestrian Centre, operated by George and Diane Tidball concentrated on hunter and jumping for all levels. Their daughter Laura began her career as a western rider with Quarter Horses, and became a two time Pan American Show Jumper for Canada.

Our four centres arranged a monthly schooling series throughout the winter months, meaning keen riders could show in the area each weekend. Naturally the competitive spirit became strong, riding improved, and we all had a great time. Heritage had the smallest shows with all the different disciplines, but we had the most boarders and soon increased our trainer roster to six.

Eventing and jumping were gaining in popularity, so after completion of the 75 x 150 indoor arena, we designed a hunter course through our woodlands and paddocks. We used large tree trunks to create twenty inviting jumps, including one which required jumping into the run-off from our lake. It was more than three feet deep and twenty feet across. This obstacle was very challenging, and with help from Penny Martin and Pamela Arthur riding clinics, many of our students became the nucleus of the B.C. fine eventing scene.

My friend, Bette Young from West Vancouver, came down to Heritage each Wednesday, and I taught her to ride Star. She was unsteady for a while, and nervous, but one day I convinced her it was time to hit the roadsides and see some other places. She trotted merrily alongside Shafter and me for a couple of miles, and then, just before turning home, Star recognized where he was, putting in a few excited short steps. That unseated Bette, and she tumbled harmlessly to the ground, rolling into a grassy ditch. She remounted laughing, as a passing motorist paused to help, and we continued toward home.

Along the way we passed the pretty hobby farm of Barry and Donna Cline, stopping to say 'hello,' but no one was at home, a pity since Bette now needed a washroom urgently. Unable to get into the house she opted to take Star to a stand of trees behind their little barn. While waiting, I could not resist taking Shafter into their riding ring jumping over seven large fences.

We took the first round quietly, and well, but went much faster and higher the second time. Shafter nervously reverted to his original ungainly, unbending frame, rapidly counter cantering, so was unable to negotiate a corner. It looked a though he would unavoidably crash into the solid outer fencing rail. I swiftly and forcefully, urged him to jump the fence, at least 4'6 at this point. We were approaching from the wrong angle, but the big horse obeyed me unquestionably. We soared through the air, and as we came down, plunged into six upright oil drums parked on the farm roadway beyond the ring.

Bette, horrified by the thunderous clatter, ran out of the trees, jodphurs down around her ankles, Star in tow, to see me lying motionless beneath huge Shafter. I had briefly lost consciousness. Had Shafter moved, he could have crushed me, but according to Bette, he was trembling all over but did not move a muscle.

I came to with a feeling of dizziness and a sharp pain in my side, but managed to crawl out from under Shafter and somehow remount him. We rode quietly home, keeping the horses to a walk. On the way were a number of fallen cedar trees, which John had only that week hauled out of the bush with a tractor to build jumps. Bette was shocked to see me take Shafter over three of them. I explained is was essential we both regained our confidence. I earned a slight concussion and three broken ribs from our plunge over the barrels.

A few weeks later the Fraser Valley Hunt met at Heritage. It was perfect for John now riding Star. I was better and there was no excuse for me not to join in on big Shafter, for I had mended enough.

Of course, Shafter was excited by the appearance of the new horses at the farm, but he was capable enough during the first run. On the second, hounds were moving on well with a number of horses competing to take the panel jumps. Ahead was a solid five strand barbed wire fence, with a hunt 3 foot solid panel, about twelve feet wide, between two posts.

The Master, in his scarlet coat, was ahead, but I was rapidly overtaking him, not being strong enough to hold Shafter back. He had set his jaw and neck, having a grand old time. No one was really looking out for the others at this stage, just closing in tightly to take the jump in order, and no one noticed Shafter was running away with me, coming ever closer to the panel jump.

I put all my weight onto one rein, hoping to pull him away from the other riders and the wire. At the same time he fell into the same wild jumping pattern he had adopted when he plunged into the barrels. I could not stop him. It seemed we were in the air forever. We not only jumped the barbed wire fence, but a scarlet coated rider on a pinto pony as well!

During the hunt breakfast the Master beseeched me to leave Shafter at home. We began taking part, quite seriously, in hunter trials at Livingstone Park, singly and in pairs, with Louise Hemmingway as my partner, where we negotiated more than twenty field jumps. I could not help loving the big horse for the swashbuckler he was, but Star claimed my heart, and I longed to know more about this special breed known as the American Quarter Horse.

I asked Donna Cline, who had a beautiful mare, to introduce me to the leading Quarter Horse breeders in the district. She took me to visit the A Bar E Ranch in Cloverdale, just ten miles away, owned by Art and Eileen Petersen, on May 21st, 1970, a date never to be forgotten.

Eileen was a very beautiful woman, with wide clear eyes and a wondrous smile. She obviously loved her horses as much as I had always loved mine. We clicked immediately, so she took me to meet their exciting young stallion. Sir Quincy Bob. He was a deep sorrel (chestnut), standing 15.2 hands high. I was impressed by his bold eyes, balanced conformation and proud presence, but found his heavy muscles and short canon bones very different from those of Irish hunters.

The Petersens had purchased Quincy from a top breeder in Oregon, Dan Opie, whose Quincy Dan, father to Sir Quincy Bob was an AQHA Champion sire, a grandson of Supreme Champion Sire the immortal Three Bars, a Thoroughbred. The bottom line of his breeding was equally prestigious, littered with more AQHA Champions, led by King Fritz. Breeding to prove conformation and athleticism. Carefully studied breeding had produced conformation and athleticism with outstanding results.

Sir Quincy Bob was not to be denied his parent's breeding. He had been winning Halter and Grand Championships wherever shown in the West. I could not stop analyzing him. His muscles screamed the power this type of horse must have. His handsome head demanded respect and attention.

Several of Quincy's mares had produced his first crop of foals, all strong and handsome with flashy white socks and blazes. I could not get over the incredible muscling and huge quarters and forearms on the babies. Two of the mare were due to foal very soon, and I was particularly drawn to one. Her name was Whispering Lady, a dark sorrel with a Thoroughbred's classic head, a well set up athletic body, and I understood she had been very successful in the roping arena. Her legs seemed longer than the others in Quincy's band.

144

She was by Whispering Smith out of Diamond Taylor, a fine line of racing and halter horses. The match seemed likely to produce an outstanding baby, more of the kind I had ridden in England.

Lady was carrying her first foal and had looked me directly in the eye several times whilst I was viewing her. I thought she was trying to tell me something, perhaps some kind of special vibes passed between us.

Eileen invited us into her house where we consumed many cups of coffee in her livingroom while she proudly displayed Quincy's trophies and ribbons. I had never seen so many collected by one horse. Eileen also introduced me to the world of the American Quarter Horse Association, telling me about their AQHA Champion and Superior Awards, their Registers of Merit. She explained how she and Art, along with other Quarter Horse enthusiasts, had founded the British Columbia Quarter Horse Association under AQHA's umbrella.

I learned how the AQHA point system worked - points being awarded to winners in their recognized shows only with a minimum of six or more entries in each class. The Association had categories covering racing, western and English disciplines, trail classes, western riding, barrel racing, pole bending, cutting, roping, reining, hunter hack, etc., with emphasis on a horse being recognized in halter as well as performance in order to fulfill requirements for the coveted AQHA Champion award. I learned about halter futurities, how important it was to win them for establishing a young horse.

Futurities are not part of AQHA Achievement Awards, being run only by State any Provincial Associations for their purebred young horses. Outstanding judges are chosen for this prestigious evaluation. Sometimes there are three, presenting a consensus of the finest animal. Winning assures instant recognition for the horse's future potential.

It seemed complicated and such a lot to train the horse to do, but what a challenge for horse and rider, and what a challenge for me.

At the time I visited the Petersens no breeder, owner or trainer had made a gelding AQHA Champion in British Columbia or Canada. Perhaps the stars had decreed an Englishwoman would be the first to do so! But how could I do this? Those beautiful animals would surely cost a great deal of what I did not have - money. Our monies were tied up in improving Heritage. Purchase, care and eventual showing of an American Quarter Horse seemed impossible to manage financially. Still, I saw no harm in dreaming, and asked Eileen to write down in her 'order book' the special foal I wanted from Quincy's crop the following year. Perhaps by then I could discover a way to find the necessary money.

I told Eileen I wanted my Quincy foal out of the English-looking mare I had admired, Whispering Lady, for it seemed to my eye the Quincy/Lady cross might produce excellent conformation in an offspring. The foal had to be a colt I would later geld. I wanted the affection and strength of character seldom found in a mare. Since I felt I was dreaming anyway, I went all the way, saying he had to be a red sorrel with flaxen mane and tail, with a star and strip on a pretty head, along with three white socks for luck!

On the way home, I considered how remote chances were of seeing any part of my dreams come true.

Sleep was slow coming to me that night.

The morning after my visit with Eileen, the phone rang at seven o'clock. When I picked up the receiver Eileen did not wait for me to say 'hello' and did not say who she was. I knew.

"Your baby arrived just after you left last night," she said quietly. "Quincy's red sorrel son from Whispering Lady. He has the star and strip and three white socks."

Long moments passed before I was able to speak. This could not be happening! You do not order a foal and have him appear exactly as you specify! Even if such a miracle had occurred, I could never afford him.

"Eileen,' I finally said, "you know I just have no money for this year, it was supposed to be next year."

"We'll work something out," she said. "Come over and see him in a few days."

There was no way I could wait, of course, and freely admit I did not have safety in mind during the fifteen mile drive from Aldergrove to Cloverdale.

Eileen and I did not waste time with words when I arrived. We went straight to the paddock, close to the house, where the proud young mare stood, with her first foal - he was tiny - curled up in the grass at her feet. even then he had a commanding presence. He watched me. He seemed to be saying, "Well, here I am for you. Now what?"

Even more dramatic, the way the newborn foal looked at me, were Whispering Lady's eyes. As the night before, they looked straight into mine. It was a unique connection confirming the promise she had made the night before, only I had not known what she was trying to say the first time: she was bestowing her firstborn

146

to me. What an honour. I would never let her down.

As we walked quietly toward the pair I realized something was drastically wrong with the baby's ears. They were set very far forward. One was cocked perkily toward me. The other lay squashed flatly on his head. What a horror nature could have done such a thing to this exquisite little creature. Eileen quickly consoled me, saying both ears would be perfect in a few days. It was merely a lazy muscle. Standing in that paddock, looking at the foal, it was as if a giant magnet twisted his little soul into mine. We were destined to belong to each other. I dropped to my knees, crawling to the baby, so as not to intimidate him by towering above. As I stroked his little face he moved slightly toward me, and I sat on the ground, embracing him, for quite a while.

My 'order' had miraculously been filled to the letter, one year in advance. Tremulously, I reminded Eileen of my bleak financial situation.

"We're going to work it out," she said.

There was a construction strike in B.C. Art hauled gravel for a living, and the work had totally dried up. With four children and fifteen horses to feed, the Petersens needed money and food. It was agreed I could have the baby for $1,000 on the understanding he would be gelded, or a further $1,000 paid before his second birthday. Prior to the strike they had valued this foal at $5,000. I agreed to expose him in the show ring to promote Sir Quincy Bob. Though showing horses was second nature to me, and I had commendations to prove it, I had not shown Quarter Horses and agreed initially to follow all of Eileen's advice. Our terms were simple. I would pay the Petersens $100.00 per month, tapping the grocery money to do it, for seven months, and select one of our young steers for her freezer, to be valued at $300.00. What a deal for us both. Eileen imposed one condition upon it: she had to approve of Heritage's layout before final signatures were drawn. Fair enough.

That afternoon Eileen came over to inspect our farm and obviously approved, for she swiftly agreed the foal was to be mine once he was weaned. She processed the registration papers with AQHA the following day.

My pilgrimages to A Bar E Ranch began. I could not keep away, and several times weekly managed to drive over and visit my little foal, who seemed aware of our future together. Many friends shared my enthusiasm and came with cameras to record his progress, the first being long time pal Mavis Dayton, who had ridden Star regularly with me from Heritage. She had encouraged me over the years in my various endeavors, and was very excited about this beautiful foal.

Whispering Lady was a sweet, contented mother, giving a generous milk supply daily. Her son also received a supplemental mixture of oats, corn and calf manna. He grew, and flourished. The recalcitrant ear soon righted itself, as Eileen had promised. Three other mares and their foals roamed in the pasture with Whispering Lady and my colt. Though my little fellow was the smallest, he never lost for pluck and was always into the games with the others, daily growing more adventurous, bucking and racing around in circles.

He would let me get close so long as I continued to creep slowly with my head bent lower than his, so as not to tower above him. He would tire abruptly from his games and lie down, welcoming my advances as I crept on all fours to his side, when he laid his head in my lap whilst I softly stroked him. These were magical times often lasting half an hour.

There was only one name for him, of course. Being from Great Britain, I had been raised amongst the gentry. The "Sir" from his sire, and the "Lady" from his dam decreed gentry. The Petersens used "Hyline" as first names for all their homebreds.

Hyline Gentry, he became.

When Gentry was a week old Eileen and I slipped a small leather foal halter on him. He was curious, but did not rebel. We left him with his mother for about an hour before catching him and snapping a lead rope onto the halter ring. Quite a battle ensued when he planted his little feet firmly in the grass, refusing to move other than taking an occasional backward step.

He reared a time or two, and I kept him gently straight as he came down. His resistance was strong, and I realized there and then, I would have to assert my authority. The next time he reared I did not hold him forward, but slackened the rope, allowing him to fall back gently onto the grass on his side, being careful by allowing enough rope so as not to twist his neck.

Gentry lay there with a "what happened?" look in his eyes until I patiently coaxed him to his feet, stroking him and speaking quietly. I again tried to lead him forward, when he gave an stronger rear, with both feet well above the ground, whereupon I pulled him even more strongly to one side, forcing him to the ground again, where he lay, glaring balefully at me.

I let him stay there a few moments before tugging him back to his feet, again speaking very quietly and encouragingly. He decided to cooperate and walked sedately beside me for a few steps. He had accepted my authority over him. Several days later I took a rump rope down to the field. It was constructed of heavy cotton, with a small loop at one end through which the other end was pushed, forming a larger loop to fit loosely over his tiny quarters.

With the shank in my left hand and the rump rope in the right, I urged him forward. He did not budge immediately, but after a few insistent tugs from me, obeyed the pressure and moved with me.

When Whispering Lady came to inspect what was happening to her baby, I attached the lead shank through her halter, and she led him forward as I continued gently tugging with the rump rope. It barely took a minute before Lady and I were able to keep Gentry straight and moving forward happily.

Lady assisted me for several days. We would take a few staggering leaps and ambles for fifteen minutes or so. Within a week the mare lost interest and resumed her grazing whilst Gentry and I wandered off happily together inspecting other parts of the paddock. It was no problem teaching him to trot beside me. When he tired, I sat beside him while he rested in the grass. Strangely, he seemed not to miss his mother at all.

Eileen and I had agreed lady and Gentry would stay together at A Bar E Ranch for about five months. As the days passed by the impressive presence I had seen in him, when he was scarcely a day old, became pronounced. It was all there - the proud thrust of his head on an elegant neck, his sharply pricked, closely forward set ears, the bright "Here I am" look in his eyes.

Although Gentry was still the smallest in the crop, one could not miss his well formed quarters, strong stifle and gaskin muscles, or his deeply forked little chest, all traits of a fine Quarter Horse, plus the slightly sloping croup, which I knew would produce a jumping horse later.

My frequent visits to the A Bar E Ranch continued, but by the time Gentry was three months old I think the Petersens had grown tired of me. Eileen surprised me one day asking if I might like to take Lady and Gentry to Heritage, and let Lady stay until Gentry was weaned. She said she had never made such an offer before, but was certain I would look after the pair as well as she, and my facilities were better.

No one's "yes!" ever came faster than mine.

John and I scoured and disinfected a large box stall, then

layered it with about a foot of fir shavings, and he made a small creep feed for Gentry in the corner opposite to Lady's manger. After cleaning and filling the automatic water bowl, and putting a tender flake of second-cut alfalfa for Lady in the stall, we were ready for the arrival!

I could barely contain my excitement when a wake of dust at the far end of the driveway announced their coming. Then Eileen's trailer came into view, and we were soon backing Lady and Gentry out into the yard. Both had travelled smoothly. We put them straight into their stall, watching as they inspected their new home before they relaxed and settled down.

Ostensibly to make sure nothing happened to them, but more truthfully to take every possible opportunity to be with my colt, I checked on Lady and Gentry several times that night.

Discovering the American Quarter Horse was one of the most thrilling moments of my life. I somehow knew it was a portent of an undreamed-of future. What the future would be, I could not say. I only knew Fate was pushing me on. I could not have stopped had I wanted to. The urge was too compelling to ignore.

Each dawn I greeted and fed Lady and Gentry before the rest of the boarders, taking time to place my little foal's feet squarely beneath him as he stood in his creep. He quickly understood this little request meant a great deal to me, obliging happily, ensuring for his future, he stood square naturally. However, I had not failed to notice he had a slightly turned off fore leg. This could be a serious conformation fault if not corrected whilst his bones were forming, so I arranged for a knowledgeable farrier to trim his hooves every three weeks, concentrating on the off fore, lowering the sides and front, which eventually produced a completely straight moving horse.

Kevin came to visit us in the summer, with boys he had met on the West Vancouver holiday, staying for a while at Heritage. They had fun swimming in the lake, and helping with odd jobs around the farm, playing cards and laughing a lot. We took Kevin and Bryce Ferguson to Whistler Mountain for a day, roaming amongst the wonderful high mountain scenery overlooking the blue Pacific Ocean.

Gentry was to become the greatest 'time waster' of my life. I never tired of watching him cavorting with his mother, chasing the frogs and birds, lifting his head and trotting over to see me whenever I called. By the time he was four months old he transferred his affections from Whispering Lady completely to me. He was no longer interested in her udder which filled painfully.

It was time for weaning, a sad episode I dreaded, for it meant tearing them apart. I spoke with Eileen, who came over to see the pair. Delighted with Gentry's growth she agreed the time had come, returning shortly with her trailer. It was very simple, just leading the pair into their stall whilst I held Gentry, and Eileen led Lady quickly outside closing the stall door.

Never shall I forget the sad sound of Whispering Lady's plaintive cries, calling for her first born, as Eileen loaded her into the trailer and drove away. Gentry seemed unconcerned as I stood quietly stroking him. I led Gentry out of the stall in time to see the wake of dust Eileen's trailer was lifting along our driveway. I watched the dust. Gentry stood beside me, nuzzling my arm.

This was the true cementing of the partnership between Hyline Gentry and me. Call it sentimental, call me anything you wish to call me, but then and there I vowed to give whatever knowledge and love I had of horses to the little American Quarter Horse standing at my side. More importantly, I vowed to educate myself regarding the ways of AQHA. For unless I was aware fully of the Association's rules and procedures, my little wonder horse might never have a chance.

One of my first steps toward the objectives was to use a damp brush on his flaxen mane in an attempt to make it lie flat. While I was brushing him he urinated. During the process, I remembered an old trick of English grooms to help with their stall cleaning. They whistled the same tune every time the horse staled, which they soon associated with urinating on cue, enabling the grooms to collect it quickly. My intelligent horse learned fast, so that once we were out on the show circuits, he would urinate after I whistled a few bars when unloaded, generally before putting him into the fresh show stall, making it easier to keep dry.

Many horse owners show their weanlings and I had wondered about it too, though when Art Petersen frowned disapproval, I quickly understood his reluctance, realizing how they could be injured en route or on the grounds. As no points were awarded until the yearling year it was a waste of time too.

However, that did not prevent me quietly leading him around, standing him squarely, running him out in a straight line. He was fed with great care, conditioned for correct growth with the best vitamin supplements, and after the 1st of January 1971 I gently lunged him at the trot, to increase his growing muscles, for five minutes each way daily over a three month period, always ensuring he wore splint boots.

The Petersen's other young horses were splendid, but all agreed Gentry was the shining star. He stood 15 h.h. at eleven months. his muscling and compelling personality screamed to the world he was going places. Eileen encouraged me to enter him in a major Futurity in Monroe, Washington, and helped me with his presentation, agreeing to handle him in the ring for his first important outing. We were both nervous, she because any credits Gentry earned promoted his sire; I because Gentry was mine.

Louise Hemingway, good horse friend from Aldergrove, drove us down through the U.S. border. My horse decked out in a new cotton sheet and leg wraps, rode resplendent in her red and white trailer. We three girls were excited to be taking him for his first exposure amongst other established breeders and horses.

Arriving at the huge, new showground we were somewhat dismayed to find there were not the expected wooden stalls, giving peace and privacy, but eight foot high wire mesh ones. Gentry was able to view the large building filling up with nearly two hundred young horses around him. I removed his leg wraps, brushed and fed him his usual ration, then as the overhead lights were lowered through most of the building, left him, hopefully to rest.

Eileen, Louise and I spread our sleeping bags in the back of the covered pickup, fitting tightly together like sardines, and slept fitfully for a while. Several times I slipped out to check on my young horse to find him standing quietly, but only once lying down.

I rose early to prepare Gentry. He did not want to stand still or walk quietly. I was so glad Eileen would be at the helm as they went in the ring, as she banished me, a nervous wreck, to the bleachers.

The colts entered singly, walking up to the judge, Roger Ruetenik, whose ring steward asked them to stand up square for a few minutes before trotting to the end of the ring and lining up on the far side. After eighteen it was Gentry's turn. He shot through the gate, eyes bugging, at the peak of his excitement. I held my breath, feeling so proud of my magnificent red colt with his flaxen mane, one of the tallest, yet one of the youngest out there in the ring.

Without warning, moving toward the judge, he flew in the air with a mighty leap, knocking Eileen's pale blue Stetson flying in a long arc. It landed near Roger Ruetenik's feet.

Eileen jerked Gentry's lead tight, making him stand square and still, whilst the judge retrieved the hat, returning it to her. It was a sure way to gain attention, and Gentry was duly awarded 6th place in the class of 38.

How right I had been to accept fate's challenge to get deeply involved with this breed of horse. Despite knocking Eileen's hat off, Gentry had conducted himself with much presence in his first AQHA show, a presence he would never lose.

After Monroe, under Eileen's advice, I entered my horse in the British Columbia Quarter Horse shows, spread throughout the province. Somehow I would find the entry money and persuade John to take care of Heritage those weekends. I persuaded him, with a winning horse, we could advertise the Stables as being the Home of Hyline Gentry, bringing in good horses for our trainers. He was doubtful, but some of the boarders convinced him to at least try.

Without any kind of transportation, showing certainly presented a huge problem. I eventually sorted it out from the kindness of the Clines who agreed to trailer us to Sardis, in the Fraser Valley, linking up with horses trained by Len Cooke at John Geisbrecht's J Bar Ranch. Len was responsible for three horses, and agreed Gentry could fill the fourth part of the trailer for the season, for which I bought dinner for he and his wife prior to each show and paid for the gas. I think initially other competitors were intrigued with the way this English woman set about showing her American horse, and for the first year, when I was no real threat, generously shared their advice and ideas.

The Oliver International in the beautiful Okanagon fruit growing valley became the first target. Gentry had been left at the J Bar Ranch overnight with arrangements for me, with friend Bette Young, to join up with Len on the road before 7 a.m. the following morning, the day before the show. The six hour journey through the tortuous ravines of Manning Park and Princeton mountain roads was more than daunting for me in a small car as we set off, and I was so grateful competent hands were looking after my colt.

We never came across Len. Arriving at the showground I anxiously asked around for anyone who had seen the brown four horse trailer along the way. No one had. John Geisbrecht, who had arrived before us, sensing my panic, said he had heard from another trainer they had seen one tumbled down a ravine! Perhaps it was our horses? It became a game with the cowboys, 'let's have a bit of fun with this silly woman, and tease her for a while.' I did not think it funny, but when Len quietly showed up several hours later than expected, was feverishly waiting. I was to learn this fine trainer had driven slowly and made several stops to ensure my young horse's legs were not stressed. I was in very good hands.

Gentry was developing into a strong colt and at this show had not forgotten the excitement of Monroe. He dug holes in his stall, rolled, whinneyed, reared and was generally obnoxious. Early the following morning, after preparing him, I waited outside of the main ring to make my own first appearance. My horse was behaving like a spoiled brat and I did not then have sufficient knowledge how to control him. Len quietly, as ever, asked if he could take him away behind the barn for a few minutes whilst I waited in line. I did not know what he meant, but agreed. Five minutes later a very subdued, and well behaved Gentry returned for me to lead into the ring and win his class.

The following week we entered the quarter horse section of the Chilliwack International, a five day show. It was less than thirty miles away, but Donna Cline agreed for me to borrow her trailer and go overnight. I was on my own for the first time, and after settling Gentry in a portable stall, under big maple trees, with the trailer close by, I bedded down for the night, sleeping on the floor of the trailer where my horse had ridden. I needed to be close to him on the one hand, on the other John did not give me enough money to join friends in a nearby motel. I managed.

Our yearling colt class was the first of the day at 8:00 a.m. We had begun to know the ropes and I was not surprised to be brought in first of the lineup under Mexican judge Charlie Arajua. As he walked away comparing my horse to the others, he turned. Coming back up to me, he told me my horse was 'dropping' and I must slip back a placing. I had no idea what he meant, but obliged, quickly standing him square again. A few moments later, this relentless man returned and ordered me further back, to fourth place. I was mortified, as I realized the 'dropping' meant Gentry's penis had been waving about. A lesson well learned, as I never stand a horse up now without keeping an eye alert for the problem, moving the horse forward, pulling on the lead line, snapping on his neck, or if necessary slapping the penis gently with the line. Now this has been sorted out before entering the ring. For a while I carried an icy cold water pistol which I used to shoot at the offending organ, giving instant retraction results, making the cowboys laugh.

I was preparing for the B.C. first Futurities during June, but had one more show at nearby Cloverdale where I learned another big lesson. Gentry was again pulled in first of eleven yearlings. Whilst the judge was deciding between Gentry and his brother

Hallmark, Art on the sidelines, gave me the wink he was not standing square. I backed him up a few paces, seeing a look of distress on my friend's face, but I did not understand why. In backing, Gentry had leaned back, turning his legs outward, giving an impression of cowhocks. I was pulled in second and never again backed any horse up into position! I was learning the hard way. Pull them forward gently.

My dream, or was it a nightmare, was fast approaching. The British Columbia Q.H.A. annual Show in Cloverdale, which included Colt and Filly Yearling Halter Futurities. I had worked many hours with Gentry to prepare him for that special show. He would be competing against more than twenty entries from Washington State and British Columbia.

What inhibited me most were the outstanding yearlings from the States. Their owners would not have assumed the travel and entry fees if they did not have something very special to show, not to mention as a handler I was such an amateur. Professional handlers would be in control of the lead shanks of most other entries.

My first shows had been memorable, although I had learned a lot. Regardless of the pride I took in Gentry's win at Oliver, it was not the same as winning the BCQHA Futurity. I could not imagine what the odds might be for our winning, but I dreamed of it and prayed for it.

My horse gleamed as never before. His muscles bulged from all the strapping and lunging. His movements on the shank were straight, brisk and full of pizzazz. But he was growing again. Surely at such an urgent time he would not get too high at withers or quarters! They had to grow evenly for me!

They did. I gave him long early morning runs, then daily retired him to his shaded stall. His rich, red coat must not fade, for that would reduce the lovely contrast with his flaxen mane and tail. To be honest, I cheated a bit in that direction, washing them often, adding a few drops of bleach to the rinse water. His white socks were washed daily with egg shampoo until the pink of his skin showed through, and I gave him a tablespoon of paprika in his night feed to darken his red coat.

How wise Gentry was, even though so young. He knew what I was after and stood square and bright each time I appeared. We had long before cemented an unspoken understanding of pleasing the other.

A date never to be forgotten. June 25th, 1971. I had booked a stall for Gentry overnight, to give him a chance to acclimatize, relax and eat properly, thus hopefully be easier to handle.

On the way to the showgrounds at the Cloverdale racetrack Gentry travelled quietly in the trailer borrowed from the Clines. I was driving our red Pontiac and was not nearly as calm as my colt. The moment of truth was near. I would soon view our competition, some who had beaten us at Monroe.

Arriving in the late afternoon I parked close by Gentry's assigned stall, settled him there, checking to make sure I had not forgotten any of the more crucial items - my sleeping bag, a basket of provisions including tinned butterscotch pudding and fruit juice for me, and Gentry's apples and carrots ...and the silk scarf.

I had always polished my horses with a soft silk cloth, a habit from England, so for Gentry's first futurity I had looked for one in my wardrobe, where a burgundy and cream square paisley came to hand. No other material wipes like silk. It picks up even the most minute bit of dust.

I camped on a stool beside Gentry's stall. He was immaculately turned out with not a stray whisker anywhere, looking so beautiful in his scarlet blanket. Occasionally he arched his neck and touched my head with his nose. At our first shows he had rushed around his stall, or rolled, prompting much grooming and cleaning each time. But at the BCQHA show he acted the perfect gentleman. He pricked his ears, with the tips almost touching, as other young horses passed by, but soon lost interest in them and gave all his attention to nibbling alfalfa.

I watched the parade of young horses with much interest and saw none that surpassed Gentry, but then I was not the judge who would make that decision. Eventually the barn was quiet and I crawled into my sleeping bag in the back seat of the car. Every dog barking woke me if the stiffness of my position did not. I managed about two hours sleep, before going at 5 a.m., to fetch Gentry to lunge him in the main show arena.

He was stretched out, sound asleep, but awakened at the sound of my voice. We walked companionably to the arena, past luxury campers and motor homes where others still slept. Stillness was all around us. The dogs had decided now to be silent.

In the arena, after removing Gentry's blanket and ensuring his tail bandage was sufficiently high and intact, and the splint boots adjusted properly, I urged him into a trot around me, or tried to. But he was uneasy in the pale ghostly interior of the vast, empty space, and snorted, twisted, bucked and reared.

After a firm scolding and tug on the line, he eventually settled into his regular rhythmic trot, and we worked off his tension, settling him down.

While I was lunging Gentry an able trainer, Doug Henry, appeared, leading a beautiful palomino yearling filly, Mach Gold. Before he started lunging her we exchanged greetings, each complimenting the other on his horse. Doug and I were to repeat those early meetings many times at ensuing shows, while the rest of the population slept.

Gentry thought he had never seen anything so beautiful as that glowing filly with her white mane and tail. Perhaps he fell in love with Mach Gold. She was indeed gorgeous and in later years was to become an outstanding show horse.

At an earlier show Gentry had won his first true fan, Annette Backstad, who later purchased his full sister, Hyline Special, and a half sister as well. Annette also came early to the arena and was of great help in quelling my nervousness. I thought it extremely kind of her to take such an interest. As the years passed by, other Quarter Horse people would prove just as considerate and caring to us as Gentry collected many fans.

I returned Gentry to his stall, fed and watered him, then came the grooming and rewashing of his white socks. Reverence and deep feeling went into every rub I gave him, and I suppose I overdid it a bit, a cowboy type paused in front of the stall and told me if I kept it up, I would rub my horse away before the futurity began. He was quite right. I replaced Gentry's blanket and left him to eat in peace.

The show began promptly at eight a.m. Gentry was entered in the first class, not the Futurity, but a class for yearling colts. I changed into my western suit, silver belly coloured, black boots, with matching hat and gloves, donned Gentry in his leather show halter, and we joined other handlers in the collecting ring. Everyone had left blankets on their colts, so we were unable to clearly see the competition. I took satisfaction in noting none was taller than Gentry, if that meant anything.

John and several of my non-horsey friends arrived to cheer us on, and he wisely kept everyone away from Gentry and me. I was too nervous to be civil or polite to anyone for long, although one friend, Noni Franks, did stand by, with a dandy brush whilst I lovingly gave the final polish before entering the show ring with my silk scarf, which eventually became a talisman of good luck. It was used primarily for the final sparkle on my horse's coat.

I was too nervous to enter first, though I knew how important it was to catch the judge's eye quickly, enabling him to compare the rest of the horses to yours rather than against it.

Finally, I took a deep breath, tried to put on a wide smile of confidence, slipped off Gentry's blanket and tail bandage, and we proudly entered the ring. Gentry knew something special was happening, and with his incredible inborn presence, seemed to grow even taller, flexed his long, elegant neck and strutted brightly beside me as I lead him around the ring. I could feel the judge's eye, J. Calvin Ross, upon us and tried to walk as proudly and jauntily as I could mid all those professional handlers.

We paused in front of the judge for personal assessment, then trotted sharply away. Gentry behaved perfectly. Then came the agony of standing still while the judge evaluated the remaining entries. Some of them looked truly splendid, but none were turned out quite as meticulously as Gentry I thought. But perhaps the judge was not interested in such fussiness.

We were asked to line up head to tail whilst Mr. Ross walked up and down the line of yearling colts. With one eye on the judge and the other on Gentry, to ensure he continued standing correctly, I barely breathed, then saw the judge beckon me out of the line. Gentry had won!

We received a blue ribbon and pewter beer mug as prizes, but the biggest prize of all was the ovation Gentry received by the spectators and other exhibitors.

The next class was for two year olds, which Leslie Reid's dark palomino colt Senor Rubio easily won. Gentry and I then had to re-enter the ring for the judge to decide which of the two winners would be named Junior Champion, an award usually going to the two year old. We walked calmly into the ring, standing beside the older horse, as yet undefeated in any class. He was well shown by Leslie, later to become a Pan American dressage gold medalist. However, Calvin Ross once again chose Gentry. This time we received an even larger ribbon, purple and blue, with "Junior Grand Champion" inscribed upon it in silver. That win remains an unforgettable milestone in my partnership with Hyline Gentry.

I returned my horse to his stall, well wishers enthused by his unexpected success gathered around, but I was too nervous to be much of a hostess. The Futurity was to be held at two p.m.

At lunch time I was unable to eat.

I was anxious for two o'clock when Gentry would be up against the stateside yearlings I still had not seen. Their handlers were appearing. I watched in fascinated horror as those professionals, in beautifully tailored western suits and matching hats, strutted along the alley ways to collect their horses, who had been readied by their wives or grooms. I had yet again been over zealous in grooming Gentry. Every inch upon him shone brightly, but his mistress was not in equal repair. I dashed to the washroom to right myself as best I could.

In getting there I passed the arena where the yearling filly class was in progress. In the lineup I saw, like a spot of pale gold, the filly Mach Gold, Gentry's heartthrob of early morning. She was so dainty and yet so finely muscled, and I wished her well. In the washroom I tidied myself, added a touch of bright lipstick and, on the way back to my horse, noted the judge had made Mach Gold the winner!

Gentry was tired of being confined to his stall, so I took him for a walk outside, hoping no strange noises would upset him. I wasted energy in worrying. He was totally at ease and being most professional about it. It was his turn to teach me.

Having won the Junior Halter Championship I built enough confidence to enter the Futurity class first. I don't recall entering the ring, but halfway around, I could not see, tears were blinding me. At last we were actually in the Futurity, the event we had worked for all of Gentry's young life!

Had I made a mess of it? Gentry did not seem to think so. He preened and strutted. I marched meekly beside him. I survived the same procedure that had taken place in the morning classes, then waited in line while Mr. Ross evaluated each other fine young horse. Gentry stood perfectly. Pricked ears, bright eyes, elegant neck proudly arched. He was staring toward something out there mere mortals could not see.

And then... and then... we were called out as the winners of the first Futurity ever held in British Columbia! I don't know how I stumbled forth to receive the handsome golden Quarter Horse sculpture mounted on a wooden stand, and another ribbon - this one pink and purple, with "Colt Futurity Champion" emblazoned across it.

I was asked to remain by the award stand until the other colts received their ribbons and left the ring. I could not believe Gentry had really beaten all of them, because so many had looked perfect to me.

Standing alone in the ring we were presented with yet another golden trophy for the Best B.C. Bred Futurity horse and a cheque for $300.00.

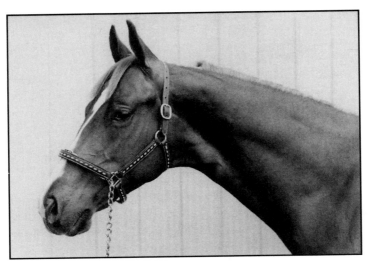

HYLINE GENTRY
Winner of B.C.'s First Yearling Quarter Horse Futurities
"Open" and "B.C. Bred"

As we left the ring a surge of friends and well wishers stood around, including American judges John Condon, and Rich Ingram, who had trained and shown against us, with very lovely young colts.

Gentry's conquests in 1971 were memorable happenings for an Englishwoman new to the ranks of Quarter Horse owners. With the Futurity winning cheque I asked John Schnurrenberger to paint his portrait. John carved on leather a marvellous likeness of my horse, then painted it to more than lifelike dimensions. John is now a famous western artist living in Westwold in the Okanagon, but I was proud for my horse to be his first major success.

Chapter Eight

"A life spent making mistakes is not only more honourable,
but more useful, than a life spent doing nothing".
— *George Bernard Shaw*

In early January of 1972, ten years after my father's death, John's enemy had become my brother, Andrew. The dividends I was supposed to receive from the farming profits had never materialized, as Andrew was too busy having a good time to manage the farms properly. Money was being squandered at an alarming rate, and thankfully, the British Government heavily subsidized farming. Without this support, much could have disappeared. More and more often I felt my father's hand on my shoulder urging me to take up arms against my greedy brother. He seemed to be saying, "You are my daughter, get in and fight for what you know I intended for you."

My mother had written to say how unhappy she was with the way events had progressed in my brother's favor, forgetting she had been a staunch ally in his manoeuvres to vest himself with virtually all legal power and ownership of the farms. I hated it all, my dilemma being tremendous. If I set about fighting through the Courts, I would essentially be fighting against my mother, who remained titular head of the family, albeit in name only. In her near senile state, living all alone at the Manor and dwelling in the past far more than the present, it was unlikely she understood I was fighting not against her, but for her rights and mine.

In true Andrew fashion his attitude towards the problem was very blase, especially since the way things currently stood were in his favor anyway. He refused to help me in my attempts to alleviate my mother's uneasiness, for anything I received would have to have come from him. He could not have cared less about his only sister.

"We're taking him to court," John said. "I want to see justice done."

I was grateful to him for taking charge. John contacted Colonel Cecil Merritt, V.C. a most prominent legal authority in Vancouver who took over the sordid situation. Ultimately I returned to England for a four day hearing at the Inns of Court in London. It was horrendous. My mother did not appear, but Andrew and Rosemary glared at me

161

throughout with hatred. The Judge ruled in my favour, breaking the Will, a practically unheard of event, castigating the family and Executors for their selfishness. I received a modest sum which went into a Trust company assuring me an interest income during my life time, with Kevin to receive the capital outright upon my death. For agreeing to break the Will, Kevin as Remainder Man, received over 25% of the money immediately.

As the months passed I would gaze at Gentry's youthful likeness and think how marvellous it might be if he could have remained that way. But each day he became more and more stallion minded, attempting to bite, rear, kick, being totally overbearing, I disciplined him, but it had little effect. If horses can laugh, Gentry was laughing at me.

I had terrible battles with him at the next few shows. We won each time, but I earned bruises each time. On two occasions, whilst rearing, he knocked me to the ground in the ring. Many friends, and my own common sense, told me even if I survived 1971, I would be in far graver trouble the following year. I was urged to relinquish Gentry to a male trainer, not only giving him the chance to excel as a stallion, but to prevent my being mutilated in the process.

I had not purchased Gentry to turn him over to someone else. I had purchased him with intentions of enjoying the work and fun involved in taking him as far as he and I could go together. In addition, I was to give Eileen Petersen an additional $1,000 if Gentry remained entire after his second birthday, and I did not have the money.

My horse was growing stronger and much larger than the horses we showed against. Usually I daily lunged him at one end of our jumping ring with plenty of room to spare. On one occasion he decided he had had enough, after the regular twenty minutes, for he shook his head, pulling the lunge line through my hands, then took off at a strong gallop away from me. I did not let go, but the speed toppled me from my feet, so like a water skier, I was towed around the side of the ring, surface wood shavings spewing up on either side like water spray. Eventually he stopped, but the time had come for my headstrong horse to be more firmly controlled.

Thus I made the decision to geld my colt and felt treacherous when hauling him to Dr. Bill Saunder's clinic for the surgery. Was I doing the right thing? Even now, I cannot say. Had he not been gelded his personality might have prevented the many successes he later recorded, but he might also have established a most royal family in his own image.

Within a month after Gentry returned from the clinic he became sweeter, even more affectionate and more obedient wanting to please than I ever could have imagined. The bloom that seems to come only to a stallion was still there, and it remained for many months afterward. Strange how those male hormones work.

Gentry was awarded the High Point Yearling Stallion trophy at the BCQHA banquet in November, first of those he won every year of his show career in three countries.

It is said by many knowledgeable horse people, a horse has one year out of the first three, which is not up to the same standard as the others. This was very true for Gentry. His hooves began breaking up and chipping. Whatever feed, hoof dressing or careful trimming he received, nothing worked very well. I think he had grown too big on his small Quarter Horse hooves which were not ready for the weight. It meant careful, limited high protein feed, certainly limited time in the pastures, and no lunging. The latter disturbed me particularly as I knew this big horse to be, must have his muscles growing in proportion to his height growth.

When people saw the success I had with Shafter Spud, others wanted to send difficult horses for me to work. My time was far too taken up, but when Diane Tidball from Thunderbird Equestrian Centre offered me a Tennessee Walker for nothing, I was tempted. This horse had been through Bob Grimshaw, the western trainer's hands, and Alan Brands' at Thunderbird for jumping, unsuccessfully. Amigo was a strong chestnut gelding, to whom I became attached very quickly because he tried so hard to please. I did not understand why the others had given up on him, other than perhaps their patience was short, and he was not meant for western or jumping.

I clipped him out and took him hunting, where I soon found he had a dead mouth. As I pulled the reins, he set his jaw, and from people watching I heard his gums and mouth turned purple, not the pink they should have been. I was run away with a few times, quite out of control, in spite of using a hackamore and thick twisted snaffle bit together. I had to agree, perhaps for the better part of valor, he, like Shafter, was not meant for hunting. So what to do with him?

Amigo's long rhythmical stride must be used for some useful purpose. I had light shoes put on Gentry and ponied him beside Amgio up and down our winding, slightly hilly quarter-mile driveway. Trotting firmly at a regular pace we went up and down eight times each morning with Gentry cheekily trying to bite my knee as he trotted along beside me. My gentle kicks did not deter him. I had to muzzle him or put on a tight dropped noseband. It did not harm Gentry's hooves and certainly encouraged his long extended trot which was to be so effective over the years.

The roadway workouts developed Gentry's muscles naturally, as no amount of treadmill work or simple lunging could ever have done, without stress to other parts of his body. Best of all, he developed long shoulder muscles through keeping up with Amigo.

Although a certain thrill quite like none other comes to one who faithfully conditions and fits a halter horse and see him take his first Grand Championship, I have never understood the mentality of owners going for halter and nothing more. A horse is not bred and born to stand still and look pretty, and I had no intention of asking Gentry to do so.

To me the most important elements in bringing along a young horse have always been to help them soundly develop in both minds and bodies, and on the physical side eight crucial items on a horse hold my attention from the animal's birth: feet and legs. I want them strong and sound and feel the best way to encourage that is proper exercise and diet, which in my case was the introduction to the supplement Drive, by fine trainer friend Rich Ingram from Washington State. Gentry's hooves strengthened almost immediately so that I realized I would have a horse for the future after all.

I have never considered myself a training ace, but do have common sense, working with all young horses to give them confidence. If you rush a young horse, or do not explain clearly what you want, they can develop phobias. They are by nature inquisitive. When a horse shows interest in something new, stop and let him look, scratch his neck, speak softly, urge him forward when he is ready, be patient. Once he discovers for himself that the 'new' thing is not going to hurt him, he will most likely accept it the rest of his life. That has been one of my reasons for always working in an arena the night before, or early morning of a show. Let the horse see the flags flying, the large billboards, the bright jumps. Let him hear the grandstand boards creak as people walk by. Let him investigate peacefully and quietly accept. He will enjoy showing, performing to please. The results from manners point of view will be happily controlled.

However, my horse's two year old year was to prove my nemesis. After his birthday in May he became lethargic and was losing his sparkling personality. We had been so successful during his yearling efforts, with great things forecast for him in horse magazines, so I was not happy with this turn of events.

I called in my veterinarian, Dr. John Twidale. He drew blood and ran a profile finding Gentry had slight macrocytic anemia, with high blood urea nitrogen and low albumin, suggesting he was not utilizing protein to full advantage. John gave him an anabolic hormone injection and I added a cup of skimmed milk powder daily to his feed.

We quickly saw a change in his condition. Our cross ties were near to Gentry's stall, where the farrier invariably worked on the horses at Heritage all day on Thursdays, shoeing or trimming. It was a good way of keeping my young horse amused, seeing the work going on. However, the hormone had such a strong effect he began behaving like a stallion again, honking loudly and pushing against the front of his stall. One filly was abruptly brought into estrus directly over the poor farrier, Bob Scheres, as he held up her hind leg. This was Gentry's first experience with the steroids, and certainly his last, I do not agree with horses having them.

After this we continued our lunging sessions, and one morning I left him in the round pen to answer the telephone. Upon returning moments later, I found he had caught his left hind foot in the fencing and was struggling to get free. I shouted for help, and one of my trainers, Karen Walt, came on the run.

In attempting to free Gentry we discovered a nail had pierced his fetlock! His foot was already swelling as I hobbled him to the hose, spraying cold water on the wound. I continued hosing until the vet arrived, who quickly determined Gentry had also stretched the ligaments around the sesamoid bone. We wondered about hauling him to the Pulman Veterinary Clinic in Idaho, reputed to be the best leg hospital in the west, but X-rays revealed Gentry's bone was displaced, and the stress of the journey would only add to the problem. Was I to lose my horse?

We chose to rely on stall rest, and pent up for the first time in his young life. Gentry was irritable and impatient. In an effort to distract him, I spent more time with him than usual, giving his foot frequent cold baths, ensuring it was bandaged firmly. He was already deeply attached to me, and his feelings magnified during his layup. He often slept with his head in my lap, as I sat in the bedding of soft wood shavings.

Gentry and I had hitch hiked and borrowed trailers throughout his yearling year. Len Cooke had been especially generous, hauling us throughout the province, as I paid my way by keeping his gas tank filled throughout the journeys, and bought he and Donna dinner the night before each show. I had all but finished paying for Gentry in April 1971 and went back to the Petersens to strike a new deal. Art made superb horse trailers, usually christening a new one each year for themselves, selling the used one at a fair price.

My 'new' trailer was a wide two-horse, with a seven foot dressing room, in beige and brown. I paid for it on the installment plan, as Gentry had been. We fitted a strong hitch with equalizers to our family red Pontiac convertible, which did not match, but in those days I did not care.

I felt very proud, after the sesamoid layoff, when we cruised onto the various showgrounds where Gentry was entered in two year old halter classes, which he won each time. In his short life he had become the horse to watch for by both professional and amateur handlers. People no longer offered to help 'the little English woman who knew nothing about Quarter Horses or western ways' for I was now a major opposition.

I did not travel to the shows alone. Good friend, Joanne Dixon, who boarded at Heritage, had a tight financial problem similar to mine – a skinny wallet. Her beautiful filly, Miss Jolee Jaguar, was her pride and joy, but she found it difficult to cover showing costs. We pooled our meagre resources, making sure our horses had proper feed rations, often subsisting on cheap fare ourselves. We allowed people to think we were staying in a motel somewhere, same as many others. Actually I slept in the front of the car, and Joanne spread out on the back seat.

I drove the horses in my own trailer the first time in early May 1972, to the Okanagon Circuits. Travel was easy from Aldergrove to Hope, then for about forty miles we climbed higher and higher, winding around the mountainsides, often looking over straight drops of several hundred feet. No rails existed then to prevent vehicles toppling over.

The scenery was magnificent, but I dared not look too closely at anything but the road ahead. Joanne did not drive then, so that chore was mine. It took courage I had not known I possessed, holding tightly to the steering wheel with clenched hands as Joanne, seeking to divert my tenseness, chatted about all manner of things. I drove for over five hours to Oliver, being exhausted on arrival, as were the horses, having had to brace themselves around the many twists and corners.

We had two exciting days, both horses winning firsts, with Gentry claiming his first Gelding Championship at Kelowna in the pouring rain.

The return journey was through the Fraser Canyon where gold had been discovered during the nineteenth century in the wildly surging waters. The road we travelled had been designed by English Engineers and constructed by Chinese labour. Camels and mules had carried the equipment along the Caribou Trail, winding through the mountains where many prospectors had struck it rich during the Barkerville Gold Rush.

It was quite a year for we novice handlers learning to negotiate the drives through the province with our fine horses. After the Okanagon it seemed relatively easy taking in the Vancouver Island Circuit. The two hour sail across the Straits of Georgia through the magnificent Gulf Islands, so famous for salmon fishing, by huge ferry to Nanaimo pleased us all. The horses dozed contentedly aboard the ferry. We both won at the Nanaimo Show and then at Alberni on the Walton Ranch, so were on quite a roll.

It was hectic, but exciting, and once the momentum began the treadmill for us kept turning. Driving to new venues, unloading, stalling the horses, settling them in and grooming, was all taken care of before thoughts of ourselves. Registration, number collecting, chatting with friends, grabbing meals on the run, ensuring tack and clothing were ready for the following day, before collapsing in the car for the night. We loved it.

I recall the Courtney two day show was carried on in deep, driving rain, where all of us were soaked. After our classes we had to drive nearly eighty miles down island to Duncan through the swirling rain. I drove as fast as I could, and when we finally arrived found, to our horror, the horses, and inside of the trailer, were totally soaked, as we had forgotten to put up the leather curtains at the rear of the trailer. Novices still!

We dried Gentry and Jolee, threw our dry sleeping bags over their backs, taking their sodden blankets to the nearby laundry mart.

The following morning the sun shone brightly, our horses were fresh, spotless and immaculate. Joanne and I had made ourselves look presentable, but we were going on heart alone. That too is horse showing. We were awarded first placings again with both horses.

In spite of careful feeding Gentry, as a late two year old, had still packed on too much weight. He was quite sound in October, with strengthening hooves, and I entered him in the final show of the year, the Northwest International in Vancouver. He won his class and his first Reserve Grand Championship, behind Phyllis MacDonald's

Colonel's Turn. The judge, Leonard Milligan, told the show manager he had never seen better hind legs on a young horse, and had considered making him Grand Champion. Although having missed six shows during the year, Gentry was to win the B.C. High Point Two Year Old Gelding Award.

A horse's bones do not mature until they are five or six years old, depending on the breed. Yet many Quarter Horse and Thoroughbred owners break their horses as long yearlings, just before their second birthday. It is a wicked procedure as the bones are far from finished growing. Various parts of the legs do mature before the two year old year, but the major joints such as the fetlocks, knee, or hock and the shoulder and stifle may not reach their limit until three or four years later. No wonder many young horses break down permanently, often from greed of the owners who 'want to win big money' and refuse to understand the impossibility, for the undeveloped bone structure, to stand up to the rigors of hard work. It is often a smart move to educate the horse's mind as a two year old, teach him at a walk to move quietly, to turn around, even to trot and canter very slowly under complete quiet control. For thoroughbreds, to show them how to break from a starting gate quietly and to canter happily beside other horses for a brief while, then to return home for the rest of the year. They will not forget the education, so that when taken back the following year, it will be accepted quickly again, enabling training to progress with far less stress to the body, meaning greater opportunities for the horse.

In mid November 1972, I sent Gentry to Len Cooke at John Geisbrecht's J Bar Ranch in Sardis in the upper Fraser Valley. Gentry's hind foot was completely sound again, and the time had come to break him to saddle. That, I would not trust myself to do, and Len Cooke, because of his gentle, methodical ways, was the trainer I chose.

Under Len's guidance Gentry was taught to accept tack and to move properly under a fifty pound western saddle, but Len did not push him in any way, for a month.

Gentry celebrated New Year's Day, 1973, his official third birthday, at home with me as a green-broke young gelding! As a reward for having behaved himself with Len, he was given a month's rest in which his only duty was to enjoy being a horse. He continued to grow on his good feed programs, oats, alfalfa and the Drive supplement.

In mid February I decked Gentry in my best English saddle, a

Steuben Parzival, and snaffle bridle with a copper-mouth D-ring bit to encourage salivation for a light mouth. He looked so mature and grown up for his now daily lunging, and long rein driving around the various jumps in the outdoor ring. After a couple of weeks I took him into our outdoor lunge ring asking Karen Walt to give me a hand. I intended to go aboard Gentry for the first time without Len, not knowing what would come of it, I might add.

Gathering the reins, leaving his head free from restraint, Karen legged me into the saddle. I sat motionless while Gentry accepted I was there. His comrade, usually beside him on the ground was on his back! He did not argue at all as I collected the reins, squeezed his sides firmly, but his ears shot forward in the manner peculiarly his when in deep thought – the tips of them practically touching. What did the pressure on his sides mean? He decided to go on a hunch, moving out in a walk, taking long, firm strides. As usual, he got it right the first time.

At long last I was riding my horse in full, regular tack, and he was enjoying it as much as I! We had a long way to go before the show ring together, but we had taken the first steps. After two weeks of daily rides, trotting well forward to achieve rhythm, suppleness, contact and straightness with impulsion, I gave him his first chance to canter. It was a rather stumbling effort, but by squeezing with both legs, loosening my hands a little but maintaining the contact he was learning to rely on, I clucked, whispering 'canter'. He knew the word from our sessions in the lunge ring, immediately diving into the gait, head too high, having a fine old time of it going faster all the time. Stopping him with light half halts on the reins came quickly, as I sat back deeper into the saddle murmuring 'whoa'. For a while I took a weekly lesson riding western, but English would always be my preference. One of the part-time trainers, a Frenchman named Michel, worked as maitre d' of the Hotel Vancouver. He had received a solid dressage training prior to emigrating to Canada, and talking with John and I in the restaurant one night, was invited out to Heritage. Michel soon began teaching us basic dressage, with others of the boarders, and we became more adroit and confident.

With the popularity of dressage beginning in B.C. instigated by Inez Fischer Credo, we brought leading trainer Klaus Albin, who had developed Olympic riders in Germany, from near Seattle each weekend to Heritage.

We were still green when I entered Gentry in his first performance class at the end of April, 1973. Western pleasure for junior horses, four and under, at the Oliver International in the Okanagon. Gentry had won his halter class in the morning, and it was time for him to be working with other fine young horses in the ring under saddle. I had no illusions of winning, but Len Cooke was there, and I did want him to be pleased with our efforts.

Len tightened the cinch just before we entered the ring, wishing us luck as I had become very nervous, not because of anything Gentry might do incorrectly, but because we had at long last reached the point we could actually compete with me in the saddle.

Gentry walked into the ring with his usual pride and presence. Judge Don Burt was soon evaluating the junior horses around us. We received more than his fair share of attention, and I knew my horse was looking good although certainly not polished. We were asked to move into the lope, and as we moved forward I felt confident, but pride does go before a fall!

I doubted we could win the class, Bob Grimshaw, Art Graves, and other trainers, rode their horses far better than me, but I hoped we would place somewhere. We loped proudly down the long side of the ring as I felt Don Burt's eyes following us. Suddenly the whole world seemed to give way. The ground literally sank. Gentry and I sank with it, finding ourselves falling into a pit several feet deep. It was no problem for my horse, cool customer that he was. He gained a foothold on one side of the deepening pit, scrambling out with his bewildered rider managing somehow to stay in the saddle.

Gentry and I had fallen into the septic tank, located under one corner of the sand ring. The day was very hot leading spectators to consume more cold drinks than usual. The overloaded septic tank had rebelled, breaking apart, leaving the ground above with nothing to support it.

We won no ribbons, but it marked the second time we had received a standing ovation, reminding me of his Yearling Futurity win. Once spectators realized we were unhurt, they rose as one, laughing while they cheered. I briefly wondered if the unusually loud reaction of all those humans in the grandstand might be the last straw for Gentry, who was wearing rings of white around his eyes for the first time since I had known him. Instead, he almost pranced out of the ring displaying filthy legs. I suppose he had already determined he was born to inspire accolades of some kind!

Gentry's three year old year was important toward seeking the much valued AQHA Championship goal. We were collecting halter points, although classes were small due to other owners refusing to compete against my outstanding horse. We had to beat five horses to earn one point, which for us had meant going Grand or Reserve Champion Gelding, so that Gentry, a Junior horse, was awarded one more than the highest won in other individual classes. The AQHA Championship is awarded to a horse who earned a total of 35 or more points in five or more shows under five or more different judges. 15 points must be earned in halter, including two Grand Championships. 15 points then have to be won in at least two categories of performance events, with the final 5 chosen from many working categories such as roping or working hunter.

In the summer of 1973 the Vancouver Art Gallery arranged a "Tour of Country Homes in Langley and Aldergrove". Five homes were chosen ranging from the Consul for Monaco, Fritz Zeigler's Castle at Fort Langley, filled with 16th century antiques and plated armour, to the Tidball mansion, with a fine indoor horse arena, built with no expense from George's sale of the MacDonald hamburger chain he had brought into Canada. Our Heritage was later called the favourite, for apart from viewing the home, they visited with the horses in the immaculate barn area, being served coffee and sticky buns. Nine hundred people, travelling in tour buses, walked through our homes as Art Gallery hostesses welcomed them explaining special features. I had been happy to be part of the Day in the Country, for it had ensured finishing the 90 foot terrace in front of the house, and setting out garden furniture. We had been so busy with the horses it had been left unattended for far too long.

My life has been a roller coaster – highs and lows. One of the lowest, which ought to have been the highest, was Kevin's wedding. He had been involved with a girl from London University when working for his PhD in Microbiology, who had definite marriage plans on her horizon. I had flown over for his 21st birthday party which I gave from the Manor House, being so thrilled with him, but somewhat horrified by a very dominating girl awaiting an engagement announcement. I have never been an interfering mother, probably as much as anything, because I was seldom around. However, on his birthday morning we had a wonderful mother/son talk when I took him breakfast in bed. He chose to delay an announcement, and after considerable thought, none was ever made.

Life goes on and Kevin became very fond of Louisa Cant, whose cousin John had been at Oakham School with him, making the introduction. Louisa had been educated at Lowther College, and furthered her studies at a Teachers College, receiving her junior teaching certificate. Her father owned a fine chain of butcher shops in Leicester, and her grandfather had been a contemporary of my father, owning thoroughbred racehorses, often meeting on the racetracks. There was a definite affinity between us all, especially as the Cants had been like parents to Kevin with me so far away in Canada.

At the end of 1972 he wrote to tell me they were going to be married in January and wanted me to be there of course. It was a terrible decision for me. Of course more than anything else in the world I did want to be with my son to share his wedding day. How to get away became my dilemma. We were running a business which was dependent on my being on hand to personally feed 60 horses three times a day, along with the constant care and surveillance. John was not capable enough. Nor did we have the money to hire anyone else or to pay for my journey at that time. I never forgave John for this, my heart broke yet again, not being with the son I loved so much on his special day.

However, after considerable thought, I rationalized had I been able to fly to England I would not have seen much of either bride or groom, enmeshed in wedding preparations and then away on their honeymoon. So why not bring them out to British Columbia for a second honeymoon during the summer months, when I would be able to enjoy them both for a longer time?

Eventually that is what happened. I was so happy to welcome Louisa into our family, strange though the Canadian part might be, and we had a wonderful six weeks at Heritage during July and August. They fitted in so perfectly. Loved the ferry ride to Vancouver Island, exploring through Victoria and the Indian Museum where we offended a guide, as I took a photograph of them in front of a diorama, of a wild horse standing in the northern tundra, flashlights being forbidden in the Museum. The newlyweds had a marvellous time exploring the foothills of Mount Baker in Washington State where they picked a cedar seedling, eventually returning back to Leicestershire planting this piece of the American West in their garden.

Two years later, when hostilities between John and I were at a very high peak, Kevin and Louisa returned, accompanied by her parents, Winnie and Ron. I did my best to make them welcome, being delighted with their visit, showing them around Langley, Vancouver and the Island, after a ferry ride through the Gulf Islands, but John was jealous of their being with us, my family.

It was obvious the Cants and Felthams saw through John. His rapid mood changes, his incredible rudeness to the senior members of my new family. I was so embarrassed, making up ridiculous stories to explain his attitude. they saw through it all of course, but chose not to discuss my situation, although years later recalled every moment.

At the year's first shows we kept collecting halter points, although classes now were often small due to other owners still refusing to compete against Gentry. Progress was slow, but we kept collecting those valuable points. The more we won, the more valuable he became.

We needed ten in one event to earn a Register of Merit, so I chose English Pleasure, although we were working western too, where I was having the problems, not my horse, with his headset. I found it difficult holding the romal reins correctly, on too severe a bit, without over bridling him.

Gentry won the Junior English classes at the first shows in the Lower Mainland, cementing the ten points in mid June for his Register of Merit. AQHA's envelope bringing the certificate is still amongst my momentos. I expected to finish his required 15 halter points during the year, which would assure the High Point Year End Award too, but we needed more working points before contemplating his final 'working category' for the AQHA Championship. At that time there were less than two thousand horses who had achieved the distinction in the whole of the Association's 2,000,000+.

My ambitions were high, now that Gentry was mastering English and western I dreamed of winning High Point All Arounds too. That meant teaching him trail, where the horse has to be calm, to think for himself. Obstacles have to be negotiated with the horse instantly obeying the rider, with the head carried comfortably, not too high, enabling him to see where he is going.

We rigged up some simple obstacles in the arena, four logs spaced a foot apart to begin with. I rode him up to look, stopped before stepping over, waiting for him to settle, then tapped his poll lightly, encouraging him to lower his head to check where he would plant his feet. With help from someone on the ground, one foreleg was quietly lifted over the first log and place in the next space. I asked him to stand motionless for several moments, quietly patting him. Then my helper stroked his other foreleg, and it was placed in front of the first. More praise, then the hind legs in similar fashion. He was never afraid, always confident and wanting to please.

The time came when we needed additional help at Heritage, and obtained it from a Halfway House helping men trying to throw off drug or alcohol addiction. I fetched two or three men from seven miles away each morning, when they mucked out our stalls and completed other simple tasks at Heritage. The physical stamina of the men was severely lacking, and mostly their mental faculties were compromised. To an extent, we were helpful to them. Instructions on how 'to keep your head down, shovel the manure and wet spots into this barrow,' plus 'push the barrow into the next stall and do the same thing before emptying it onto the manure heap,' were not too difficult for them to follow. Physical exercise in the open air was good for the men, but they were so out of condition their sweat was profuse and their breathing laboured, after only a few minutes at work. They needed many rest periods. Still the work they did lightened my load considerably, and they did not demand too much remuneration.

In early August, Joanne Dixon and I drove the final portion of the five hundred miles to Prince George for a one day show. It had been linked in as part of a quarter horse major circuit with 100 Mile House, (heavy with huge black flies biting the horses) and Williams Lake Rodeo (complete with dozens of beer drinking Indians in their tepees) en route, so it meant being away from home for an exciting week.

The road was exceptionally rough due to huge frost cracks and pot holes that appeared each spring and grew more numerous mile by northern mile. On the outskirts of Prince George the abrupt change from stark, wild rangeland to boom-town atmosphere was startling. The tall buildings, wide roadways, modern homes and apartment buildings seemed totally out of place in the horizon-to-horizon wilderness.

Needless to say the Fairground was not ready for us, but we banded with other newly-arrived exhibitors to clean stalls and lay wood shavings. Once the horses were comfortably settled in a rambling barn, we gave them a chance to rest before bathing and sprucing up for the morrow. Not long after they were dozing in neat, calm surroundings, a show organizer arrived to say we would have to move into tie stalls, as the ones we had secured were reserved for futurity colts!

None of us accepted the announcement with flawless grace, but our rebellion was moderate and did not last long. Horse show people, if they are to survive the circuits, must learn to accept unexpected snags with good humor, and rely on unconquerable resourcefulness to overcome them.

We did not intend for our horses to stand in outdoor tie stalls all night. Our solution was to collect old gates discarded in a haphazard heap on the fairgrounds, round up some hammers and nails, then build our own temporary stalls in an unused barn. We located some bales of straw left from an earlier show and appropriated them to make comfortable stall beds. Our horses slept well that night

Next morning I took a bouncy Gentry into the aisle to clean his feet, wash his socks and groom him. He stood quietly as young Judy Cunningham, a bright youth rider, stopped to say 'hello'. Gentry's feet, due to their weak walls, were being held together by odd-looking shoes, with strong side clips securing the hind ones.

Curious, Judy leaned down to examine a clip. Gentry, who had never kicked at anything in his life, opened his eyes quickly. Perhaps he felt a fly on his flank, for his off hoof lashed out in a mighty swat. The noise it made when it struck Judy's cheek was shocking. Blood spurted from a nasty gash beside her eye.

Everyone rallied round whilst Judy was transported quickly to the hospital where she received three stitches. In due course she sported a black eye but never laid blame on Gentry, as he had not meant to harm her. In spite of the inauspicious start to the day. Gentry did win Grand Champion Gelding and was readied for the All Ages English Pleasure class. There were over 30 horses entered from three years of age upwards, so the challenge was very strong.

Entering the ring dark clouds hovered menacingly above us, and before we finished our first trot, hail stones the size of golf balls splattered around, soon creating a 4 inch slippery, white footing. The judge quickly abandoned the class and we rushed for shelter in the barn stall area. Twenty minutes later the sun came out, the hail slush melted, and we resumed the class.

Gentry won. The long journey had been worthwhile.

I was in charge of rehabilitation at Heritage, for no matter how busy my days were, how tired I became, the satisfaction of restoring confidence and good health in animals, who had been mercilessly abused and neglected, brought to me an immeasurable degree of satisfaction.

My first trainer helping at Heritage was pretty Karen Walt who lived on a small farm about three miles away. Her background had been in showing jumping prior to marriage and two small children.

Karen helped me a little with Gentry's initial breaking, being the first to leg me up in an English saddle on my lovely young horse.

Inevitably we talked of her jumping career, when she had ridden and worked with Bo Mearns, one of Canada's elite jump riders.

Karen asked me if I knew of any young horses with a jumping potential which could be purchased cheaply! What an order, but I began thinking about it, remembering Lloyd Warland from Richmond who had shown his yearling colt, Par's Pug, against Gentry. I knew Lloyd had handled many horses who were doomed for killing. He brought them up from Washington State into British Columbia, prior to a tedious journey into Alberta to a killing plant. All so sad, but there are many horses who were better off dead than left in the hands of unscrupulous people to starve to death or worse.

We visited Lloyd at his Steveston Farm one afternoon. He had about thirty sad horses milling about in a couple of paddocks, scrambling for the hay he threw them, endeavoring to improve their weight before the inevitable shipping.

We both noticed a bright bay mare nearly 16 hh whose conformation appealed to Karen, and she agreed to purchase her for $500.00. Leaving the paddock I noticed a very forlorn dark brown thoroughbred gelding, with his bones sticking out everywhere, covered in lacerations. In spite of his condition, I recognized beautiful conformation. Lloyd told me the horse had been on a race track and thrown several jockeys, being extremely high strung and nervous. Now the other heavier horses in the paddock were beating him for the hay and it looked as though he did not get much. My heart beat fast! Poor animal, surely I could fatten him up, calm him down and make a useful addition to Heritage for me to ride. Gentry was still a baby requiring only limited work, so this horse could fill my riding void. He was five years old and I welcomed yet another challenge.

"Lloyd, I will give you $50.00 for that pathetic creature, but I want both horses delivered to Heritage this evening. He haggled for a few moments, but I believe he thought he had a good price for the mare so he might as well get rid of the gelding too. We eventually called the horses Happy and Go-Lucky quite appropriately.

We drove quickly back to Heritage, and prepared two of the original stalls I had for Shafter and Star, hidden away from the rest of the barn. After the horses arrived, we carefully fed them and began bathing Happy's 64 lacerations. He was so appreciative of the loving care, soon realizing we only wanted to help him. For weeks I slowly built him up physically with limited, but increasing grain mixture and good alfalfa hay, continuing bathing his sores, applying furacin and comfrey. Karen was soon able to begin training Go-

176

Lucky who made her a good horse.

Happy, with sores healing, was turned out daily with Star in the front paddock by the lake, placidly grazing the lush grass, dozing under the cedar trees. I spent stolen minutes with him as often as I could, gaining his love and confidence, watching the pounds creep back on his body, molding an even better frame than I had initially imagined. The gleam deepening in his coat told me his health was returning fast. Perhaps even more than at any time in his life.

I believed he was ready for a new phase. He did not object as I tacked him in a light snaffle bridle and my English saddle, then lunging him quietly. After about a week it was time to move on. I asked Karen to leg me up on him in the outside ring. A few of the boarders, now quite intrigued with the reclamation process, turned up to watch. And watch they did, for Happy had no intention whatsoever of my mounting him, spinning away as I grasped the saddle above his withers. We tried several times with another friend holding him on the off-side, all to no avail. I climbed to the top of the ring rail, holding Happy close to me. In the end I sat there for nearly three hours, his head finally lodging in my lap as I gently massaged his ears and neck. Needless to say our audience soon drifted off with better things to do.

It was a warm, sunny afternoon, and we dozed companionably together. I had no intention of giving in, but found it impossible to plan a way of getting on Happy's back, he was just too scared. Then a thought struck me. Leaving him in his dozy state, I eased my legs quietly beneath me until I was kneeling on the top rail, then slowly rising higher, I gently slipped down onto his back. Of course he awoke very startled, grabbing the bit between his teeth, flying wildly around the ring. As I closed my legs to his sides he went even faster so I had to raise them away. Thank goodness for my gymnastic training, horse vaulting, when at Malvern Girls College so many years before!

Happy and I raced around the ring, while I tried quietening him, using my voice when my legs no longer urged him forward. It was very wild for I had no control, but strove to stay mounted. The previous audience returned to watch proceedings, but although I slowed him down eventually, when both of us were very weary, he would not stop. He was going far too fast for me to consider bailing out. I called for two of the girls to grab his bridle on either side and I would attempt to manoeuvre him between them. They did, we slowed, all piling eventually to a sliding stop. How to get off was still a big problem for as soon as I put one leg up, the other must have squeezed him, and his terror returned as he trembled, showing white rings around his eyes. Back to the old gymnastics, I leant slightly forward, then quickly pulled both legs together, lifting high above his back, vaulting neatly to the ground. What an adventure! I persevered.

Strangely, several weeks later, Lloyd Warland called on the telephone. "Joy, I am worried about you. Please do not attempt to get on that horse. My conscience has gotten the better of me. The horse was warned off the race track because of his temperament, injuring several jockeys and frightening other horses at the starting gates."

Lloyd continued, "He was then banished to chariot racing, where again he caused problems, resulting in chariots overturning and men being severely injured. In fact, I believe he was responsible for killing a man." "The killer market became the only option, which is where I found him. I beg you not to try getting on him."

I took quite a bit of pride in telling Lloyd I had been riding the horse for two weeks, although did not admit to the mounting and dismounting problems which had gradually improved!

After a few weeks with Happy, eventually being able to ride him around our fields, I began to take regular basic dressage lessons on the little thoroughbred with Inez Fisher Credo. Her barn was only two miles away and Karen used to ride down with me on Go-Lucky, for company. I believed in going to the top for this instruction and Inez was certainly the finest rider in Western Canada at that time.

We worked hard together for over a year, during which period I entered my 15.3 hh glossy thoroughbred in a variety of schooling shows, riding in Road Hack, English Pleasure and Show Hack successfully, even pulling in a couple of Show High Point All Arounds. The following summer I entered him in the Pacific National Exhibition in Vancouver when we took a number of the boarder's horses along for three days. I think they all thought my head needed examining, taking Happy into such a noisy environment only reminding him of race track days!

We were to ride in the Open Show Hack Stake at 2 pm for the opening afternoon performances, so to help his peace of mind I took him in overnight, which was a good decision. He was very nervous upon my early morning arrival, so after his breakfast, I decided to calm him down with lengthy exercise in the quiet warm-up ring. The cattle, their mooing, the horses all around, unsettled him for a long time. In fact, I camped on him for over five hours in the end, climbing wearily off just a little time before the class, for us both to freshen up briefly and take some slight nourishment.

We had an incredible ride. Happy more relaxed, trusted me, loving what he was doing, gave a surprisingly polished and rhythmical performance. However, whilst trotting, I noticed a thick reversed pyramid of foam hanging from his mouth which he could not seem to shake off. The show ring had been decorated around the inside with a few small cedar trees, and somehow I directed his head across one of the lower branches, transferring the thick foam. It was to remain there, white and sticky, for the next two days! I proudly received the second placing in the Open Show Hack Stake, an award never to be forgotten.

Tragically Happy became even more sensitive shortly after our return home, with two veterinarians, Dr. Bill Saunders and Dr. John Twidale, declaring he would have to be permanently drugged if I was to ride him safely amongst other horses. Sedatives or narcotics would have to be administered more and more frequently to keep his nervous system controlled and prevent seizures. He was now just teetering on the brink of severe mental trauma. He foamed at the mouth in any stressful situation. He was becoming a danger to me and himself. I put him in a different barn away from Gentry, who was showing increased jealousy for the time I spent away from him. I once put them in the same paddock, but my young Quarter Horse chased Happy away with barred teeth and an evil look in his eye. It was a very sad time, but after much pressure I agreed to put Happy to sleep in kindness to him. Both vets declared he was an epileptic and incurable. I always felt had I been able to shrink him down to mouse size and keep him in a cage on the kitchen sink, he would have been a wonderful friend.

Gentry's jealousy of Happy was when I truly realized how close Gentry and I had become, and the first time I had proof Gentry was, if you will "human" same as I, susceptible to many of the same emotions.

Gentry, of course, was pleased with the outcome.

In this year, 1973, beloved Star developed a serious sinus problem and had to be put to sleep. King had gone to another farm where he carried four or five young children on his back at the same time, whilst Shafter remained in retirement. I took solace in Gentry as his show career had developed beyond my wildest dreams. The bonding between us had been incomparable throughout his life and we were closer than ever.

I continued working Gentry systematically quietly, but not over doing it, after all he was only three years old. We began to jump, working over low fences, in smooth style. We attended a fine clinic conducted by ex-quarter horse trainer Gene Lewis from California, who was training hunter/jumpers at Thunderbird, implanting a firm basis for the rest of his life.

I was approached by the Director of the British Columbia S.P.C.A., Mr. Jaworski, to become a Horse Inspector for the Fraser Valley. During the following two years I helped to rescue a number of horses from neglect and cruelty.

Dr. John Twidale, our veterinarian, who had trained at Cambridge in England, and then practiced with thoroughbreds in Australia and New Zealand, had come to Aldergrove in 1971, joining Dr. Bill Saunder's Clinic. Dr. Twidale had made Heritage his main responsibility with the then 40 horses, but now nearly sixty. One morning he appeared with an interesting proposition. A pair of wealthy Americans, Richard and Lori Cavallo, were boarding eight horses at another stable being kept in a deplorable condition. They were of mixed parentage, emaciated, needed worming, good feed, proper care and conditioning. Dr. Twidale, knowing we were just completing a new block of stalls adjoining the smallest arena, suggested the horses be moved to Heritage, and we agreed.

The Cavallos were to prove most interesting. Richard had been with the Chase Manhatten Bank in New York until moving to Vancouver two years previously as a developer. Lori, tall and blond, had been a show girl in Las Vegas before returning to Canada. It turned out she had been born in Saskatchewan, where she had spent most of her life as Lawrence Pearson before becoming "Lori". She and Richard had met in a Vancouver nightclub shortly after the final surgery completing her sex change.

Once the Cavallo horses were in good condition both Richard and Lori started taking riding lessons with our trainers, who soon convinced the pair they ought to sell their horses and buy better ones. I tried steering them towards Quarter Horses, but Lori loved the more dramatic Arabians, and they purchased six marvellous purebred Egyptian ones from Wayne Newton, the popular singer.

The Cavallos drove out from West Vancouver daily in His and Her Mercedes cars – Lori in the mornings in her jazzy sports model with the trunk crammed full of carrot treats. Richard in the afternoons in his powerful sedan. Impressive as these automobiles were, I was proud of my new wheels, a yellow second hand Pinto, an unexpected gift from John.

We were paid well for the boarding, training and instruction in both English and western by the Cavallos. John was impressed with them and for once did not complain when I spent time with customers in the barn. He thought I was paying special attention to the Cavallos, although I was not, everyone received the same attention from me.

Other friends, wealthy boarders of three horses, Ernie Kehler and his family, were impressed with the Cavallo horses. Ernie and his wife, Annette, often visited Las Vegas where Ernie gambled heavily at the crap tables, often coming away a big winner. Usually he gave the money to Annette, who added to her jewelry and fur collection. Their horse-mad young daughter, Susie Denise, took regular jumping instruction showing great promise. Not to be outdone by the Cavallos, Ernie purchased two stallions, Higher Ground and Bramus, also from Wayne Newton's Arabian breeding farm, along with two comely fillies.

All of these lovely horses were very valuable. My increased responsibilities taking care of them were tremendous. I seldom dared leave the farm even to shop for groceries. When showing Gentry I had to plead with John to run Heritage along my lines, and strangely enough, he did.

On my birthday in 1973, October 5th, John presented me with a wonderful set of show jumps he had had especially made. We arranged them in the large outdoor ring enabling us to put on monthly jumping shows bringing in additional boarders. We hired more boys to come in and help after school.

Even with the additional help, I was under pressure. The boys had to be constantly overseen, and although John was helping with some of the feeding before he left for the office in Vancouver, I still had to turn out all of the horses into the paddocks, bring them in at lunch time, often changing their blankets. I had to be especially available for the clients when they came out to ride their horses often from over 40 miles away in Vancouver. John was earning well in his managerial position at Burns Bros. and Denton. In fact, in 1973 I remember he told me he earned more than the Premier and minister of Finance of B.C. put together. We purchased an adjoining 20 acres and built another indoor arena, 100' x 200'.

My help in the construction of the new arena was to hold the survey tape to ensure sizes and depths were correct. Then, after the holes were dug for the support poles, to hold them steady while the concrete was poured. Sometimes while engaged in such jobs I would smile, thinking of my mother who was to the manor born, and knowing how appalled she would have been had she seen me so engaged.

John always slept for a couple of hours after returning in the afternoons, wanting his evening meal served promptly after awakening. He became very irritated if his meal was late.

"I am not super human," I told him. "I can't do everything at once. I have been on my feet all day and still had not time for lunch let alone to shop for your meal."

"I should think you could prepare a simple meal on time," he countered.

The typical old British attitude, where the man earns the money, and the woman looks after the home, children, daily meals and everything else, was paramount with John. He seemed to have forgotten that we were in Canada and that my endeavors had always contributed as much as his, and often more, to our bank account.

Unfortunately my chats with the clients were usually at their peak when John wanted his evening meal. Often, if I were late, he stormed into the barn area, rudely interrupting whatever conversation I was involved in, grabbed me roughly by the arm propelling me toward the house. Strangely, he could do that in such an apparent good humoured way, no one seemed to take offense.

Inside the house, however, he released all his venom. On one occasion he threw a bowl of fresh raspberries at me. I dodged, the crystal bowl hit the wall, with the deep crimson juice of the berries splashed across the wallpaper, seeping into its pores. Another time he destroyed four antique oak ladder back chairs, by dashing them against a Seventeenth Century table and over my shoulders.

During other tirades he broke most of our good china and glassware, glorying in my anxiety when he dashed tureens to smithereens which had been my parent's wedding presents from my grandparents. I watched the chips falling around me. Angry at not having the guts to stand up and fight him, knowing how fast we were going toward disaster. He took malicious pleasure in frightening me, kicking me to submission, making me sweep up the debris on hands and knees whilst he smirked. Several more years would pass before I understood this is the standard pattern of battered women. For reasons she cannot define, a battered woman tends to stand by the man who abuses her until the proverbial straw breaks the woman's back, or worse.

The straw breaking mine was a long time coming. In the meantime I merely wished I knew how to rid him of the mental torment compelling him to lash out over something as trivial as not serving a meal on time. But, I told myself, things could be worse. At least John was in Vancouver during the week.

This was not to last, however. Yet again John ran into trouble on the job. It was the same old problem. He had to have an enemy in his world at all times, someone to pick on, scorn and deride. He began antagonizing some of the stockbrokers. His Toronto Directors grew increasingly alarmed with the disruption he caused, asking him to leave!

"They're all fools, I'm as well to be out of it," he told me. "Besides, I'm needed here."

As he spoke I wondered if I could bear his erratic ways all day long every day, and he must have sensed my thoughts. "I love you so much," he said. "If you should ever try to leave me, I think I would kill you first and then myself."

Years past, on the cliff at Torquay, he had threatened to jump should I leave him. I had left, he had not jumped, as I had known he would not.

But I could no longer read him accurately. Could he do such things? Kill me? Kill himself? I would now be his enemy.

Upon leaving Burns Bros. John sued them successfully for six months severance pay, a nasty way to leave the industry. It left him in mental turmoil worse than before. Into the bargain I now had him around me 24 hours a day. I was too exhausted to do anything about the situation, my priorities being in caring for 60 horses.

Some of the boarders often rode in the indoor arena until 10 or even 11 pm, sometimes forgetting to put out the overhead lights. Either John or I made a trip to the barn to douse them and for a final check on the horses.

One night John was shouting at me because I had purchased the wrong cut of beef at the market, informing me he had had enough. He showed me a loaded gun, telling me he intended to shoot Gentry, then me and himself, as soon as the last riders went down the driveways.

God has an incredible way of looking after me. I had only that evening chatted with some of the girls, Margaret and Chris, and said if they were leaving late, after 10:30, to pop in on their way back from the barn and I would make them a hot chocolate; never to go past the house under any circumstances if I flashed the kitchen lights. It was a strange invitation to ask anyone to visit so late at night.

John had gone into the den sitting in silence. I heard the girl's car come down towards the house, moving into a higher gear. They were not coming in! In desperation I rushed to the switches by the door, flashing the lights repeatedly. Thank God, the girls honoured the signal, swiftly parking their car, coming into the kitchen.

John shouted through the intercom, "what the devil is going on? Get those bitches out of here NOW!"

Chris and Margaret heard every word. I quietly whispered to Margaret to return back to the barn phone and ask Dr. Bill Saunders, who was a counselor, for help. In the meantime chatted to 'both' girls about their horses as I made the hot chocolate. John's impatience mounted. He kept calling through the intercom for me to "Get rid of those fucking bitches," over and over again. He must have forgotten, or perhaps did not care, we could all clearly hear him.

"Clear the house," he yelled, "I demand those f...ing bitches go!"

Margaret returned, both girls bravely staying with me. Car lights twinkled up the winding drive, past the lake, with John now screaming, "Who the f... is that?"

The car pulled up quietly by the back door. Bill Saunders walked in saying, "I saw your lights on and wondered if you had the coffee pot perking away?"

Since we were three quarters of a mile from the main road such a statement was somewhat unlikely, but John bought it. I quietly whispered to Bill the scenario, that John was alone in the den with loaded guns.

Bill found him in the den. The girls left. I waited and prayed a lot. Bill did a masterful job of calming John, eventually bringing him into the kitchen. John's mood had totally changed. Bill took the guns away with him under his coat, whether John noticed or not I have no idea.

He would not kill anything that night.

He had intended shooting Gentry, my horses, and then turn the gun on me and himself, of which I had no doubt.

The Northwest International, Vancouver's then most prestigious horse show, was held in the new Agrodome Building in Exhibition Park at the end of September, 1973. I had entered Gentry in all of the Futurities as they came along during his life, but none was to give more motivation than for the highlight of this show. I had dreamed for a long time of Gentry winning the British Columbia Quarter Horse English Futurity, and worked my lovely horse to greater levels than other owners of three year olds. Hours of training, commitment and dedication had brought my horse along so far. This for the time of being, would be his crowning glory.

Gentry was taller than the other eleven horses entered, and as

I had won the Halter Gelding Grand Championship in the morning under California judge, Richard Deller, I knew he would be looking for us. The Futurity was scheduled for the evening performance which meant all the seats in the building would be full, and the young horses would probably be tense and inclined to act up.

As usual, I groomed Gentry till he shone like a newly minted penny. I braided his mane better than ever before, putting tiny white wool bows at the top of each braid, and five more down his tightly braided tail. I changed into my cream breeches, black coat and black bowler hat, ensuring my tack gleamed to match my horse. I had ridden him earlier down in the cattle barn for nearly an hour, working quietly in basic dressage movements as usual, ensuring he moved perfectly straight, but bending his body at my softest leg aids and gentle finger pressure on the reins.

All the exhibitors were female, and as 9 pm approached, we were tense showing nerves we did not know we had. Each one of us rode beautiful horses who had been successful during the year in one way or another, so winning the Futurity was not a walk over.

It was time to enter the ring. Decisively Gentry eased us in first, with a little help from me. Those initial impressions are so important to a judge.

We had shown so well all of his life, but this was a major milestone I wanted him to claim. The announcer, Jack Webb, introduced the Futurity as the main event for the evening, stating all of the three year old Quarter Horses had achieved success during the year, that they were born in British Columbia, Washington or Oregon. Gentry's march into the arena with his head and eyes alert, his beautiful 'rabbit ears' nearly touching. and his trademark elevated, long strides, certainly gave the impression he was the star and there to prove it. I rode quietly, barely daring to breathe, letting him take the limelight, not wanting to interfere with his thunder. I gathered later the other horses never really stood a chance. for when we were asked 'to trot on' I pushed him into such a strong extension, without increasing speed, his hoof prints over stepped by more than twelve inches. A remarkable action for one so young – all on a light rein – with his head a little in front of the vertical. He moved quietly, smoothly but dramatically. His canter was round and elevated, whereas the other horses moved flat with their heads stretched out in front in the usual Quarter Horse fashion. Richard Deller could not keep his eyes off Gentry. We reversed direction, performing the gaits in the same manner before lining up for the regulation back up. Gentry was glowing now, moving straight with his head and neck lightly balanced. The horses all performed well, and it was probably difficult to choose the other placings, but my Hyline Gentry had stolen the show, yet again living up to his name.

A red carpet was unrolled for the presentations. Riding up to the President of BCQHA, Jack Cunningham, we were awarded the largest cheque, a big bottle of champagne, a bouquet of flowers and the purple and gold First Place Futurity ribbon. All of the other horses received their ribbons and cheques as they proudly left the ring. I asked Jack to temporarily hold our champagne and flowers, when we were invited to stand beneath the clock at the south end of the darkening arena. The announcer introduced us, the spotlights were turned on, and we executed a spectacular sitting trot across the ring to the exit. Thunderous applause rang in our ears, turning Gentry 'on' as never before. He knew he had won. His English Futurity was well deserved.

The following day a beautiful bouquet arrived from our first mentor, Len Cooke, saying how really proud he was of our success. Len had been instrumental right from the start with Gentry's show career, and had remained a good friend.

Gentry winning 3 Year Old English Futurity
N.W. International

186

Although we had great successes at the Vancouver major shows, there was a near tragedy too. At the Pacific National Exhibition in Gentry's fourth year, we won the Gelding Halter Championship in the morning and were pleased to be third out of 21 in Junior Western Pleasure. He was entered for two high prized Open Stakes, competing against horses from other breeds, Appaloosas, Arabs, Thoroughbreds, as well as Quarter Horses, during the afternoon and evening. I had prepared him for the Open English Stake, leaving him in his stall close to the arena as I watched an earlier class. I was aware visitors to the Exhibition often wandered through the barn to watch how we prepared the horses.

Gentry was walking round and round his stall when I returned, soon trying to rub his face against my shoulder. It was so different to his usual behavior, but I did not sense a problem. Putting on his bridle carefully, as usual, I led him into the collecting area and mounted. We entered into the arena with the other horses, quickly being asked to trot. Gentry, stretched his neck out, striking high with one hoof, seemingly attempting to brush it against his face. He did this repeatedly and I noticed heavy foam pouring from his mouth. Obviously something was very wrong. I slowed to a walk and rode towards the judge, requesting we be excused from the class.

Back in his stall, Gentry pawed at his face which he lowered towards the ground. I summoned the Show Veterinarian at once. He recognized there was a major problem, but after examining his mouth could find nothing. There had to be something wrong! I asked for a pain killer to help with whatever pain Gentry was suffering. This eliminated me from further competition for the remainder of the show, as all drugs are forbidden, and these would stay in his body for at least 48 hours.

I remained with my unhappy horse, desperately worried, for he refused even an apple or water. The vet hovered round but seemed powerless. Gentry was sweating from pain and now near panic, all so alien to him. I stroked him, tried cooling him with wet cloths, all to no avail. I asked the Show Secretary to find another vet immediately, for it appeared obvious to me my horse was sinking rapidly.

This vet was aware at once of the trauma. He tranquilized Gentry, and perhaps ought to have given me the same shot too, for I was beside myself. He put a gag in my horse's mouth, holding the jaws apart, gently feeling the entire length of the gums and tongue with his fingers. Suddenly he stood straighter, but did not let go of the tongue, as he asked for a blunt ended set of pincers from his

187

veterinary bag. After a few delicate manipulations he grasped a foreign object lodged in one side of the tongue close to his throat.

The vet withdrew the pincers holding a four inch white wooden stick! It appeared someone visiting the horses must have given my horse a toffee apple, which no doubt he had chomped with relish, driving the stick into his tongue. After removal Gentry rapidly returned to his usual self, but of course I was unable to compete in either of the Stake classes due to the drugs forbidden for competitors. Someone's unthinking generosity had nearly killed my horse.

Gentry soon recovered, but the disaster brought home to me how nearly I could have lost him at the Pacific National Exhibition. It was time for some fun for us both, away from the dedication we had so far put into my beautiful horse's life. Of course horses do get tired of showing, especially Quarter Horses, plodding repeatedly round the show rings, in class after class on the same day, unable to give life and animation to their gaits, having to move precisely and correctly, according to AQHA demands. Most of us give the horses two months of rest after the hectic seasons, often having attended thirty or forty shows on the west coast, with huge mileages covered in the horse trailers often stressing their legs. They need a good rest if they are to remain sound years ahead and to maintain their happy dispositions.

Four years before, when I had purchased Hyline Gentry from the Petersen's Home of the Hylines, I had vowed at the time, to hunt him with the Fraser Valley Hounds at the end of his fourth year on my birthday, October 5th. The time had arrived!

Bev McShane with her sorrel Nowgo Leo joined us on a brilliantly sunny day, with bright blue sky overhead, at the Hall's Emerald Acres in Aldergrove for the Meet. Our two young horses loved the change of pace, safely jumping their way over about 25 fences and panels, placed over barbed wire, most over three feet high. We followed the drag hunt for over a ten mile course. Both horses were very fit and excited but behaved well in true Quarter Horse style, returning home without a bump or blemish. It was a dream accomplished for Gentry, and I promised him in the future we go again. And so we did three years later, in another country.

Newspapers and horse magazines had been writing articles about "Hyline Gentry Going Big" in August 1971, listing his outstanding yearling accomplishments. They knew more than me at that stage, but he did collect 37 Halter Grand Championships in British Columbia and Oregon, with comparative limited showing, with four eventually from the P.N.E.

Chapter Nine

"Those who say it can't be done,
shouldn't stand in the way of those who are doing it"

In 1972 I had been elected to be a Director of the British Columbia Quarter Horse Association, with monthly meetings in Langley. There had been a small newsletter initially written by Dorothy Todhunter, a knowledgeable horsewoman, judge and trainer, who had found it difficult finding time to continue. I took over the position, a curious place for me as a new Canadian in charge of reporting news to the membership as their new Editor.

For nearly three years I wrote all the Quarter Horse member's gossip for the Association, of the four and two legged varieties, thoroughly enjoying being a useful portion for the Directorship. I wrote about show results, special achievements by riders and their horses, foals born, new babies and decisions made at the monthly meetings. I loved it, typing information and opinions onto fifteen to twenty skins monthly, I organized five or six members to help run it off through an old fashioned Gestetner, stapling and addressing for despatch to all members, from my kitchen. Days later, pleased with the arrival of my efforts, members would put the coffee pot on, and sit down for a peaceful hour or two catching up with the news. Above all I felt I was giving something back to the Association which had taught me so much.

I so often wanted to leave John. There was no affection left in our marriage. He kept me trapped ensuring I had only $10.00 weekly for personal spending. I loved my horses far too much to walk off and leave them, their comfort came before mine. John rationalized, correctly, I would never be in a position to place the horses elsewhere without money. When a woman becomes totally exhausted with hard work, and is subjugated to a man's superior strength, she becomes a pathetic shadow of her former self. My normal strong cheery personality was lost. I was incapable of intelligent thought, or working matters out. Like the past drunken men working for us, I kept my head down and carried on with the work. My thoughts were only of the horses in my care. Who would give them their next meal if I did leave? I struggled on, accepting the abuse. I lost all respect for myself, but somehow around the horses I found hidden strength and courage.

My main concern was insuring the Heritage boarders were happy. The majority still lived in the Vancouver area, arriving in the late afternoons for their rides or training classes. After their more than one hour drive to the farm, particularly if the weather was bad, I believed a warm, personal welcome was essential.

I enjoyed telling each owner some little story about their horse's day, for they were all happy at Heritage, with some horses building special relationships with others. Such stories were considerate and personal.

Dorothy Neville, an elegant woman working as a counselor with the Department of Indian Affairs in Vancouver, owned two outstanding saddlebreds. A palomino, Leaders Gold Ruler, and a dark chestnut, Whispering Winds Commander, who lived up to their names. They frolicked happily together, with Ruler firmly keeping his young companion in order. Dorothy especially relished stories of the episodes, such as Ruler prancing across the grass paddock, head high, tail flowing, showing off.

Another palomino, Ace, a thoroughbred owned by Abigail Brown from West Vancouver, was particularly kind to Gentry, encouraging him to take long stretching strides as they galloped playfully together in the eleven acre gelding pasture beside the lake. It is so necessary for horses to have fun, especially if in training when their daily work can become very demanding.

I had a difficult responsibility keeping the now six trainers from trying to steal one another's customers. They would listen to a lesson, criticizing the procedures in front of other owners, claiming they could make them Olympians if they changed allegiance. I would not tolerate it. I found it necessary to schedule times for the trainer's use of the indoor arenas and outside ring, ensuring they fitted around the boarders own time tables. Keeping the peace was not easy!

One western trainer forced the horses into submission in a variety of cruel ways, offending us all. I instructed her to change her ways or leave, so she did tone down for a while, but her temper tantrums resurfaced. If she arrived in a calm frame of mind she achieved miracles with the horses under her instruction, otherwise we loathed her and I made it known her time with us was running out fast as I would not tolerate abuse of any animal on my property.

However, she established a relationship with Lori Cavollo achieving some success with her and the Arabian horses in the local show rings.

Parents of the girls from West Vancouver asked if their daughters could stay overnight before the monthly schooling shows. Entertaining them as house guests was more than I could cope with so we created a clubhouse of sorts, in the barn overlooking the small indoor arena, where they showered and slept, coming down to the house for meals. During the summer months the girls rode before it became too hot, then swimming in the lake with their horses in the afternoons.

John created massive breakfasts of braised lamb kidneys or smoked kippers, which the girls hated, but dared not refuse. Cold cereal alone in the clubhouse, would have been far more to their liking. John had a limited selection of recipes, which he learned to cook well for an audience, sadly to cook just for me proved to be beneath his dignity.

Our six trainers kept busy schooling and training Quarter Horses, Arabians, eventers, hunters and basic dressage, but increased their incomes with the Cavollo and Kehler horses especially, soon claiming ribbons with them in the local shows. Obviously there was rivalry between these families, who in their individual ways, were accustomed to winning whatever they undertook. Susie Kehler was tiny, refusing to eat properly at home. She was incredibly determined when on her jumping horse, always insisting on lessons and local show appearances. To make her eat, I encouraged her to stay at Heritage from time to time, on the understanding she ate the same meals as John and I, or no riding.

Throughout all of this my sights were set on Gentry's AQHA Championship. Inspite of my being abused in the house, once outside with my beloved horse, I found energy and, with support from many of the boarders, maintained a high standard of training with them. Whenever Gene Lewis gave his jumping clinics at Thunderbird we were there.

Gene was aware of Gentry's special attributes, making us work correctly at all times, I had to ride a spirited young horse around the arena with closed eyes and arms extended directly from my shoulders. We learned to jump through a small combination under the same conditions. It was unnerving, but it taught me balance, to keep off my horse's mouth, leaving his head alone. Gentry and I grew closer, reading each others thoughts and moves. Gene advised me to get another saddle if I was going to ride successfully over jumps. Fine rider and instructor, David Rogers, whose family owned Stampede Feed and Tack, the largest tack shop then in Canada, generously sold me his German Somner, which improved my position and safety.

Perhaps my system was different to the majority of riders, who rode round and round the riding rings and warm up areas until the poor animals were bored to death and looked it, seldom showing any animation. Certainly I trotted, but on a long controlled rein at first, around the warm up areas, not forcing my horse down into an unnatural gait, with humped back and excessively unnatural head and neck carriage as we see so often. I asked Gentry, and subsequently all my other horses, to trot out long and low until I felt them relax, which often came with a sign of a slight drop from beneath the saddle. This was the message to me they were now ready to work. A quiet walk for a few minutes to gain their breath back and then constructive work began, collecting the reins comfortably with light, still hands, never over bridling. Riding 20 meter circles at the trot, then moving into canter, I ensured my horse moved off the hocks, keeping calm. Changing from six strides of canter, a half halt down to trot for about four strides, then back to canter, is a wonderful repetitive exercise engaging the hindquarters. Sometimes I walked from canter, always quietly and controlled, keeping in a rounded frame, then back to canter. These movements shorten the horses frame giving natural collection, and furthermore he enjoys it! I often played waltz or march music when schooling, producing a calm and responsive willing attitude. The work has to be enjoyable for horse and rider. Certainly Gentry and I welcomed our daily sessions together.

Our wins had been impressive, Grand Champions, the Yearling Colt Futurities, English Pleasure Futurity at the Northwest International in Vancouver, his Register of Merit, Class wins, Show All Arounds and many Year End Awards, which we received at a Dinner Dance Award evening each fall. Trophies began to fill the house to such an extent we built a Trophy Room by the office. We won English and western pleasure, trail and working hunter classes, a many varied collection of points, but by the end of his fourth year Gentry still needed the five points in a working category to secure his American Quarter Horse Association Championship, which I had vowed to do the day I purchased him from Eileen Petersen. To my knowledge there was no B.C. bred gelding who had achieved this top status.

Although my experience of roping was very limited, knowing Gentry's mother had been very talented in this category, I felt he should follow in her footsteps. Proving my horse's versatility in this tough stock saddle competition, along with my working hunter efforts, fascinated me. I could never be any kind of efficient western trainer against the professionals, but I wanted to prove him in the world of cowboys.

My immediate problem was to find the right trainer. As usual, I wanted the best. It was now the last show in British Columbia for 1974, the October Northwest International, so I had to decide Gentry's future quickly enabling him to have the appropriate training during the winter months. I had become quite adept at buying and selling tack to pay his past expenses, wondering how on earth I would cope with the final round, but I knew, with my heart set on it, I would manage somehow.

Gentry was in demand by several trainers who fancied themselves finishing an AQHA Champion, a major achievement in those days. Bill Collins, from Cardsholm in Alberta, a talented and kind man, wanted him for his speciality, cutting. When I asked "How would you feed my horse?" he straight faced replied, but with a smile of his lips "With moldy hay and snowballs" of course not giving the answer I wanted, although I think we both knew Gentry was perhaps too big for cutting.

Well known Alberta western trainer, Bob Grimshaw, who I had competed against many times when he worked from Richmond, B.C. was anxious to train him reining. I had seen Bob ride brilliantly, but knew one of his systems was to work the horse in various parts of the reining patterns, then shut him back in the stall, with darkened drapes so the horse could see nothing. According to Bob the horse had to stand there remembering what he had just learned. Not for my Gentry, it would shatter his personality, apart from his again being too big, and I doubt in a horse's makeup if they can recall previous lessons that way.

Two other trainers approached me during the same show, but I was not inspired. His size precluded cutting and reining, then why not utilize it to the fullest? I still felt he should rope like his mother Whispering Lady. I knew I would find the right trainer somehow, and quickly, perhaps from the United States.

I found him during the lunch break in the Agrodome Members Lounge of the Agricultural Building! I had been invited with friends for a drink after tucking Gentry into his stall after a successful morning at halter, and although only 2nd in western pleasure, picked up 3 points myself against tough competition.

Hank Alrich, a very knowledgeable cutting judge, would be assessing those classes in the evening. His pretty new wife, Pat, had accompanied him from Oregon, and was momentarily sitting alone at a small table whilst he chatted with old buddies. I joined her to ensure welcome in our midst.

In the course of the conversation I told her I was searching for a special trainer for Gentry, and mentioned I had been impressed that morning by the handsome young man who had won the western pleasure. I was especially aware of his quietness and gentle hands.

Pat smiled proudly, telling me I was talking of her son, Bob Avila, beginning his training career. She explained he did not yet have a barn to work from in Oregon, but soon hoped to rent a little place in Tigard, near Portland. While speaking, into the lounge walked Bob. Joining us, I told him about Gentry, when he asked me if he could have a look at the horse. He had not been aware of him inspite of my successes in the morning, as he worked with the mare, Sparky Girl, for Sport Laughlin from Yamhill.

As we approached the stall, Gentry pricked his ears alertly as always when he saw me coming. As usual, they almost met at the tips.

"Hello, Rabbit Ears," Bob grinned, patting Gentry's neck.

Bob quickly assessed my horse, his wonderful size and conformation built to rope. Our mutual decision was for me to take Gentry down to the Pacific International in Portland, Oregon, the following month. Bob stated if he did well there, he would give him a roping education.

Our Heritage western trainer, Heather Innes, had helped me with Gentry, especially with trail endeavors, and she quickly agreed to help with him at the P.I. where the showgrounds stretched along the banks of the Columbia River. In November it was damp, cold, and shrouded in fog. Thank goodness we arrived prepared with enough warm blankets and leg wraps.

The Pacific International, or as it was known, the P.I., was a major show for open and various breed classes, like the Pacific National Exhibition in Vancouver. I was fascinated with the Tennessee Walkers, flashy Saddlebreds, dramatic Arabians and top-flight Quarter Horses. Many famous Quarter Horse personalities I had read about in the Quarter Horse Journal would be my competitors.

Despite the dreary weather and impressive quality of competitors, my spirits were tinged with sunshine. I just knew in my heart Gentry would acquit himself well. I was further heartened by remembering the judge was none other than the illustrious AHSA and AQHA adjudicator, Don Burt, who had been very impressed with Gentry at the 1973 Chilliwack International in May where he had won his first High Point Horse award.

Gentry winning the All Ages English Hunt Seat at the Pacific International in Portland, Oregon. November, 1974

Gentry took the Grand Champion Gelding honours, winning the Junior Western Pleasure, a huge trail class with Heather on board, and an even larger English Hunt Seat for All Ages, with me. Gentry was High Point Horse for the show. he appeared to have collected 15 AQHA points and I was ecstatic in that company. But we should not count our chickens before they are hatched, I learned too quickly. When I requested from the show secretary the Halter

Champion silver horse usually given out in the ring, I learned with horror, she had not applied to AQHA the required 90 days before the show for their approval. Technically the show was unapproved, therefore no points would be awarded to anyone. A major catastrophe for me, but I did have the trophies, though not the silver halter Champion horse, and ribbons with photographs of their presentations.

Despite the disappointment over the points, Bob Avila was thrilled with Gentry, agreeing to take him immediately to his small barn in Tigard to train him as a roper during the winter.

I had had one unpleasant experience of entrusting Gentry to the wrong person for a week shortly after he had turned three when, due to a filthy girth previously used on another horse, he became infected and closely escaped founder. I had promised myself I would never make that same mistake of entrusting him to anyone else again. There was something very compelling about young Bob Avila. He was a total unknown, but I knew had been instructed well by his father Don Avila, a good judge and trainer. Bob was beginning his career and desperately wanted an outstanding horse to prove himself. With knowing his mother, too, I felt confident Bob would look after Gentry nearly the way I did. At the time Bob Avila agreed to take him, he did not enjoy the brilliant world headline status he has today. I shall always be proud to be the first to "find" Bob giving him the opportunity to shine. He was just beginning his career. I barely knew him yet never doubted him. Gentry went home with Bob.

I believe the custom of finding reasons to throw victory parties on the show circuit in British Columbia began with Art Folliott's pride in his talented children, Stephen and Susan. They took six American bred horses to Youth AQHA Championships.

The first victory party I remember was one of Arts, in which he broke open a few bottles of rosé wine, inviting friends to toast the winning horse. Other celebrations came regularly after that, for futurity winners, special stakes and triple circuit grand champions.

All the time Gentry logged his successes I dreamed of giving a party for him too, but by the time I covered his monthly training and maintenance, along with show expenses, there was little cash left in my teapot. However, I made a resolution at New Year 1975 to establish a party fund, contributing a little each month.

A sum of five dollars went into the kitty in February, due to my splurging on extra gas to make several trips to Yamhill, seven hours away. Bob, no longer satisfied with the Tigard stabling had moved his operation to the ranch of Sport Laughlin, top Quarter Horse breeder, and grandfather to his girlfriend Chrisity. By now Gentry had turned into a cowpony, proving his pedigree bloodlines were rich in cow sense, which really surfaced when Bob took him into the roping arena.

Bob's initial working specialty was heading and heeling, with Gentry proving equally good at both. Exceedingly fast, he loved chasing cows which were in his blood, moving in for the throw. When awaiting the barrier to drop as the cow left the chute, he would rub his hind quarters against the back bars, building thunder, as the old saying goes. Pushing away from the bars when the barrier dropped, put an extra zing into his explosive getaway, but also rubbed hair off his powerful hindquarters. We used a lot of vaseline to encourage new hair growth! Gentry broke numerous roping record times.

Oregon has a huge population of competing ropers. More than a hundred heading and heeling teams were entered in open competitions in McMinnville, where Gentry made his debut in late February. He came away with a first-place belt buckle for the novice event, which I happily gave to Bob for his efforts.

Despite tight finances, Heritage was humming along with now sixty horses and six trainers. My days were filled morning till night, but I missed Gentry dreadfully. Whenever possible I rose before dawn making the seven hour drive to Yamhill. I never told Bob I was coming, but Gentry knew. When I was possibly half an hour away from the Laughlin ranch, he would become fidgety if Bob was working him in the arena, or if in his stall, he persisted in craning his neck to look out. If in the cross ties or alley way, he would turn to check all vehicles driving into the barn area. If on the hot walker, he often tripped over his own feet while peering down the driveway. On one occasion Bob had left him on the hot walker with the bridle hanging from the saddle horn, Gentry grabbed Bob's favourite expensive reins in his mouth, chewing in frustration. My horse received quite a scolding when Bob returned seeing the two ends dangling from his mouth!

Sometimes during the visits I would saddle him up, taking him into the hills to escape the boredom of training. Bob was concerned for me, as Gentry, conditioned to a peak, would cavort and buck in exuberance once we were on our way. I never scolded, but sat quietly reveling in his love for me until the escapade was finished, then going wherever I decided. He especially loved climbing to the tops of the hills to stand looking down at the tiny, silent automobiles far below.

I cherished those shared moments in the Oregon hills, woman and horse away from the rat race, problems and toil, with majestic trees and soaring birds in a quiet sky for company.

It is not always sunny in Oregon. This western state, with its magnificent coastline and heavily timbered forests, has the highest precipitation in the Nation, especially encouraging hazel nut orchards in the Yamhill area. One day I decided Gentry and I should explore some of the local country. We meandered for nearly three hours, occasionally picking up a sharp trot when climbing the higher reaches, whilst I looked for a return route. It had seemed simple to me, or so I thought, to keep taking a right hand turning, but there were none. I had to admit I was lost when the skies opened, drenching us with rain. I had not taken a raincoat, so within moments I was soaked to the skin. Gentry shook his head to remove the rain from his ears, but I did not worry unduly, for it was not cold. Turning back, the way we came, for a further three hours seemed ridiculous; there had to be a faster route if we continued. Had the sun been out, I could have determined the direction, but it was asleep until the rain stopped. We kept following the winding road, which we had enjoyed with no one on it earlier, but began anxiously looking for someone to help.

In the meantime Bob and Christy were looking for us deciding to call in the police to organize a search party, when they came across a straggling, waterlogged pair, about two miles away from Yamhill.

"Do not ever do this again," said Bob emphatically. Had I discussed the route with them earlier, I would have been persuaded to take another.

I meekly promised I would not distress them that way ever again, although I knew Gentry needed time away from his constant schooling.

In April, Bob entered Gentry in several events at a large Quarter Horse Show in Spanaway, Washington. Best of all, I was to ride Gentry in the bridle path hack class. I was anxious to watch them together in other classes, but Bob firmly asked my not to.

"Please stay away out of sight," he said "You know how "Rabbit Ears" is when you are around. He looses all concentration with me."

Bob often called Gentry 'Rabbit Ears' as he had the first time they met at the Northwest International in Vancouver the previous October, because of the way his ears, set more forward than any other horse we had known, almost touched when he held them to attention.

Joanne Dixon came with me to Spanaway, and I stayed hidden as requested. Gentry only came third in the Halter Aged Gelding class under judge Paul Horn, earning two points. Basically "gated" for the first time in his life, we decided the judge's vision was hideously impaired, or he preferred the bulky type of horse rather than an athlete! His decision in any case.

Bob's first ridden class with my horse was trail, and he had been so anxious Gentry showed well for his first appearance near the Canadian border, over which many of my friends were bringing their horses. I continued to obey his instructions for keeping away from the barn area. We sat at the top of the bleachers, behind a big post. Gentry was outstanding in this class normally, and his owner, who was struggling to pay his bills, intended having the pleasure of watching him win one. There was no way he would know I was hidden amongst the many spectators, or even on the showground.

But he did, as he kept looking toward the bleachers in my direction, where I sat hardly daring to breathe. In spite of Bob's strong leg pressure, Gentry was not cooperating. After entering beautifully through the metal gate, he negotiated the backup ell well, not touching the poles, but instead of moving slowly and carefully, as AQHA rules require, reversed at full speed.

The next obstacle meant the rider dismounting within a chalk circle, hobbling the horse, who was supposed to stand still, whilst the rider walked across the arena, around a barrel and back. Bob told me later he had no hope "Rabbit" would get it right. He was fidgety, somehow deducing I was somewhere close by.

As Bob walked off determinedly on his route, Gentry hopped with front feet firmly hobbled together, straight to the ringside, looking directly toward me, whinneying a loud 'hello'.

Bob retrieved his mount and rode out of the arena.

I let quite a bit of time pass before joining everyone in the barn. Bob was waiting.

"Unless you are riding him," he said emphatically, "Do not be in any arena where this horse is performing. Ever again!"

I meekly promised not to, staying miserably in the barn while Bob and Gentry competed in western pleasure. When they returned, Gentry was ambling happily beside his trainer, but Bob was walking with his head down.

"Rabbit" went exactly as a pleasure horse should," he said glumly, "but the others minced along, going nowhere, with their heads hanging too low, in my opinion...we got the gate."

I said nothing. It was a disastrous day now. The judge obviously did not like my horse.

Gentry and I were entered in the bridle path hack class later in the afternoon. Christy, riding a sharp little horse, Taylor, was also entered. We suspected the way things were going, neither of us would place, so agreed we might as well have a good ride and trot on properly when asked, not slink around dejectedly, like many of the others.

We pushed on with lots of impulsion. It was a cheerful ride for me, being with my beloved horse again, knowing we made no errors as he glided out with his long, beautiful stride. I was astonished to be called in third.

Bob, waiting at the gate, gave us jubilant Thumbs Up sign. I do not know who preened more, "Rabbit" or his owner, who was feeling somewhat vindicated after the morning trouble she had so unwittingly caused. It was a highlight of my day then, be it rather humble.

I had been working very hard at Heritage, seldom leaving the property, unless it was to show Gentry. John did not object to the time I spent away with him strangely, filling in briefly to look after my jobs. We were constantly in the news, Gentry was practically invincible, and I know John was proud of our achievements, aware of the fine reputation it gave to Heritage and our horse management. Great free advertising!

All the same I missed my Vancouver friends very much. Initially they had visited us for dinner parties I gave, or to collect me en route for their days shopping in Seattle, but invitations to us jointly never came. My friends were not prepared to tolerate John's rudeness amongst their other friends or his disgusting sexual jokes. I did not blame them.

However, I must have been in their conversations from time to time, as good friends are. Jean Long phoned one day asking to speak to me. John replied I was unavailable to speak with her; I was just too busy. He did not add he had forbidden me to contact any of them. Jean, knowing John's unpredictable behavior from the months we lived with them, was very concerned. She told him firmly she wanted to see me and unless I could talk with her soon, on the telephone at least, she would be sending the RCMP to investigate!

Obviously Jean had discussed this with my other special friends, for three days later Annette Kehler phoned to say she was arranging a luncheon and wanted me to attend. John must have been shocked when Jean had spoken so strongly, because he spoke reasonably with Annette, saying he knew Joy would be delighted to accept. It was such a long time since I had seen these special old friends, and Annette's home was only about ten miles away, in White Rock not the hours long journey into West Vancouver where the others lived.

The Kehler home, Fircrest, was situated on ten scenic acres overlooking the Gulf Islands off the Ocean Park bluffs. Jean Long, Delia Puttkamer and Gerry Barregar were waiting with Annette to greet me. We lunched by an open window in her elegant dining room. I was in another world, the quiet peace of one of those incredibly beautiful pastel days, only seen on the coast of British Columbia. Under the soft blue sky the sound of our mutual enjoyment of being together once again surrounded me, helping me to laugh a little. We were surrounded with the sweet perfume of a thick hedge of pink roses enclosing the terrace, quite enchanting and I was in another world.

The crunch came with coffee, when I was told the reason for the gathering. My friends were gravely worried about the situation between John and me. They could imagine what happened behind closed doors. They felt sure my life was in danger and wanted to help me shed my marriage and get on with life again. A little cash in hand, they said, would start things rolling. Each presented me with a cheque for one thousand dollars. Tears cascaded down my cheeks, my heart nearly burst with emotion. Friendship is a two way street, what had I ever done to earn theirs to this degree?

I was profoundly touched by their generosity, but at once returned all but Annette's.

"Who knows when I can repay you, Annette," I whispered, between shaking lips, "but I promise I will."

"Don't worry, just get out of the mess. Make an appointment with Ed Mortimer. He's one of the leading divorce lawyers in Vancouver. He'll know what to do."

I rang Ed for an appointment from Annette's home, agreeing to see him three days later. Ed Mortimer's advice was brief.

"Leave the bastard." He agreed I should sell the farm quickly.

I had every intention of doing so, but until the farm was sold, horses under my care had to be safely put into capable hands, and Gentry and I found a safe haven. A week after the Mortimer visit I had a long telephone call from Bob Avila. We had agreed he would show my horse until he achieved his five points in Heading and Heeling roping, and then he would be returned to me. But life takes unexpected twists and we have to be ready. Bob told me there was not another horse in Oregon who could touch Gentry for halter and pleasure. His roping was coming along superbly. Could he not take him along with some of the other horses if he kept show expenses for me to a minimum? He believed Gentry had a marvellous opportunity to become one of the leading horses in the Quarter Horse Nation if he was campaigned fully during the rest of the year, and he should be High Point Horse for Oregon and of Jefferson County, inspite of missing crucial classes at the early shows. It meant financial sacrifices for both Bob and me. The dream continued.

We had been campaigning Gentry lightly because of my financial problems, but I felt he deserved the chance Bob wanted to give him. Somehow it seemed a chance for me to soar too. Gentry had been kept in superb halter flesh and amazingly it had not hindered his roping speeds at that time.

"Go for it, Bob," I whispered, not knowing where the expense money would come from, but knowing, as before, I would get it somehow. Bob loved Gentry nearly as much as me, planning those successes for him. His care and outstanding riding skills with Gentry would cement his future as a top trainer too. Leaving John would have to be put on hold until the end of the year. What were a few more months in the long run after all I had been through?

Gentry carried on collecting halter championships, and winning in western pleasure, trail and both heading and heeling roping. If I was unable to be there Christy rode him very successfully in English. He won many Shows All Arounds, sometimes even running the barrels to collect an extra point. He was practically invincible and I am sure the friendly Americans many times wished the Canadian horse would go home along with his English born owner. In the middle of May at Yreka, Gentry won every class in which he was entered, (five), under the judging of Millburn Barton.

By mid June he had four of the five roping points needed for his AQHA Championship. I was in turmoil, desperately wanting to be with my horse for his crowning moment. The work, constant vigilance and upheaval left my memory, for it had all been a labour of love, yet I knew if my story were to have a happy ending, I must not be there to witness Gentry's glory. His speed, power and intelligence were being talked of in the horse world everywhere. I believe some of the pleasure trainers in British Columbia doubted this big horse, competing against the finest ropers in the Nation, could pull it off. Many had rightly scorned his efforts at Spanaway in April.

Bob took six horses to Hermiston in Oregon for the June show to be judged by Duane Green. Gentry rode in comfort across the front two standings of the big trailer, for he hated the constriction of a single stall, scrambling up the trailer walls around some corners. This would have injured his legs had they not been securely wrapped. Bob gave him the added luxury.

On 21st June 1975 Gentry was second and reserve champion at halter, Christy rode him to second place in Senior English Pleasure. I do not think anyone even stopped for a bite to eat or a can of beer, the tension in the Avila camp was tremendous. Gentry was second again in the heading, but he won the heeling! When Bob called from the showground he said Gentry's time was so fast he received a standing ovation! I had not been there to see my horse's triumph in the flesh, but my spirit had been with him all along. Gentry had his AQHA Championship.

Gentry's final roping point for his AQHA Championship.
June 1975

I had been feeding horses in the barn when the telephone call came through. I tried to continue with reasonable efficiency, but for a few minutes most of the grain landed on the ground instead of the buckets.

Messages of congratulations came in from everywhere. All were warmly received, but one was more special that the rest. Mailed from Gentry's birthplace it read:

Congratulations Joy and Gentry
To our "First" Hyline Gentry
First Futurity Winner
First Grand Champion
First Register of Merit
First Superior Halter Horse
First AQHA Champion

from your parents:
Sir Quincy Bob and Whispering Lady
and all the Petersens
at the Home of the Hylines

Chapter Ten

Seneca:
"Real joy, believe me, is a serious matter."

The time had come for Gentry's Victory Party, but I did not intend to schedule it until Bob and Christy could attend, for so much was due to their wonderful efforts. The time and place I aimed for was late August at the Pacific National Exhibition in Vancouver.

One of my first steps preparing for the celebration was to create a collage with many of Gentry's better photographs, on a huge sheet of red cardboard, then to address, but not mail, invitations for about fifty friends, holding back fifty more to hand out at the show.

John did not know how to handle the situation, happy and proud on the one hand, but jealous on the other. He watched my excitement, becoming incensed because I was a few minutes late in putting dinner on the table one night. I had finished with the horse's suppers and going down to the house about 5:30 pm to prepare John's meal, telling him I still had to make up all their breakfasts. Would he help me later? I was quite unprepared, when without any warning, he grasped me around the throat, swinging me wildly into the kitchen cupboards, then loosing his grip, and I sank onto the floor. The impact with the cupboards caused my top teeth to bite through my lower lip, and I briefly lost consciousness. When I came to I was sprawled on the floor with John standing over me. He grabbed me by the hair, dragged me into the living room, slung me into a chair, refusing to let me move. The blood from my mouth was sticky on my neck, soaking into my shirt. I was too numb to feel pain for a while. He sat in another chair, glaring at me. I begged to go into the bathroom to mop up and attend to my injury, but he scornfully refused.

Mercifully, a knock came at the door. I escaped, running to our bathroom locking myself in, whilst John answered the door. He stopped later, outside the bathroom door, calmly telling me everything was alright. His mood had changed.

I stayed in the bathroom all night. Before dawn I slipped out of the house quietly driving the pickup past the house, to a doctor in Langley, who attended to my wounds. After hearing my story, the doctor wanted both of us to undergo psychiatric evaluations. John categorically refused, but I visited the psychiatrist the Emergency doctor recommended.

He turned out to be an East Indian who thought wives should be subservient to husbands in any case! After the initial visit, I did not return. However, I called up John's doctor, Mike Neilson, who was able to talk him into a general checkup. As a result, shortly after, he went into the Langley Memorial Hospital for thyroid gland surgery. I was pitifully glad his doctor had found something seriously wrong, trusting he would behave a little more normally once it had been corrected.

Ten days later, the day John was to be released from the hospital, I was rushing through my horse chores when the Cavollos arrived. Lori in her Mercedes, with Richard minutes later, in his. She stormed up to me saying they were unhappy with their bill. They could not understand why some of the lessons were for $6.00 and others for $9.00

I patiently explained "Some were for training your horses, and others were for instructing you and Richard on them."

They were not satisfied, so I suggested they wait in the house while I fetched John from the hospital. To make themselves a hot drink and to read the horse magazines on the coffee table, until I returned.

I was exhausted. It seemed so unnecessary at this time, and I wept all the way into Langley, six miles away. To my dismay, John was waiting at the entrance, furious because I was a few minutes late. He said nothing when I explained the situation on the way home. When we arrived, he instructed me to drive past the house up to the main barn. The Cavollos were waiting near their cars. Richard walked over politely inquiring after John's health, but he ignored the remark.

"Richard," he said, "your wife has upset mine once too often. Your bills are straight forward, and I'll explain them to you now if you wish. But in view of the inconsideration you've shown after all we've done for you, I'm giving you one month's notice to take all your horses and yourselves away from Heritage."

He put his arm around me, and we walked to the house.

"You don't have to tolerate such nonsense," he said.

John Richardson will forever be an enigma.

Shortly after I had comfortably settled my husband with a cup of tea, Richard Cavollo appeared asking for reconsideration. John refused to give in. We called a knowledgeable realtor, John's doctor's wife, Sharone Neilsen, asking her to quickly find the Cavollos another home for their horses. In the meantime, we told Richard and Lori, we would loan them a trainer on a temporary basis and I would instruct them how to feed and generally maintain their horses.

Two days later, an exhausted Sharone Neilsen called from a phone box in Aldergrove to talk privately with me. She had taken the Cavollos to every possible horse property in the entire Fraser Valley. Many efficient farms were available, but they were satisfied with none. They wanted Heritage! John, at this precise time, was working on the roof of the large arena and knew nothing of our conversation.

Of course this surprise turn of events demanded some serious consideration. None of the Cavollo horses would have to leave, my established trainers were all in place, and best of all, the boarding horses could stay where they were.

My share of the money from the sale of Heritage would be ample to give Gentry and me a new start. Now and again in discussing the sale of Heritage, John and I had never agreed on a price. He thought $250,000 was fair. I wanted $400,000 and up. Consequently we never did anything, and I knew we would probably do nothing again if I consulted him.

"How much would your commission be if we sold for half a million?" I asked Sharone.

"Thirty thousand," she replied.

"We will sell Heritage for $530,000 firm," I said. "The contract must be signed tonight, along with a down payment cheque of $100,000."

Within half an hour Sharone's car came up the drive with the Cavollos. We were most cordial with one another, and I invited them into the house. We all felt a satisfactory agreement had been reached. Then John appeared.

"I thought I told you people to get out!" he said angrily and would have continued the tirade had Sharone not swiftly taken him into the kitchen explaining the new situation.

John returned all smiles and affability and for the next few days was in his element working out financial arrangements with Richard.

We arranged to hold a First Mortgage at 12%, then an attractive level, and the cheque for $100,000 was safely deposited in our account. It was a very good deal in 1975.

The Cavollos would give a new name to Heritage: "Neetriht," thirteen spelled backwards, Lori's lucky number.

We agreed to be out of Heritage in early October. Since preparing our departure left little time to manage the farm properly, I struck a bargain with one of our trainers, Brenda Sloan. She agreed to direct operations until the Cavollos took over. Brenda's event horse, Muffin, had a companion, a ridiculous goat with wandering tendencies. He left a pellet trail wherever he roamed. All I had to do in return for Brenda's cooperation was to stop complaining about the goat!

The three-week Pacific National Exhibition, a fair sponsored by the Provincial Government for all farm animals, opened in Vancouver the second week of August, and the hottest item in barn talk everywhere was the sale of Heritage. Fourteen horses from our barn were competing in the show. Gentry's party was scheduled for the evening of the twenty-seventh, after the Opening Ceremonies of the Quarter Horse segment of the show.

The new owners of Heritage spearheaded the Ceremonies. The Cavollos entered the indoor Agrodome arena, seated side by side in an open landau pulled by two grey Arabians, driven by well known trainer Freda Gunst, continuing in a sedate parade to the red carpet and official guest seats. Richard was dressed in a black tie and dinner suit, Lori was wearing a clinging white gown edged with emerald green ostrich feathers around the flowing hem and sleeves. They were so proud to be the new owners of Heritage, and of course this was an excellent way of advertising their acquisition, in the spotlights, being introduced to the full house by the Official Announcer Jack Webb.

Shortly after the dazzling entry ceremonies, I rode Gentry successfully in the English Stake, and his party, held in the main alleyway near to his stall, amongst the other fourteen horses showing from Heritage, was soon under way. Both John and I had managed to purchase cases of sparkling white wine, and the Cavollos in their excitement of new ownership, had contributed a case of champagne. John, never at ease with horse people, was quiet and polite, revelling in the celebration. Gentry, always at ease with horse people, was endearingly courteous and gregarious when I brought him from his stall into the alleyway. He seemed to know the wine toast, led by Andy Rees, was for him. Andy gave him a bright red quartered apple too amidst the loud applause from our guests.

The wine put all of us in a heady mood, and the evening rolled on with much camaraderie and high spirits. Susan Folliot's horse, Bucket Jack, also earned his AQHA Championship in 1975, and we were later presented to the thousands attending the show. Susan entered the arena first, looking quite beautiful and distinguished, leading her fine horse beneath the spotlights as the announcer, Jack Webb, spoke of their many accomplishments.

Gentry and I were waiting at the end of the darkened arena. His mane was meticulously braided. I wore my best English outfit, smiled too much and blinked far too much. Frankly I was slightly inebriated from too much wine.

I rode Gentry proudly into arena as the spotlights followed Susan and Jack's departure. The spotlights swept across the sand footing, beaming directly upon us. Gentry already invigorated, trembled, rising above his usual brilliance and presence, seeming to teeter on his toes.

I never heard what Jack Webb said about Gentry's being the first BC Bred Gelding Champion, or all the kind things he said about me. The applause was deafening as Gentry and I attempted to present a smart sitting trot diagonally across the arena to the out gate.

"Gallop him!" someone shouted from the crowd. Others lifted the same cry, until it rang throughout the building.

My co-pilot, the wine, had rendered me incapable of intelligent behavior. My beloved horse, more than ready for a caper, was in a full gallop on the first stride. The boys manning the spotlights were taken by surprise. Their beams danced wildly as they valiantly tried to keep up with us as we galloped twice around the arena, to cheers and applause. Veterinarian Dr. John Gilray, in vain, tried to stop our electrifying behavior, waving his arms to halt us by the exit gate. To this day I do not think he has forgiven us as he hopelessly attempted to keep the show on time.

Whether American Quarter Horses wear English or western tack, whether they appear east or west of the Mississippi in their own country, wherever they appear, cheers in their name are dominated by 'yahoos', the call of cowboys in the old west. Yahoos were abundant for Gentry in the Agrodome that night. I felt accepted by the Quarter Horse world for the first time.

Upon leaving the ring and dismounting, I was surprised to see Lori waiting, filled with enthusiasm for the show, the world, her new ownership of Heritage, and Gentry's honoured turn under the spotlights. Before we knew what was happening, Lori had taken Gentry's rein away from me and strode on her long legs, her white gown and green ostrich feathers, rippling and billowing about her ankles. Gentry, ears sharply pricked, nickered in surprise but retained his composure.

I meekly trotted behind. After all, I could find no fault with anyone who admired Gentry and wanted to be seen leading him. I assumed we were marching toward his stall, but we passed it.

"Wait a minute!" I called.

Lori marched on, with Gentry extending his beautiful trot to remain abreast of her and all those drifting ostrich feathers. I was falling farther behind all the time, but managed to keep the pair in sight by extending my own trot.

They marched out of the barn into the bright night lights spreading across the adjacent fairgrounds, continuing to the sunken arena where the dust of the recent demolition derby had not quite settled.

To my amazement, Lori swung onto my beloved Gentry, and I could tell by the way his muscles gathered he knew a romp was in the making when Lori reined him toward the slopes of the sunken arena! He might loose his balance, fall and break a leg! Her horsemanship was far from good.

"Don't do that!" I shouted.

But they were already off, and as soon as Gentry began his first lap around the sloping sides a cheering crowd gathered around me. As the circling dash continued, I perceived my horse was on the wing, in total control, enjoying every minute of the lark. On occasion he gave a mighty buck just for the fun of it. As his leaps continued, my allegiance switched to Lori, for Gentry's free spirit, unleashed, was daunting her original bravado. She had never ridden such a powerful animal, including her expensive Arabians, for she was still very much a novice. "Hang on, Lori," I found myself screaming, "you can do it..."

And she did, though her gown and ostrich feathers were somewhat askew at the end of the fun, and she was breathless when she swung off Gentry, giving him a pat on the neck, handing me his reins.

"He's all yours," she said smiling, taking a deep breath at the same time.

Lori and I would never be friends, but in that moment we briefly communicated.

God Bless free spirits everywhere.

At the close of the PNE in Vancouver, Gentry returned to Oregon with Bob for final preparation before the last show in San Francisco, the Nationals. I set about making final plans to leave Heritage. I had been successfully selling the horse supplement Drive all over the Northwest for the past three years. Most of the final order of 40,000 lbs had gone, but some buckets and sacks were still stored in the garage. Buz MacDonald, a successful Quarter Horse exhibitor from Nanaimo, Vancouver Island, had shown interest in taking on a dealership from me. At that time I held the largest distribution areas in the country, Washington State, British Columbia, Alaska, Alberta, Saskatchewan and Manitoba. Had John been more supportive we could have made a wonderful business from it alone, for Gentry, as usual, had proven its many attributes. Since Buz was a special friend soon to retire, I was anxious to encourage and help him with a new venture. I rang him, saying I would give a special deal if he purchased the remainder of the stock, asking him to meet with John and me the next morning.

That night John and I tried discussing our future. For the first time, I told him I intended to leave forever and was totally unprepared for his reaction. To be sure, it was the same old song...he could not live without me, he loved me desperately, he would never beat me again, I was his world. The same old song, but never had he delivered it with as much feeling.

I gave him no answer that night. He assumed I had acquiesced. The following morning I awakened knowing John's fervent plea had confused me, knowing I needed some quiet time with Gentry to think things out. I was very tired mentally and physically. I had to make a step of some definitive kind. I did not know what the step would be, or where it would take me, until Buz MacDonald arrived. Everything suddenly became clear then.

"John," I said casually, "why don't you take Buz over to the Drive dealer in Aldergrove and give him a first hand look at their operation?"

Both men agreed this was a good idea. As soon as they were gone I managed to hook up the trailer to the pickup, a task I had never been able to complete alone. Unexpected courage made me strong. I backed the trailer as close as possible to a side door of the house, and quickly packed a bag. All of Gentry's trophies and ribbons were already safe in cardboard boxes, and somehow I managed to lug each one outside, loading them in the trailer; hundreds of trophies were leaving Heritage.

Thus I drove away from Heritage with a few dollars in cash and the Visa card John had forbidden me to use.

Imagine my panic when I saw John's car returning up the drive. My courage held. I pulled off the road, waiting for John to stop beside me. Casually leaning out of the window, I said I was taking the trailer down to Aldergrove to get air in the tires. He believed me, and why not? The tires looked somewhat low, considering the load they were carrying!

Not looking back, I drove on, pausing at the US Lynden border. When the Custom's Inspector asked where I was going, I smilingly said, "just down to Oregon to fetch my horse from training."

He tipped his cap and waved me on. He was not interested in the trailer! Three hours later I entered the afternoon rush hour traffic in Seattle, being at once intimidated by the noise and congestion. No doubt I disturbed other drivers because of my slow pace, but I dared not travel too fast. What would I do if something went wrong! I was in a foreign country, had very little money, had run away from a husband, and I was alone.

My head ached fiercely, and my vision blurred from all the tension. I followed the traffic flow until a motel sign loomed near the SeaTac Airport.

By flashing the Visa card, I secured a room and slept twenty-four hours of my new freedom away. On awakening I ordered two poached eggs and some chocolate milk, then called Bob Avila to tell him I was on my way.

"I thought you might be," Bob said. "John has already called."

I briefly explained, asking him to make reservations at a motel near his home.

"You'll stay with me." he said. "So come on."

Virtually all my newly found self confidence wilted on returning to the trailer. I had forgotten to lock the doors! Anyone could have stolen Gentry's trophies!

Bob and Christy were waiting for me when I arrived in Yamhill, several hours later. They asked no questions and made no comments, though the trembling in my arms and hands was surely visible. We unpacked my strange trailer load, lifting the boxes through a bedroom window, storing as many as possible in the clothes closet, stacking the others against a wall.

Once those mechanics were completed, I went to my beloved horse. Gentry nuzzled me excitedly, giving little squeals of delight. I sat with him for a long time, stroking his gorgeous hair. He was the panacea I needed.

I felt reborn.

The feeling was not to last.

Bob, Christy and several horses, including Gentry, left the following morning, bound for a show in Eureka, Oregon. I was too

212

weary to accompany them. As the day wore on, I realized again I was alone, truly alone, for the second time in my life. It was a horrible feeling. I tried to plan my future but could think of nothing sounding remotely sensible. I was, to keep it brief, in a void.

My spirits sank even lower when the entourage returned from the show. During a heading class, Bob and Gentry had raced down the ring after the cow. It had been extremely hot and dry so the organizers had arranged for a heavy watering of the ring. The top surface dried quickly, leaving it slippery beneath. At the throw of the rope, in a fast gallop, Gentry lost his footing, crashing into the cow, and Bob came out of the saddle. All three hit the dirt.

Fortunately, Bob was not seriously injured, although Gentry pulled the superficial flexor tendon over his hock and had to be rested. He never went lame, but the tendon never really went back into place properly. He developed a thoroughpin, but after my massaging him several times daily with a healing stimulant to encourage the circulation, the injured area was drained and treated promptly. We were very fortunate to have the services of an outstanding leg veterinarian, Dr. John Metcalfe, who was practicing then at nearby Beaverton, ten miles from the Laughlin ranch. The thoroughpin eventually disappeared.

John finally located me in Yamhill by telephone, sounding desperate, not wanting our marriage to end in such a manner. He asked me to lease a large motor home in Portland, return to Canada with it, collect him and some of our things, then spend a leisurely month on the Oregon coast.

"Give us this last chance," he said. "Then if you still want to end it, I'll not stand in your way."

No matter how tormented I had been in the marriage, leaving it with a peaceful goodbye rather than the hasty evacuation I had executed, would make a far better memory. Besides, as long as we could get him better, I had nothing much to do until Gentry's final show, the American Nationals, at the Cow Palace in San Francisco, scheduled for the end of November. I knew Bob would look after him for we had great plans for his final show of the year there.

I rented a Winnebago of questionable vintage, a forty foot green monster, that bullied me all the way to the Canadian border crossing at Lynden. The Canadian Customs would not let me drive the American vehicle across as I had not brought the appropriate papers. I begged parking space at a nearby farm, Edalyne, and phoned Joanne Boyle, a good friend whom I had known through my decorating days in Vancouver. She and her retired husband, Pat, a lumber executive from MacMillan Blodell, lived close by on a 40 acre farm, just north of the Canadian border. Joanne collected me within twenty minutes.

On the way back to her farm she gave me startling news. Not knowing I had left Heritage, she had gone over to see me. John had asked her to help him dispose of my clothes, my antiques, personal cosmetics, nearly everything I owned! Apparently the Cavollos had offered him an extra $1,000 to get out by the end of the week.

Joanne said, over her protests, he had taken most of my clothes to the garbage dump, saying he did not like to see me dressed up anyway. Our antiques and furniture had been sold very cheaply at Maynards Auction in Vancouver and some of the boarders had been invited to take what they wanted from the house. It was intolerable.

I no longer cared, but it was something else I could not forgive.

When I called John from the Boyles' and told him what had happened, he asked a neighbour to drive him to the border, where he obtained special permission to take the Winnebago to Heritage to pack, and return there within two hours, early the following morning.

Two hours was ample time. There was little left to pack. Our steps sounded hollow in the empty house. At the end, as we were leaving, we paused and looked at each other. John reached for my hand.

"We'll still make it," he said. "You'll never be sorry."

I did not reply. I had nothing to say.

We drove down through Washington State to the magnificent Oregon coast, stopping occasionally to watch the sea lions gaming with the seals mid the wild rocks and pulsing waters. We had planned a leisurely trip, but for a reason neither of us could define, we wanted to keep moving and did not stop long anywhere.

The big vehicle was difficult to manoever around the hairpin bends. Often I peered through the window thinking we were about to meet our end while John tugged at the wheel. He had driven trucks in England, but that was years in the past. He had neither the knack nor the strength to dominate the motor home, his temper soon frayed, and he vented his anger by shouting out of his window.

When he shouted like that, to no one, I sighed. Sometimes he grinned sheepishly. Sometimes I feared I could not help contain my hysterical laughter.

We stopped frequently at enchanting bayside restaurants but spoke little during the meals. We gazed seaward instead. Sometimes we purchased fresh shrimp and sourdough bread, munching along the way until we grew tired. We would pull over, sleep for a while, and be on the move again. We never had the urge to make love. We had not done that in years.

John would not stop to read the map, and I was certainly not a good navigator on the twisting roads. We did take one wrong turn, ending high on a cliff overlooking the Pacific and San Francisco. There was no where to turn around. John was furious. For a moment I expected his fury would propel us over the cliff to destruction below, but he controlled his anger, and we made is back down, although the brakes heated alarmingly and the Winnebago engine steamed.

We made it to the historic Cow Palace in San Francisco. I found Gentry in his stall, and my heart ached when he whinneyed his special welcome.

I remember little of events taking place at The National Show in November 1975. Gentry was third in a huge aged gelding class. I sat in the bleachers with Rick Johns, Hank Alrich and two other top flight judges, who all said Gentry should have won and taken the Grand Championship. The judge, Richard Shrake, had placed constantly behind Gentry all year with a client's horse from Oregon. This was his revenge. Gentry and I were tenth in Bridle Path Hack after three elimination rounds and nearly forty horses. I do recall glimpses of the Grand Entry during the Opening Ceremonies, the darkened arena suddenly brilliant with dancing spotlight beams, the colorful sheriff's poses and riding clubs with their waving flags, a vivid recollection of four Palominos carrying ladies dressed in green velvet, riding sidesaddle, American and Canadian flags proudly borne all over...the stirring music... "whose broad stripes and bright stars through the perilous fight"... "God Save the Queen".

After the first part of the show we had planned a leisurely trip, when Gentry would not be exhibiting, during the middle of the Nationals, to Reno, then down through the Nevada desert, past the huge ammunition supply areas. It was an interesting part of the world to visit, but we were very tired with the strain of driving the old vehicle, and the stress of the past weeks. It would have been fascinating to have stopped and seen Death Valley, but it was hot and obviously we could not take our blundering bus down, so we pushed on, eventually pulling into a Las Vegas R.V. parking lot close to the MGM Hotel.

This was more to John's liking. Civilization to him, away from winding roads by the ocean, away from horses, just colorful people wandering in and out of the casinos. I was happy for him and decided to enjoy the bright lights myself. We showered in the adjoining facilities, changed into fresh clothing, and then wandered along The Strip for several hours, into the incredible hotels we had seen on the television or in movies, watching excited people working the slot machines. We ate in elegant restaurants, as waiters brought delectable meals we had not had to cook ourselves, a luxury in itself. But three days was enough. It was time to continue on to San Francisco and the final events of the Nationals.

Throughout the entire journey in the Winnebago, John had been reluctant to do anything basic in the way of normal maintenance. Gas consumption had been horrific, demanding deficits from the Visa card daily. Instead of the 40 foot monster he had insisted I rent from the Portland dealership, it would have been so much better to have taken a 28 foot Canadian motor home. He would not listen. He had wanted a home away from home as we no longer had one, enabling us to take whatever clothes we had, some files and the pathetically few items left from our arrival in Canada in May 1957. As far as I was concerned he was welcome to the Queen size bed at the back of the vehicle whilst I curled up in the little dining table area.

John's statement as we left Heritage "We would make it" became ever more remote with each mile we traveled. His frayed temper became out of control again after we left the glamour of Las Vegas. Conversation between us was nonexistent. Both of us wanting to go somewhere, but we knew not where. Tension kept building. His ever increasing shows of anger, fault finding, and demands, kept me increasingly hypersensitive to his every gesture and mood.

It was a long, hot road back to San Francisco. In Bakerville John pulled into a supermarket parking lot, shut off the engine, declaring he wanted to rest for a while. I suggested it would be a good idea to stock up on a few groceries if he would let me have a few dollars. He grudgingly gave me a twenty dollar note, saying it would have to do. I wondered where the $1,000 had gone from the Cavollos, who had given it for the hasty, unnecessary departure from Heritage, and was quite sure our slender resources were gone. I had not been consulted. I would not have moved out under those conditions for less than $5,000. John certainly had not thought out what our needs would be for the month before we left.

I purchased eggs, milk, sourdough bread and a steak. Leaving the store I noticed a police car parked outside and walked up to inquire, as a Canadian, how long it would take to drive back to the Cow Palace and which route to take. John must have been watching, for when I tried opening the door it was locked. I knocked several times, when eventually he screamed through the door - "go back to those f.... police, you are not coming in here." The police car had pulled away. I sat on the step of the Winnebago. After a while he opened the door, instructing me to climb inside. He would not speak one word to me.

John drove off searching for an RV site in which to park. He drove in and around three sites during the next two hours, but none had empty spaces. He was red in the face, looking ready to explode, I dared not let him see me looking at him. I was very frightened of the tension building up in him. It was getting dark when he turned into a quiet lane turning off the main road. Obviously we could not remain there taking up the entire width, but soon a big grass area appeared. John steered us away from the lane end and turned around in a big circle, ready for departure at day break.

We muddled through a meal of sorts without speaking, then he pointed at the table, ordering me to clear it quickly because he was going to bed and wanted the lights turned off. I did as I was told whilst he went for a walk in the grass. He returned shortly with his shoes covered in oil and grease, defiantly wiping them on the green shag carpet. I remained silent and we settled down for the night.

We were wakened to bright lights, and an enormous engine revving. John raced through the vehicle, started up the motor, driving back the way we had come the previous night. Looking out of the window I saw a huge plane rushing by. We had parked on the end of an airport runway! Our problems could have disappeared forever.

We joined Bob Avila's entourage for the final day of the Nationals, then helped load the horses watching them depart en route through California back to safety in Yamhill. We slowly wound our way behind, intending to take a week exploring the Redwood Forests, and then on to Eugene, to attend the Oregon Quarter Horse Association's Year End Awards Banquet. Driving along Interstate 5 should have been simple, even in the cumbersome Winnebago. As we made our way up the mountain pass around Lake Shasta in Northern California it was obvious we were in trouble. The vehicle made terrible groaning noises, slowed down, and refused to change gears effectively. The wide road stretched ahead with the summit appearing farther away with every groan of the motor. When I had reminded my husband he must fill up the oil in the engine, he had sworn at me, ignoring the obvious maintenance requirement.

John pulled to the inside lane, just managing to struggle onto the soft shoulder. The engine was steaming. He climbed out to investigate, noticed remnants of oil dripping to the ground and went on a cursing spree.

We flagged down a passing motorist, a woman, requesting her to ask someone, at the first garage she came across, to come to our rescue. She promised she would, and a tow truck eventually arrived. The mechanic informed us we had wrecked the engine. The repairs would take at least three days. The awards banquet took place the next evening.

The most economical plan was to lift the engine and carry it to the nearest town, Reading, for repairs. A gaping hole was left in the front of the vehicle, through which anyone could climb in and steal the few belongings we had left. We decided to spend the night in the RV, with the driver of the tow truck promising to send a cab for us the next morning, when we could gather our belongings and proceed to Eugene.

We spent the night, as usual, sleeping at opposite ends of the Winnebago, not speaking. It was very cold high up the mountain pass with the gaping hole where the engine had been.

I thought of Gentry and his conquests in 1975. Granted earning his AQHA Championship, plus a Superior Award in halter, fulfilled my longstanding dream. But I was also aglow with pride when considering the salvo of trophies he had lifted in halter, roping, Western and English pleasure and trail in Washington, the State of Jefferson B.C. and, especially, Oregon.

In spite of the late start in serious campaigning, and the unfortunate accident layup time, he was a contender for High Points honours at the Awards Banquet. In close pursuit were two game horses, Skipawambus Bars, owned by Ron and Judy Doyle of Myrtle Point, trained and shown by Arlene Cloepfil, and the inimitable Sparky Girl, Sport Laughlin's favourite mare.

Bob Avila had kept a close record of Gentry's points knowing the race for Hi-Point Gelding and the magnificent Gibson western saddle would be very tight. They had competed in the barrels sometimes, never winning, but adding a few on now and again. At the last O.Q.H.A. meeting before the Nationals, Bob had nervously attended to hear who had won. He was horrified to learn we had lost out by only one point to Skipawambus Bars. Bob was totally confounded when hearing the point keepers tally. He did not agree, immediately demanding a recount by all of the Directors! This was a serious matter and dutifully they fulfilled his request.

The cabbie appeared on time, and with one of those tolerant smiles seemed to accept the failures of all mankind, helping us load our belongings and selves into the taxi.

We checked into the Country Squire Inn in Eugene just in time to bathe and change, taking our places at Bob Avila's table in the ballroom shortly before dinner was served. I ate, tasting nothing, waiting for this most important of awards ceremonies to begin.

When they did, my Canadian-bred Hyline Gentry swept the board! His most sentimental award was the Hi Point OQHA Halter Horse Trophy, in memory of Ursula Mathias Opie, whose husband, Dan, owned Quincy Dan, patriarch in Gentry's male line of decendency. He won Hi Point honours for OQHA All Around Horse, Trail Horse, Halter Gelding and Senior Halter Gelding. He was Reserve Hi Point Working Horse, being beaten by Skipawambus Bars, and in Steer Roping Heeling when Beau Jag, owned and ridden by LeRoy McCay, beat Gentry by 1 1/2 points.

We held our breath for the announcement of the Hi-Point Gelding of Oregon Quarter Horse Association for 1975. Hyline Gentry had 262 1/2 points and Skipawambus Bars 262. Bob's own meticulous point keeping, and insistence on the recount, had ensured we took the saddle!

The month before, at the State of Jefferson Awards Banquet, Gentry had won the All Around Horse roping saddle with 141 points over Jim Bar James, owned by Carol Butts with 86 points, which I gave to Bob for his outstanding dedication with my incredible horse.

Gentry with trophies won by me, Bob and Christy Avila.
November, 1975

We were delayed several more days before the engine was made ready for our return drive to Portland, and a very angry man who had rented his motor home to us. We managed to escape unharmed, and quickly retired to a motel to discuss our futures. I knew they should be separate and said so. I wanted to remain in Oregon somewhere near Gentry and suggested John return to Canada alone.

For the first time since our marriage we actually had some money, and John had been saying he did not intend to work hard very much longer. His plan, it appeared, was to live off the money from my father, and then his father. After which he expected our earnings from the sale of Heritage, properly invested by him, would be sufficient to take care of us. I was disgusted.

Canadians are permitted a home in the U.S. for six months, less a day, provided they maintain a residence in their home country. John suggested we have a condominium in both Portland and Vancouver. For me to remain with Gentry in Oregon where I was so happy and had made many fine friends. He would establish our official residential requirements by living in Vancouver and he would occasionally drop down to visit me. Perhaps it was the best way to get rid of him, and to satisfy Immigration at the same time.

It sounded simple enough to me.

John rented an apartment on the twenty-third floor of the International Plaza in North Vancouver, and we purchased an elegant condominium for me in Portland. It was on the thirteenth floor of the Lincoln Centre with a magnificent view. In the daytime I saw a range of mountains with Mt. Rainier and the Three Sisters standing starkly white against the nearly always vividly blue skies. At night the darkened glass windows reflected twinkling lights of the city.

Living in Oregon was like coming home to me, considering the many friends Gentry had made there. I enjoyed the simple condo life for the time of being, especially dips in the pool after a day of riding my beloved horse in the Yamhill countryside.

My albatross reappeared. John came down to visit early in 1976, stayed two weeks, then returned to Vancouver staying for a few days, establishing his residency. He returned again, although he hated the routine. Our arguments resurfaced. What were we doing in this country anyway? He was incapable of staying away, did not know what he wanted.

I had grown braver with a certain amount of independence. I stated I did not intend to return to Canada with him. He kept coming down to Portland while I spent most of my time in Yamhill. There were times when John struck me again. Part of me cringed and cowered, but the other part refused to acknowledge what was happening. I took the blows, and then forgot when I was with Gentry in Yamhill, my Camelot.

Bob's mother, Pat, and her husband, Hank Alrich, brought Camelot even closer. They owned a charming small horse farm on a dead end street across from the Willamette River, thirty miles south of Portland. They had several empty stalls in their barn and suggested I board Gentry with them and ride around their local lanes and hazel nut orchards. Our year of campaigning with Bob had finished on a brilliant note, but I now felt my horse and I must curtail further training.

Pat and I became firmer friends after Gentry moved in, when we rode often together. The relaxed lifestyle appealed to me. There were just twelve homes along that part of the river, all with private access for water skiing or boating. Pat introduced me to many of her congenial neighbours and I thoroughly enjoyed the new life.

Even Pat knew little of the problems I had with John, it was a matter I did not want to discuss with anyone. She and my new friends told me how lucky I was to have an affluent, retired husband willing to give me freedom to be with my horses, though he really had no interest in horse related pursuits himself. There was no need for them to know the truth.

Bob Avila and Christy Skuzeski had a beautiful wedding in a Roman Catholic ceremony in May 1976. John and I attended, and as always in the presence of horse people he was quiet, outwardly easy going and pleasant. I sat beside him, viewing Christy in ivory satin and lace, with Bob in a cream-coloured tuxedo and matching shirt. How utterly beautiful they were, encircled by the sort of happiness I had permanently lost.

Shortly after the wedding Pat called, excitement in her voice. A cedar home, surrounded by cottonwood trees on Eilers Road, on the banks of the Willamettte River, opposite to her farm, was going up for sale.

"If you could manage to buy it you'd be only a hundred yards from us!" she told me. "Gentry could remain where he is, you could walk over whenever you felt like it, and even watch his grazing in the front grass paddock from your house." It was an ideal situation.

Strangely, John was favourable, and after viewing the property, agreed to purchase it. Selling the condo did present a few problems, but we were able to revert it back to the original ownership. John then gave me the cash to buy the home on Eilers Road, but insisted both our names be on the title. I was not happy about that, but if he really was going back to B.C. it would work out! Famous last thoughts.

"As soon as you're settled," he said "I'm going back to British Columbia. I've had enough of Oregon." He had not made a single friend, so it made sense.

At last! A final and amicable parting!

During the next few weeks I was busy putting the house in order, choosing new carpets, painting the kitchen and bathroom cupboards, creating a warm and pretty home with some new furniture linking well amongst my few antiques. John became apprehensive. He was afraid the American Immigration Department would evict us from the country on 24 hours notice, and we could loose the property. He returned to B.C. each week to purchase gas on his Visa to prove residency. He made no effort to be friendly with the kind neighbours, who were beginning to think I was not so 'lucky' after all.

Gentry and I took many solitary rides. We rode for miles along the river. I always gave him free rein, and he often paused to watch the water skiers, small boats and occasional float planes by the private docks.

During one of our rides we passed a stable for Saddlebreds and Morgan horses. We rode in to say 'hello' finding they were mainly training driving horses. They were very friendly, and, noting my interest, invited us to return for a lesson the following day.

Thus Gentry was introduced to a pair of shafts with one end on wheels. We rigged him up in driving harness, finding he was quite tolerant of the eye blinkers hiding much of his vision, especially from the wheels following closely behind.

I hitched him up and took the long reins behind the wheels, and calmly drove him down the arena's long side. He stopped at the end, unable to negotiate the corner as a shaft pressed into his shoulder. I quietly backed him a few paces, then walked up to his shoulder, urging him to take small steps as if he were sidepassing. He understood very quickly, and in this his first lesson, we transferred to a light buggy with me riding behind.

Hitching him to a buggy had not distressed Gentry in the least. It was probably easier than carrying, say, a fifty pound western saddle with a heavy rider on top. His spine was not taxed by weight, it was easier thrusting forward to pull this simple vehicle.

My habit of setting goals and achieving them persisted. Driving would become a new discipline for Gentry and me. I noticed an advertisement from a member of the Amish faith who was selling oak driving carts, with large rubber bound spoke wheels, in a kit of parts to be assembled. I soon bought one and had a great time building, staining and varnishing it. It was substantial and, to my eyes, far more appropriate for a Quarter Horse than the light sulkies.

Once the cart was finished Gentry and I had great times driving along the quiet river roads, but playtime ended in mid August. John walked in one day unexpectedly, declaring we were selling the house and both returning to Canada. There was no reasonable explanation. There was no discussion, just another order.

It was to be a bad period. He beat me several times and on one occasion hit me over the head with a chair. Somehow I managed to escape him and seek refuge with neighbours, Charles and June Mason. As I pounded on the door, praying they were home, I heard John coming. He was only yards away when June opened the door, saw what was happening, pulled me inside, slamming home the bolt, just as John landed against it.

I spent the night with the Masons, with John quietly walking around to claim me the following morning! He told the Masons I was having a nervous breakdown, was in need of treatment, and he would look after me. Somehow his ingratiating manner convinced the three of us, and I returned home with him, where he locked me in Gentry's new trophy room until the evening.

Through the door John coldly told me he would see I had no money of my own, that I was living in a foreign country illegally, and I was indeed suffering a nervous breakdown. I lost all confidence when he was around again, being totally unable to stand up for myself. After all half of the money from Heritage was legally mine.

I believed him. The flutterings in my heart had told me the same thing whenever he was around.

"I'll be alright if you'll just leave me alone," I managed to say.

"You're staying in that room until you agree to do exactly what I tell you to do, or you'll never see that bloody horse again. I'll kill him."

"No!" I screamed, terrified. "No, I'll do anything! Don't touch Gentry."

"That's more like it," he said slyly, opening the door, giving me a fierce kick.

"We'll have you right in no time," he said. "I have been talking with Dorothy Neville who has recommended her psychiatrist in Vancouver. Your first appointment is already set up."

"Thank you," I managed to say not wanting to antagonize him further.

Perhaps those two words turned the key. Or perhaps God in his mercy at last revealed to me how battered women can become spineless, fear-ridden and subservient to their abusers.

The tea I drank that day was the most bitter of my life. After nineteen years refusing to do so, Joy Cooke Feltham Richardson, finally admitted she was a battered woman. After less than eight weeks of ownership, we sold the house quickly and made arrangements for returning to Vancouver.

From that day forward I would travel a slow road back to self respect.

That road was long.

Chapter Eleven

Psalms 126 verse 5
"They that sow in tears shall reap in joy"

Selling the Eilers Road property was simple, especially after the improvements I had done to the house and grounds. I think, even now, John had planned the whole scenario to get us out of Oregon. My entreaties to stay fell on deaf ears. I had repeatedly told him I could never live in Canada with him again. My friends were understanding, but at the same time disgusted with me for having succumbed to his manipulations, and I feared they would wash their hands of me altogether if I returned to Canada with him. It was impossible for anyone to understand why I still lived with, what had become, a monster. When we left Heritage, I had stated my future would be either in Oregon or back to England with my family, and of course wherever I lived, Gentry would be with me. John had seemed to agree, but he was always full of devious ways to get what he wanted.

John defiantly oversaw the packing and shipping of our belongings, while I watched the proceedings heartbroken. I trailered Gentry, while John drove behind ensuring we did not stray along the way. Prior to leaving, I had phoned Pat Bennett, manager of Highland Hills Boarding Stable in Aldergrove, located less than three miles away from our old property, and requested a stall for my horse. When we arrived, Gentry's stall was ready. Not quite the upscale accommodations he was used to, but it was clean and dry, and located near an open door. He accepted the down graded lodgings far better than me.

John exchanged our rented one bedroom condominium for a two bedroom in the elegant International Plaza Hotel. Our condo was on the 23rd floor overlooking North Vancouver and the Burrard Inlet, where an increasingly busy port supported a wide variety of cargo ships. In the distance stood my old friend, Mount Baker. The majesty of the mountain became a homing beacon I drove towards when visiting Gentry everyday in his new barn. I had no enthusiasm for any unpacking of our belongings, and I left some, especially my trophies, in their boxes stored in a locker in the basement of the hotel.

I wrote to Kevin, telling him all the horror stories of my life with John and he answered be return mail, asking me to return to England and live with him and his family. At last I thought, my family understands. I must go home. Now I had real place to go after my escape from John.

Regardless of all else, John and I had never violated each other's mail. However, when Kevin's letter arrived, John demanded to read it. I told him it was in the bedroom and I would get it for him later.

Fear prevented me from acting rationally. I knew if John found out I had told Kevin what was happening, he would surely beat me to a pulp, then and there. I ran to the bedroom, grabbed Kevin's letter out of my purse, and locked myself in the bathroom. John pounded on the door, threatening to break it down. I tore Kevin's letter and flushed it down the toilet. When I mustered enough courage I opened the door, telling an angry John I had simply wanted to use the bathroom. He did not believe me, guessing the truth. Incensed, he kicked me repeatedly, destroying any pretenses I had left of self-worth. Resistance was dangerous.

That night, I slept fitfully in the second bedroom and the next day, with John's eager insistence, I visited Dr. Bezerdi who photographed my bruises, patiently listening to the sordid instances of my husband's maltreatment of me. Through my tears, and the use of many Kleenex, I began unburdening myself from the horrendous weight on my shoulders. The doctor's calm acceptance of my terrors slowly began to convince me I was not a mental case. I had been consistently brow beaten, subjected to increasing mental and physical abuse over many years. The problems were John's, not mine.

Dr. Bezerdi told me he would recreate my courage over time, and inevitably I must leave John once and for all. He told me he would summon John for a discussion, explaining I was a manic depressive with extreme highs and lows. It would get John into his office, he said, allowing him to meet him to try and understand his problems.

I explained we had merely transferred our hellish life from one location to another. I was disgusted with myself for capitulating to his demands, that his degradation never let up. My strengths were undermined when he continued to call me stupid and weak. His sadistic joy in smashing my beautiful dishes, which had been a wedding gift to my mother from her parents, broke my heart. Dr. Bezerdi understood my reasons for not leaving John sooner, but said he knew the time had come for action.

Upon my return John was silent, reading the newspaper, and

attempting to act as if nothing had happened between us. He even suggested we should move from the condominium nearer to the Fraser Valley so I could spend more time with Gentry.

"We will have money coming regularly from the Heritage mortgage, so why not find a pretty townhouse in Burnaby, decorate it lavishly, and settle back into our West Vancouver lifestyle of theatre and symphony evenings again? Burnaby would suit us both, halfway to Gentry and within easy access of Vancouver's growing nightlife," he smirked.

I was appalled, but heeding my new doctor's advice, I pretended to think about it.

John accepted my doctor's invitation to discuss me, agreeing to meet with another psychiatrist, Dr. Cook of North Vancouver, who would help him. Later, I learned John had been hoping to have me committed to a mental hospital.

Several days later, John broached the subject of the money he had received from his Court Action against the brokerage company when he had been 'let go', and had returned to 'help' me on the farm. He had willingly suggested putting it into the expansion of Heritage and purchasing twenty acres of adjoining property.

"I think before the final money comes in from the sale of Heritage, the sum of $130,000 should be withdrawn legally from our joint holdings and put back into my hands. We can split the remainder between us if you like, although it should be invested for our future," he informed me.

I was dumbstruck. Throughout all the years we had been in Canada, I had worked for a pittance, giving him my cheques from The Chelsea Shop for mortgage payments of whatever home we lived in at the time, while he allowed me only small sums for personal items and groceries. He had obviously forgotten the frequent periods he had earned practically nothing and I had supported us both. The down payment for our first home in Canada, most of which had also gone to save him from bankruptcy. John also chose to forget I had sold Heritage for considerably more than he thought it was worth, and more than he would have asked for in 1975.

The strain of John's behavior and the visit with Dr. Bezerdi had taken its toll on me. I was shivering, feeling weak and knew I had a heavy cold coming on. I went to bed, telling John I had a temperature and wanted to keep warm.

I was unable to rest, a splitting headache adding to my chills.

John came in to the bedroom, surprised I was under the covers. As my throat was sore, I quietly asked if he would get me a glass of orange juice from the refrigerator.

A few minutes later he returned with an opened can.

"You want a cold drink, here you are, you Bitch!" he bellowed as he squeezed the lumpy frozen juice over my chest. I screamed from the sudden cold, which infuriated him more.

Surely, at this moment, John was insane. Nothing else could possibly explain his behavior of the next few minutes, nor how I survived. Roaring back into the living room, he removed something from his brief case. Returning to the bedroom, he pulled the sodden covers off me, grabbed me by the arm, and forcefully dragged me from the bed into the living room. I was horrified to see his hand open the sliding glass door onto the balcony.

"What are you doing?" I gasped

Without a word he pulled me, with the strength of ten men, through the glass doorway. I struggled to resist, but he was more powerful. I could do nothing, as the man I had lived with for twenty years, hung me over the iron railing as both legs dangled precariously in the air twenty three stories above the ground. I clung petrified to the railings, begging him to let me back up again.

Holding both of my wrists with one hand, he reached into his pocket to retrieve a pen and a pink piece of paper. "Sign this or I will kick you down," he snarled, thrusting it before my face. I did not know what it said, nor did I care, but I did as he asked. Satisfied, he pulled me back onto the balcony. Numbed and terrified, I crawled into the living room.

He sat in a chair, smirking. "You just agreed to my having the $130,000 before final division of the remainder of Heritage money. I scribbled out your wishes whilst you were in the bedroom!"

Shaking, I returned to the bedroom and climbed into warm clothes. I knew I had to get away from John immediately and talk with my lawyer, Ed Mortimer.

John suspected something was up when I returned to the room. "Where do you think you're going?" he demanded.

Trying to be meek, I replied "I have to get out of here for a while. I can't breathe in this atmosphere with you. I want to walk alone in the Indian Reserve behind the hotel."

"You are not leaving here," he glared back.

I buckled, collapsing into a chair, feeling dreadful from the fever, let alone the iced juice and the horrendous episode on the balcony. I knew I had to get away. I was very frightened, but somehow whenever things have been their worst, an inner strength has come over me. I know God protects me with a busy Guardian Angel, but this day I was confident there was an army of them surrounding me. Cowering down would achieve nothing. I must make a decisive move, and do it for myself.

I walked over to the telephone and picked up the receiver, not expecting John to allow me to make a call. I was right, he slammed it to the floor. We glared at one another, and then surprisingly contrite he said: "Go, but you do not take your purse or car keys with you."

I opened the door to the hallway, quickly moving outside, closing it behind. The elevator doors were less than fifteen feet away, but with 23 stories for it to rise for one of the four condos on our floor, it would be a long time coming. Afraid of John changing his mind, I fled to the concrete fire steps, running swiftly down several flights. Suddenly I noticed people leaving an elevator. I jumped into it before the doors closed, leaning breathless against the back wall.

I was still lost and dazed, but for a few moments wandered aimlessly in the hotel lobby not knowing what to do or where to go. My heart thudded wildly, and I was unable to think clearly. Wandering near the magazine shop I stumbled in, smiled at the familiar lady behind the counter, asking if I could borrow 25 cents as I had left my purse upstairs and needed to make a phone call. My Guardian Angel looked after me again, for the sales lady handed it to me unquestionably. I must have presented a desperate picture with an unmade, blotchy face, wild hair and a conglomerate of clothing. Quickly I located a telephone booth, dialing Ed Mortimer's number. For once he was available. Tearfully, I related what had happened, instructing him to draw up a disclaimer, saying I was dangerously threatened into signing a "pink piece of paper" under duress, about an hour earlier, regarding giving John $130,000. I said I hoped to be in to sign it sometime tomorrow.

Leaving the building I wandered out into the fresh air towards the Indian Reserve. Rounding a corner I saw John coming towards me! "You should not be out here with that cold" he said, taking hold of my arm propelling me back towards the hotel again. I could not believe his timing. He had not seen me using the telephone obviously, but I knew I must keep up the charade, for it was essential I sign the disclaimer document, I had instructed Mortimer to complete, as soon as possible.

I knew that the document would be essential when the divorce proceedings began. That could be a long way off my lawyer had told me, there would be delays, long waiting periods to book Hearings in the Law Courts which were very full and over booked. There would have to be Discoveries of us both in a mini court, apparently saving the Divorce Court time, but I never understood, for what was the difference where we were, or what was being said, in the long run? To divorce John would be easy with many witnesses to his cruelties. All I wanted was my legal half share of Heritage. He would want his $130,000 off the top before division! In 1976 it was a lot of money, and the Courts and lawyers would have a field day prolonging a decision, which should never have been necessary in the first place.

Now he had his 'precious' piece of paper signed I suppose John felt confident his crazy fantasies would not fall apart. He thought he had beaten me. He would no doubt rely on that money to fight me for the rest of Heritage money, for I knew he would not just fade out of my life at that time. I don't think he particularly cared anymore if I was around either, although his pride would not let him face the future easily with a wife who had deserted him. For him to remain in Vancouver, with me dead or alive, he intended to come out smelling like a rose.

Both Ed Mortimer and Dr. Bezerdi stressed I should leave the country with Gentry as soon as possible. They agreed John would do all he could to hinder me, believing the divorce would be delayed a long time if I were not on the local scene, slowing down his future plans. If he thought I was finding a way to escape, they both agreed, my life would be in jeopardy. In fact anything to thwart John must be avoided at this time. There was no guarantee he was taking the prescribed heavy doses of valium to control his paranoid schizophrenia, which meant I would be at the mercy of his split personality.

I had begun my escape legally, but I still had to find the wherewithal, a long road lay ahead. We had a small joint account, but if I were to take even one dollar John would have become suspicious. Somehow I had to find the money to fly Gentry to England safely with me, a problem at times seemingly out of reach. I continued to fear him.

There were no abuse centers in those days that I knew of to turn for help, for John had isolated me from my community and friends, I would have to struggle through on my own. I had not one to confide in and ask for help, other than the lawyer and doctor, whose constant advice was to leave John, an option I could not choose because I would not abandon Gentry.

With John believing the $130,000 would soon be his, he became somewhat more considerate, insisting I spend more time with Gentry at Highland Hills, in fact he welcomed my being away nearly all day. I sometimes considered what he did when I was away, thinking perhaps he was meeting someone else. If I inquired, he said everytime he had been for a walk, lain down for a rest falling into a long sleep. It sounded so false and dull, but I was not interested.

John suggested one day, to my great surprise, he thought we should move out to Burnaby into a townhouse. That was going to confuse my escape plans horrendously, but then on thinking further, I did see some merit. I had no way of then finding our escape monies, perhaps I could get that home put in my name and he would go off somewhere else? A long shot perhaps. It seemed essential, to me, that the money we had left Heritage with be tied up into property, until our marriage was dissolved, although I did not dare tell him so. John would soon spend the remainder of the Cavollo down payment; a new fancy car, a cruise, a visit perhaps to see his father in England, and an elegant new wardrobe, along with a very expensive taste in wine, when eating out several times a week in top flight restaurants.

I had not trusted the Cavollos ever, and now received frightening premonitions that their tenure in Neetriht, our Heritage, would not last. Their knowledge of horse management had been deplorably low and we knew expenses had been colossal with them hiring a top flight trainer, new horse trailers, a fancy motor home and many more new horses, show tack and equipment. I could not see them making any profits from the boarding operation the way they ran things either. How were they going to pay our first mortgage monies? Richard had financed four more mortgages behind us, involving members of the Lion's Football Team. I shall never understand how he convinced football players to invest in Arabian horses out in the Fraser Valley! But that was how he became such a con-artist no doubt. It looked a definite possibility they would renege all around and we would be forced to foreclose and claim our old Heritage back. I think John was wondering this too, but we did not discuss the matter. After all, he had laboriously worked on the financing with Richard after I had made the sale. He could not admit he had left a loophole.

The last thing I wanted was to retrace old steps. Much as I had loved creating Heritage and bringing my horses along, the last thing I needed was to return with John. Hence his idea for us to move nearer into Burnaby, to be available for a swift take over.

Individually, neither of us wanted to loose our financial achievements since arriving in Canada in 1957. I knew I must have some income wherever Gentry and I lived. I had been responsible for so much, I rationalized, I would be a fool to leave everything in John's hands, for he would have a field day working out how to manipulate the remaining money away from me. I would temporarily postpone the escape, for in reality what choice was there?

We purchased a three bedroom townhouse in Village del Ponte, Burnaby. John encouraged me to decorate it well with good wallpapers and to line one bedroom with cedar planking making an attractive trophy room. It was only a matter of weeks before we had moved from North Vancouver and become reestablished. I felt a total hypocrite, knowing I had no intentions of staying. I reassured myself with my wholesale connection's help, I knew the place should easily sell.

John's life continued with morning runs, keeping an eye out the bank mortgage rates came in regularly, and taking me out dinner, where we sat in uncompanionable silence, either in the Vancouver Hotel Timber Club, The University Club or one of Umberto Menghi's fascinating restaurants. John still enjoyed belittling me, frequently making me return groceries if I had not purchased the finest cuts of beef for him. He was striving to give the impression we were wealthy retirees wherever we went and whatever we did. Who cared? I suppose his mental health was kept in check by his psychiatrist, Dr. Cook, and the drugs to some extent, but I was constantly afraid of his eruptions.

Not unexpectedly, the Cavollos began getting into arrears with their payments to us. Many excuses and procrastinations. Alarmingly we heard they had fled to Northern British Columbia, taking some of the horses with them, who eventually perished in the frigid winter outdoors. Wayne Newton was not receiving his payments on the horses bought through his mortgage arrangement either. Richard had transferred the property into financial holdings in Winnipeg, Thompson Valley, who, we were informed, would continue our first mortgage payments.

Now John did become excited, for it began to look very doubtful we would receive our sale money after all. For a while he still pondered on foreclosure, with us returning to the old place, trying to sell once again, after the mismanagement had been properly restored. That was furthest from my thoughts!

Although we had two bedrooms, with the trophies in the cedar room, John insisted I sleep in the kingsize bed with him. Not that he touched me, it was a matter of his pride in case anyone visited, and he could keep and eye on me too. I lay on my side, facing away from him, in never more than ten or twelve inches, whilst he spread across the rest. If I, in my fitful sleep, moved out of my space, he kicked me viciously. Many nights I waited until he was sound asleep, snoring, then slowly and quietly rolled out onto the floor, squirming my way out of the room. Heart in mouth I tip-toed to the trophy room, quietly removing some trophies and ribbons from the walls, packing them into cardboard boxes I had stored in the wall closet. I dared not take too many all at once, in case he noticed, but I knew I should remove some to a safer place. My friend, Joanne Boyle, had kindly suggested I put anything I wished at their farm in the large basement.

Fearfully, in the darkness, each night I lugged them out of the room, down the stairs, through the front door, eventually to my car in the parking lot nearby. I wonder what would have happened if I had been seen in night clothes carrying boxes surreptitiously away? Police at best. I did this for weeks, each morning dropping off what I had taken, enroute to my ride with Gentry. John never made any restrictions about my few mornings hours with my horse, but woe betide me if I was back later then I had agreed earlier. Obviously he was not interested in visiting the trophy room.

Leaving John was not easy, there was so much to do. For my protection I had to arrange with at least two friends to be with me when I told him; I had to arrange with the furniture packers the removal of many trophies, half the furniture, and my personal belongings, to put Gentry somewhere safe away from Highland Hills where he was currently boarded, and above, all to hide myself. I also had to make plane reservations, arrange the difficult piroplasmosis blood test for Gentry, to sell my trailer, sell my car, and to ensure there was enough money for the whole audacious escape.

I was the consummate actress, keeping John unaware of my tension filled activities before the final moments of departure.

Making plans to fly back to England was not easy either. Prices through various airlines had to be investigated and of course I could not leave phone numbers where I could be contacted. I ought to have employed the services of a horse transportation agent, but I thought it would have cost me more. There was no direct route from Vancouver, and I had never flown a horse before, so I was totally unaware of the procedures, although it soon became apparent there were a number of crooks in the flying trade.

233

I stressed to the furniture moving company, half of the contents we possessed would be shipped to England when I gave a date, and that it must also be confidential until the last moment. Some nights I went through the dining area and kitchen cupboards moving our possessions into equal shares, putting red stickers on some shelves and blue on others. A waste of time, for it all belonged to me but I felt, illogically, John should have his half - a decency he never deserved.

Dr. John Twidale took care of Gentry's necessary health regulations. I wrote to the Ministry of Agriculture in England requesting an Import License for him, which upon return would give me 30 days from issue to get him into the country. There were no quarrentine regulations for my horse, but he had to have the special authorization showing a negative piroplasmosis blood test. Piroplasmosis is a disease carried by bloodsucking ticks which infect the horse, particularly in tropical regions of the world. The ticks grow as parasites within the red blood cells causing destruction of them, resulting in hemolytic anemia, kidney dysfunction, encephalitis, and a horse may be dead within 24 hours. We had not been in any infected areas, but another animal carrying the disease might possibly have been in contact with Gentry somewhere along the way. The test was such an important measure it could not be certified from the Vancouver Veterinary Laboratory - it had to go to Ottawa, the other side of Canada.

There was an enormous amount of work ahead before Gentry and I could flee the country away from John. To allay his fears I entered in two major shows, Chilliwack International and the major Quarter Horse event at Thunderbird Equestrian Centre in Langley.

There was still time to kill whilst my plans were finalized. I wanted Gentry to remain fit and rode with the trainer at Highland Hills, Phyllis Philbreck, taking dressage and jumping lessons. One morning, pulling my stirrups up, I jumped off my saddle, tucking one rein through a stirrup leather, allowing Gentry to walk around the indoor arena whilst helping to put the jumps away. Gentry wandered over to a good friend, Pam Boulter, who had always loved him, standing close by.

She said loudly to those around "No one seems to own this good horse with its lovely saddle and bridle. Is there any reason why I should not take him home with me?"

Instant reaction. Gentry obviously heard and understood, for he awoke from his casual wanderings, racing back up the arena to me, quivering a little, with his gentle mouth twitching in great concern.

Of course I soothed him, assuring him we would never be parted, whilst everyone laughed. It had been such an instantaneous reaction to Pam's loving question.

Still unable to sleep beside a loudly snoring husband, most nights I continued slipping out of the bed, making my silent way down the stairs. Systematically I now began removing crystal, hunting prints, china, and silver from the cupboards. They went to my friend, Noni Franks in Vancouver, where we put on a garage sale one Sunday morning, to help with my escape money. I sold my trailer to John Twidale, who was so instrumental with my escape plans. He agreed to take delivery when I left. He too felt I must not alert John to the fact I was planning to leave for he believed Gentry would be held hostage in some form. Amazingly I talked John into making arrangements for us to both sign with the Royal Bank that the money from Thompson Valley, Heritage owings, would be paid into a Joint account from which neither of us could withdraw without a signature from the other. He must have felt secure that I would be unable to empty the account. We did have some money left in the Aldergrove CIBC account, about $8,000. But I did not touch it until the very last moment and prayed John would not plan on investing it elsewhere.

I sold the car for delivery several weeks later. With the sale of my horse trailer, the garage sale money and the gamble there would be enough in the joint bank account in Aldergrove, I might just scrape through. My debts were adding up quickly what with the air fare, the cost of shipping my personal belongings, veterinary necessities through the border, getting out of the country with Gentry to fly from Seattle, arrangements to board him in Leicestershire in England, and the van to meet us at Heathrow Airport. I was not sure where we would land up, and could I still manage it all without alerting John?

I booked the flight from Seattle with Flying Tigers. They were unable to tell me how much it would cost in US dollars. Their representative, Mary Cisco, told me it was to be mailed directly, then rang back several times to say bring it in cash, first in US, then Canadian and finally, in US currency. The sum seemed exorbitant. As no specific time could be given for flight departure, plans were made to spend a few hours at Longacres Race Track in Seattle.

The piroplosmosis blood test was presenting a ghastly problem. Controllers at all airports in Canada went on strike, bringing the whole Canadian flight system to a total stop. It was very hot at the beginning of August, so conveying the precious drawn blood by bus without refrigeration was out of the question. John Twidale somehow came up with a miracle - he knew a private plane that was flying across the country through the Canadian Air Force! He hitched a ride for Gentry's blood with it. There were taxi journeys at the Ottawa end to get it to the Government Laboratory. It arrived safely, but had to wait over the weekend for the culture to form before the precious negative certificate could be flown back to us again. It arrived just ten minutes before eventual departure!

My arrangements began to fall into place. John once again had another of his terrible eruptions. He screamed because I was serving a homemade spaghetti bolognaise when he wanted something else. He jumped from the table, grabbed his plate of steaming pasta, banging it over my head, sauce and spaghetti streaming down my face and shoulders. I begged him to stop, but he dragged me from the table and flung me against a door frame, hitting and kicking wildly. Somehow I wrestled free and escaped through the door, running to a neighbour, who quickly let me in. We summoned the police this time.

When they arrived I had to go back into our house with them. One man took me into the bedroom, heard my story, told me to pack a bag, and said he would take me somewhere safe. I was so shocked I put things in the case, took them out, put them back in, in total confusion. The other officer tried talking with John in the living room. He refused to say a word, would not answer, sitting in sullen silence. That officer came to talk with us, put his arm out to lead me away. I do not know how John turned the scene, but he did. He walked quietly up behind the two policemen, smiling ingratiatingly saying "It is all right, Officers, this was just a normal little marital spat, my wife does not want to leave me."

With that he ushered the policemen out and I was left gasping. John's devilish charm had worked against me yet again. But it would not do him any good this time.

I do not know where my confidence came from other than God took a firm hold of me, directing the new courage through Dr. Bezerdi. My horse was my life now in Canada, and I knew once I could get him safely away and over to England, near to my son Kevin and his family, we could assume a quiet and safe lifestyle there. Dreamer yes, but a dreamer with heart.

To ensure John was not suspicious I entered Gentry in two major shows. I was now basically on my own with a few lessons in basic dressage from trainer, Phyllis Philbrick. I knew how to look after my horse and how to ride him of course in a variety of disciplines, but it was over two years since I competed at Quarter Horse top levels in Canada, September 1974. I did not want to ruin his reputation at this stage.

So I took him to the Chilliwack International in May where we won the English Pleasure and the Halter Championship in the Quarter Horse classes. I rode him against a number of quality horses in the CEF Open Hunter Hack and Hunter classes, winning both. It had perhaps been a risk to carry on at the level we had left off, after the two years, when Gentry had been officially retired. The majority of B.C. horse owners were all equally determined to see us unseated, literally, but the challenge paid off.

Preparing Gentry for the major BCQHA Summer Show in June was the most important to me. Perhaps I was risking too much after the success of Chilliwack, everyone was out to revenge their defeats. For me it was to be a grand finale for this outstanding horse before he left the country. No one knew of my plans, least of all John.

My favourite day of trimming, washing, cleaning tack and getting to the show arrived. All was accomplished correctly, I did not forget anything. I even remembered my own supply of hard boiled eggs and tinned butterscotch puddings, stashed in the trailer for the inevitable moment I would feel weak, needing energy rapidly, having no stomach for the usual hot dog or hamburger offerings.

Thunderbird Equestrian Centre in Langley was probably one of the finest in Western Canada. It was my favourite, situated close to the Trans Canada Freeway, making it easy for competitors whether they came from Vancouver Island, Washington State or from the Rockies in Alberta. A large crushed rock parking lot held the campers and trailers comfortably, along with the newer impressive motor homes. 400 horses could be housed in fine stabling, with automatic waterers, lock-up cupboards for our belongings, plus warm horse showers and restrooms. An outstanding restaurant Keg in the Country, owned and managed by George Tidball's son Steve, provided wonderful steak and fish menus with extra large sized alcoholic drinks. It was merry place for competitors and spectators to watch the show through large glass windows.

Gentry was stabled in the main barn for 40 horses with good straw bedding and a quiet environment enabling him to rest comfortably between classes. I felt sorry for the horses in their stuffy trailers or tied outside, often in scorching sun.

The indoor arena was 200 x 100 feet with a very large viewing area at one end for the bar of the Keg Restaurant and further seating for 400 in the bleachers on one side. The heavy washed sand footing, harrowed several times a day, usually ensured the surface was easy for the horses. It was quite my favourite riding arena where we had scored so well over the years in Open Hunter and Quarter Horse classes.

Gentry and I arrived early on the Friday afternoon. After finding his stall, stowing him safely inside with fresh alfalfa hay to keep him content, I took my papers into the show office for validation and to collect my number. I had used 66 for many years, but after I finished with regular Quarter Horse shows in B.C. Jean Matheson from Langley, a very successful AQHA Amateur, appropriated it, claiming fine successes too. For this show we were given number One.

It was fun greeting old friends I had not seen since pre-Oregon days, chatting about their current horses, admiring and listening to their tales from past years. Devilishly, and frequently, I commented on their animal's condition and coat before leading them to peer through the bars at my ever gleaming and healthy Gentry. Vitamin supplements and 'tricks of the trade' have been closely guarded secrets between horse people, although as I had been selling Drive for so long, quite a few fed it to their horses whilst others thought it no better than many other vitamin supplements available. It was up to me at this major and our final show, to prove them wrong, especially since it was the fourth anniversary Gentry had been on Drive.

Whilst collecting my number from the secretary I had helped undo the many boxes of brilliant ribbons, all carefully hung on clothes hangers in correct order for each class, along with the especially splendid ones for the Futurity and Grand Championships, and most prestigious, All Around Horse. I had donated a navy blue woolen cooler, edged in scarlet for the High Point Horse of the show, which declared Drive for Horses on the near side. I wondered who would be the lucky horse to take it home at the end of the show, and whether I would agree with the judge's placings. The judge was up from California, Richard Deller, who had given Gentry his very first English Pleasure Points in his first class four years earlier, and under whom he had won the English Pleasure Futurity as a three year old, at the Vancouver Northwest International. Had we changed for the worse or better in his eyes? only time, and not much of it now, would tell.

After settling my horse for the night when other competitors had talked themselves out, I retired to the 'glory' of my trailer, pulled out the foam pad and sleeping bag, changed into warm pajamas and slept. Early next morning I awoke and had fed Gentry by six, brushing and polishing him, applying my Hi Pro Plus for extra sheen with much palm rubbing. I whitened his socks, blackened his hooves, put on his elegant Victor silver show halter and replaced his damp tail bandage, finishing with his light weight wool blanket inscribed with his name proudly resplendent in scarlet on one side.

My own breakfast! Small tin of apricot bits in a pudding. Well, it was better than nothing and nutritious to see me through the morning. I did my face, changed into my halter clothes, ensuring silver earrings were shiny and my hair tucked neatly under the black cowboy hat. Then back to Gentry again. Bless him, guzzling his hay quite unconcernedly. How pleased I was to have begun early, to avoid the confusion of other competitors stabled nearby.

I sauntered over to the indoor arena not twenty paces from our barn, watching how Dick Deller was looking at the horses. Most judges want the horse to enter for halter under their own special directions, and I was anxious to please him. The fillies and mares were judged first and then it was time for the geldings nearly an hour later. I was ready. In went the two year olds, then the threes. Gentry still with blanket and tail bandage on, and I with clean cloth in hand, to wipe away any dust, edged our way to the front of the waiting horses ensuring we were first into the ring for the Aged Geldings, as had been our system over the years. I removed Gentry's clothing, polished his swiftly all over with my now diminished paisley silk scarf, careful not to brush against his shiny mouth, lightly oiled with vaseline, shining darkly, and we were ready. "Please, God, let this be a good show for us." I prayed. The gate opened, the ring steward summoned us forward. "Walk to the judge, stand him up, then trot away, turn and line up on the west side."

A deep breath from Gentry and I, and a quietening word from me and we were into our routine before I remembered I had not practiced standing him up square for months. What a fool I had been, there had been so much time the previous night. I need not have worried, Gentry had not forgotten. He did his part beautifully, and as we trotted, me racing in step in that sandy footing, I felt an excited exhilaration. I walked smartly back to the west side of the arena, standing him correctly again. Many old friends watching from the bleachers, whispered kind comments, but I heard nothing as the other horses in turn made their appearances.

Was Gentry relaxed doing his fifth wheel dropping trick? I bent to look and he was thinking about it. I slapped him quietly with the end of the leather rein, restanding him. He shut his eyes, dropped his ears and went to sleep! The judge was coming in our direction fast. I cajoled, held his head up, pinched his cheek, nothing worked. He looked like a worn out old horse - how could he? what else could I do? That darn old horse knew more about showmanship than me! At the moment Dick Deller approached, the important moment, Gentry awoke, beautifully alert and refreshed, looking at something off in the far distance with pricked ears, arched neck and yes, a little smirk to his lips, seeming to grow even taller and more firm as the estimable judge walked around him, whilst I hopped out of the way, ensuring every muscle was noticed. We were asked to go out in first place. That hurdle was over, for we had beaten some beautiful animals. I had kept up Gentry' image as a top halter gelding, collecting the blue ribbon and pewter mug. The Championships were to be held at 7 pm, a long way off, could we reinforce our position?

My oak driving cart was propped up close to the secretary's office, draped with an old pink blanket with a rope barrier strung across to keep people away. It was close to Gentry, so I could watch both at the same time, whilst seeing much of the show in the arena.

Suddenly two small children dashed around the corner, playing hide and seek, and noticed the barrier had been temporarily removed by someone, presumably to let a horse go by. The children were screamily happily, as they chased about, and I gave them no special thought, wandering into the office where the results were beginning to come through, being swiftly written up on the AQHQ forms demanded by their rules to arrive in Amarillo headquarters within ten days.

A loud crash. I knew what it was without turning around. Someone had toppled over my beautiful driving cart. Several of us rushed outside to see it dashed to the ground, with a small boy, Jason Cramer, immobile beneath all that heavy oak and iron. Miraculously one of the shafts had pierced a door as it fell, which had prevented it falling lower. the door had a gaping hole, the cart appeared all right though one shaft tip was lodged in the door. The little boy was silent and motionless. Was he dead? My heart leaped in fear as we lifted the blanket to peer beneath. He was alive, unhurt, but very silent with shock. Thank God for that strong door which no doubt saved the child's life. Our hearts began to beat normally again, it had been a severe shock to all of us. We raised the cart, wedging it safely again. The few scratches would not be noticeable as we drove around later.

The afternoon turned unexpectedly cold. As it wore on, I realized how unusually nervous I felt. The driving exhibition I had originally agreed to give had evolved into a small class. Gentry and I had never been in a ring this way before, so I could not help but wonder if he would be disturbed with the other rigs close to us. I groomed him again, put on his elegant black patent leather, piped with scarlet harness, dusted it down, and with the help of friends, especially Doug Denyer, who had driven horse teams in his youth, hitched Gentry up. He snorted lightly and shied - then we spread the scarlet blanket over the driver's seat and Doug and I climbed aboard. I grasped for the reins and whip, sending my tolerant horse out of the barn at a sharp walk, past many vehicles onto the Centre's exercise track. I knew we were a smart outfit, with the cart matching blanket my left lapel and a swirl of red feathers jauntily flowing from one side of my black bowler hat. Perhaps a rather unorthodox dress, but I knew it would be sharp under the lights of the arena. Gentry and I were nervous, but Doug, calmed us both down for the nearly half an hour until we were on display.

A prime rib barbeque supper was being served to competitors, but I was far too nervous to participate. For the next two hours I was going to be too busy to think about my stomach anyway.

The evening performance was about to begin. Our driving class was to lead it off. My two competitors, in bicycle wheeled racing carts, joined me by the entrance gate. Waiting, I unhooked the overcheck, wiped Gentry's foaming mouth, and then, deeply concentrated, climbed back into my seat. I knew we would cause a stir in the ring, B.C.'s first viewing of Quarter Horse pleasure driving.

The arena had been smoothed down with a tractor blade during the supper break, but the sand was disturbing, nearly six inches deep, and had been watered, making it very heavy. The bleachers were full to capacity when our judge returned from his supper. We were invited to enter the ring. I swiftly rebuckled the overcheck as my competitors, Bill Irwin and Garnet Sweet, invited me to drive in first.

I was now tense with excitement, sitting stiffly in place, reins correctly held before me close together, just below shoulder height, with the whip in my right hand. The involuntary gasp from the spectators as we entered, helped push from my mind that this was Gentry's first appearance and I was immensely proud of him. He pulled me strongly through the sand and I know we made a dramatic impression. This was going to be a popular class. I was unaware of the other horses behind us, and Gentry was quite unconcerned, which was just as well. Our strong walk, gentle trot and faster park trot were executed in fine form. I do not think I had felt as exhilarated in any class before and somehow the spectators too seemed to be holding their breath as Gentry leaned more strongly into his harness, coming out with his beautiful extended trot along the ringsides. The ringmaster, unversed in the correct procedures, asked us to reverse! Fine when on top of a horse, but in that deep sand, a very difficult procedure. He ought to have asked us to change on the diagonal across to the other end of the ring. After a strong trot on the other rein we were asked to line up in front of the ringmaster to be inspected. My nemesis was to come. The heavy cart sank deeper and more firmly into the sand than the light trotting sulkies.

The sulkies were easily able to back-up, but we could not. Perhaps I should have cheated a little and driven a few paces forward to get out of the rut, and then backed up, for in our training sessions Gentry obligingly backed straight for twenty feet or more. On this occasion he tried so hard, he sat back down on his hocks in the sand. When the placings were called I understood when Bill Irwin, with his palomino stallion Sir Colonel, was in first place with Gentry second. Dick Deller, our judge, told me later it was the backup, which he knew would cause trouble, that kept us from winning the class. We proudly drove around the ring before leaving, and I believe tears filled my eyes with happiness and delight from the performance my wonderful horse had given - all heart as usual for me.

By the exit gate we were greeted by many admiring fans, one in particular, Art Folliott. The doyen of our B.C. Quarter Horses who had done so much for us all over the years. Art was in tears, too. He grabbed me around the neck, hugging me. I was stunned, for over the years we had crossed swords several times for he openly stressed the top Quarter Horses should never be risked in anything but halter and pleasure classes, and I had argued repeatedly, with care their versatility should be fully exposed. He stuttered through his tears "Well done, Joy, you have just now done more for the Quarter Horse here than anyone before you. That was a magnificent exhibition and I want to congratulate you." It really was an accolade and well worth the cigarette burn on my coat sleeve. It would mend, but I would never forget Art's genuine kind words.

Several friends came to my assistance in uncoupling Gentry, storing his harness and putting his cart safely out of harm's way. I returned him to his stall as another of his fans, Dorothy Neville, also in tears by the performance, said we both had looked "A million dollars out there." I realized the class was over at last, that we had not been disgraced, and that the three months of hard work with the new discipline had been well worthwhile.

Gentry had loved all the attention, but it was now time to wash off his legs, to wipe him down from the sweat marks under the harness, to refresh him for the Halter Championship classes which were to be held within the hour, after the colt and filly Futurities. The spectators were certainly being treated to many excitements this night, especially just then seeing the splendid yearlings with their bright futures before them. I wistfully recalled the glory I had known just six years before as Gentry, then a yearling, had won me the two first British Columbia Futurities at this same show.

Having readied Gentry yet again, tail bandaged, I left a young girl in attendance to keep an eye on him to ensure he did not roll in the dusty straw. Quickly changing into my yellow and grey check jacket, keeping on my black pants from driving, but adding my black cowboy hat and gloves, I was ready. There was little time to spare as we made our way to the gate as they called for First and Second Placed Halter Geldings from the morning classes. Gentry was excited still from his driving, so needed no waking up this time. We marched into the arena, and he stood magnificently to attention, eyes and ears pointed at something in the crowd, the special way only he could see, his glorious head drawing all eyes to him. Our judge did his duty by examining all of the first places horses, then asked us to step out in the first position. Gentry had won the Senior Gelding Championship. Then he chose his Junior Champion and the two of us once again returned to the line for comparison. Gentry was still 'turned on' and again we were asked to go forward to receive the Grand Champion Gelding award. What a day! I returned him to his stall with applause ringing in our ears. All those ribbons were now hanging from the door, what a handsome array they made and how proud I was of my retired horse. You can't keep a good one down.

The rest of the evening slid by. An English Pleasure Futurity with lovely young animals showing what way the futures would turn. A Calcutta Auction in which we all bid on the competitors entered in a Trail Stake. I was still excited, flinging my hands in the air, so it was not difficult for trainer Nick Henderson, who was soliciting bids, to get one from me. I had apparently chosen the man who was to finish fifth and the money paid out only to fourth, but

Gentry, Grand Champion Pacific National Exibition.
Vancouver, 1976

somehow I felt the $35.00 I had given to the cause had been well worth my superb day. I returned to my horse, too exhausted to attend the dance held in the arena, sitting with him in his stall, feeding a few more carrots, giving lingering hugs and endearments.

Early the following morning I gave Gentry his breakfast, laced more heavily with good oats than usual, and began putting up his mane into tidy braids, the little knobs on top being finished with white wool. A friend, Abigail Brown, had driven all the way from West Vancouver to braid his tail, which we finished with the same white knobs. I sprayed all with hair lacquer, wrapping a damp tail bandage carefully around, and left him to finish his breakfast in peace whilst we searched for hot chocolate, watching the final rounds of the trail classes, which had begun at 6:00 am.

It began to rain, but I knew from the previous week in Chilliwack when I had to work him well down, I must do it again. So, dressed in an old raincoat and hat, with Gentry's legs bandaged to keep them clean, we rode over to the training track. Nearly an hour later, after

244

many circles, shoulders in and canter departures, I felt he was moving under himself properly and was sufficiently loosened up and settled down. In for a quick bite of lunch for us both, and I changed into my ring clothes, including my yellow vest and black bowler hat, minus the red feather, and we were ready for the afternoon's work. The Amateur English Pleasure had about 30 horses entered and I wanted us to do well. Many familiar faces, who had been so kind the previous night, began to look not quite so friendly towards us, realizing we could still be a threat, and I determined to be just that.

All my hours of dressage over the past weeks were to be remembered and I knew now how to ride effectively in and out of the corners. It was time to go into the ring. We trotted smartly past the judge who was standing in the far right hand corner, enabling him to see every mistake any horse made. Gentry felt good and relaxed under me as we performed every gait smoothly. We were not asked to extend trot, which was a pity, but he must have gone well for after the lineup it was announced we were the winners.

A Youth class followed, and then the All Ages English with the trainers competing. We rode as in the first class and again came out the winners, receiving our third silver mug for the show, quite a collection along with the AQHA silver horse from the previous night's championship.

The serious part of the show was over. Lindy Townly, the resident jumping instructor at Thunderbird, was over seeing the working hunter jumps set up, with our judge correctly insisting they be measured at full regulation height. I had put on Gentry's running martingale because he became very enthusiastic and difficult to hold flying over a series of jumps, and of course shortened my stirrups two holes for a better position in the saddle. Now I had to remember the course! How humiliating if after all this I ruined things for my beloved horse by going the wrong way. Our turn came to ride the working hunter course, which we did calmly with correct speed, but a refusal at double solid cedar planks, because I had not gone wide enough into the previous corner, was a serious fault, caused by me. I ought to have ridden him harder. We whipped around and I really rode him properly this time, flying around the rest of the course faultless, to be awarded another first place, as another girl had not ridden fast enough and another knocked several fences down. Next came the jumping with all fences raised a few inches and my heart began to hammer, but Gentry watched eagerly with his beautiful ears pricked, so I ought not to have worried. Our first round was clear, but again I ought to have ridden a bit faster, as we tied with another horse. Our President of BCQHA, standing by the exit gate, told me for the jump off I must 'go for it', and I did. The first jump was a brush which we flew over as if it had been six feet high. I was so relieved to be over I neglected to ride him deep enough into the next corner and we took the following jump on the wrong lead, knocking the top rail over. My fault entirely, so we ended up with a second place.

It had indeed been an incredible show and as I was to present the Drive woolen cooler to the Hi Point All Around Horse I went to the office to find out who it was. Imagine my delighted surprise to find, at this stage, Gentry had tied for it himself.

I spoke with the other competitor and was so proud when the announcer told the crowd the major award had been tied between Hyline Gentry and Deep Commander, who had excelled in the western classics. It really had been quite a feat for us to be so high in the final point standing without putting on a western saddle at a western show! The following day, Carol Rees, the Show Manager's wife, told me they were going to award the Hi Point Championship all to Gentry as we had been in more classes, a Quarter Horse rule, and Deep Commander would take the Reserve. I was so thrilled for my lovely horse. Also remembering that when he had been three years old, like Commander, he too had tied for a Hi Point and under the same ruling been awarded the Reserve. How many similarities there seemed.

It has often been claimed by knowledgeable horsemen that an intelligent horse can be compared to a six year old child, and that they definitely do understand a great deal of our thoughts and commands, acting accordingly. Gentry and I always had a special understanding of the other, and sometimes I thought he teased me into relaxing, by pretending to misbehave with an innocent buck, to be followed by a smile on his lips.

Gentry had excelled throughout his life, winning Futurities, Championships, High Point Show All Around Championships, Register of Merit and his esteemed American Quarter Horse Association Championship competing in strong classes all the time, but none gave me quite the "kick" as our last show. Returning from semi-retirement he had given his heart again to me, and I was overjoyed with the response we received from many knowledgeable horse people.

When working on our 'escape' plans from Canada I had to also decide where Gentry should go on arrival in England. Leicestershire, where the heart of hunting country is centered, and where I had ridden as a child, drew me because Kevin and his family lived there too. In my Pony Club days I competed against leading child riders from the Bradley family of Oakham and knew they were still foremost in the horse world.

Joan had married senior veterinarian George Gibson, and was a Master of the Cottesmore Foxhounds, Michael was a veterinarian in the Gibson Clinic in Oakham, and younger sister Betty had married Robin Leyland, another fine horseman who, at that time, was the Chef d' Equippe for the English Junior Eventing Team, coaching them for International competition.

Robin and Betty Leyland ran a top flight horse livery yard at Barleythorpe, just two miles from Oakham. I remembered the yard had been built originally for Lord Lonsdale with large, warm stalls close by the house where the Leylands now lived. I would send Gentry to them, knowing he would receive the best of care, along with the fact if he were traumatized or injured during the journey, the Gibson Clinic was close by. Also I wanted Gentry to represent, when we were settled, the American Quarter Horse in England and to be recognized for the outstanding horse he was. I knew the Leylands would give the care, help and knowledge I would need. Receiving their letter saying they would accept by horse soothed many of my fears.

Years later, I heard foremost judges from California, Don Burt, President of AQHA in 1996, and Richard Deller, had been en route to a major show by plane in 1975. Sitting together inevitably they talked Quarter Horse, discussing horses they knew that had given outstanding versatility worldwide, promoting strength of the Association. Both had judged Hyline Gentry over the years, and agreed he was perhaps one of the finest exponents they had ever seen. An outstanding halter horse who excelled in all performance and many working events. They regretted he had not shown at the Worlds in Oklahoma, to have been able to prove himself before the very best. I did too, but my finances had not allowed. The plane story was told to me by Don Burt himself. There was no stronger confirmation, to me, of their opinions.

The flight was confirmed, I had only a few more days to wait before Gentry and I would leave for England. It did not take long to move Gentry over from Highland Hills, where John expected him to be, into the care of my firm friends Ann and Bobbie Hall at Emerald Acres in Aldergrove, so at least he was safe.

I rang the moving firm to come the following morning at 10:00 after first collecting the trophies waiting at Pat and Joanne Boyle's farm. Joanne, and Joanne Dixon, my friend who had a sad marital breakup, and been such wonderful company when she had shown her mare, Miss Jolee Jaguar along with Gentry and I, had volunteered to be with me when I physically told John I was leaving him. They were very brave and I was so indebted to them for their courage. The scene was set when they confirmed they would be present the following morning. As it happened I had been invited to Doug and Dorothy Denyer's daughter's wedding shower, who prevailed just as I was leaving them, facing a longish drive home, to remain overnight. I would not have to spend another alone with John! I called him to say I would be back early the following morning.

Chapter Twelve

William Wordsworth:
"My heart leaps up when I behold a rainbow in the sky."

Driving back to my 'home' the following morning I saw my two friends had arrived, with fortunately the moving van still quietly waiting around the corner. They had already been to the Boyles in Aldergrove to collect the boxes of trophies. I asked the driver to come in ten minutes and went inside. John was talking with my friends saying he expected me back momentarily. I gave the two Joannes each a hug, then put on a pot of fresh coffee. It all seemed so civilized and normal as we sat down.

I took a deep breath and said: "John, the girls are here to help me tell you I am leaving you now. I have been terrified of you for a long time and cannot put up with it any longer."

He stood up in shock, reached for my arm and tried dragging me from the room. Both girls stood up saying together: "Joy is not leaving our sight."

John ignored them and proceeded his dragging. Joanne Boyle grasped my other arm and there began a tug of war. At that precise moment a loud knock came on the front door, the movers had arrived in the nick of time! I escaped to open it when John temporarily released me, inviting four burly men inside the house.

I informed John: "I am only taking half of our possessions. Some cupboards doors have red stickers and everything in there remains for you, all else is being packed and going with me."

A few moments later he jumped to his feet, lunging for me again, but this time an alerted man inserted himself between us. Shortly after, when I had gone into another room to speak with the packer, John followed, attempting to close the door behind him, but my two splendid friends forestalled him quickly, standing on either side of me. He left the room. The packing took nearly four fraught hours. John spent most of the time sitting in his chair with clenched hands, the knuckles showing starkly white through the flesh. Now and again he walked over to see what was being wrapped removing something from a box, only to have the packer put it back when he turned.

Eventually all was finished, it was time to leave. John sat stonily in his chair by the door. The girls had moved just inches outside. I put my hand on his shoulder saying "It is so sad we are finishing this way. You terrified me for so long it has been difficult getting my courage to leave. Thank you for the good parts of our marriage and the gifts you gave me. I wish you well. I am leaving for Oregon then England. Goodbye." He did not speak a word.

Then as I moved through the doorway he asked "Where is Gentry now?"

I lied "He is in Oregon with Bob Avila." that was the end.

My fine friends took me to a nearby coffee shop for a hot dog of all things! It was something to break the tension, then we drove back to Joanne's farm where I would remain until leaving the country.

As soon as I had left, John was on the telephone apparently to Immigration at the Border, the Police and his lawyer, demanding from them all that I be prevented from leaving the country. Each told him I had done nothing wrong and was free to do as I wished.

Waiting for the Veterinary License to come through from Ottawa was torturous. We had the Coggins and Health Certificate from the Federal vet, Dr. Felius, but the most important one, essential to avert six months' quarantine in England, must arrive before our departing date of 17th August, just four days away. I was a bag of nerves inspite of my host's kindnesses to me whilst staying in their home. Days were slipping by.

I gave in to panic. Joanne Boyle was a strong and calming influence. She taught me to macrame and put me to work making her a lamp shade. Out of habit I kept wondering how John was caring for himself. It not longer mattered, I had to adjust.

A number of my friends, with whom I had been so involved in the horse world, decided Gentry and I should not leave the country without their special good wishes. Some of them knew we were actually still in the country, but all had refused to gossip or give any hints to that affect. They were extremely loyal, being well aware of the John terrorism from the past. However, through a surprisingly complicated link of phoning one another to give messages for times and venue to be passed on, a Farewell Party was arranged at Highland Hills. Just two days before we were to leave, on a brilliantly sunny, typical British Columbia day, I arrived with Joanne Boyle, expecting two or three friends. I was overwhelmed to be greeted by over thirty of them waiting for me under the apple trees. There was a beautiful cake, embossed with the words: "Goodbye and Good Luck

Joy and Gentry." Pat Bennett had so graciously organized this cheery sendoff, which finally brought farewell tears as we hugged goodbye, from many outstanding friends never expecting to meet us again.

Gentry was my anchor, the source of my strength. He was there. Depending on me. I would not let him down. Each morning I rode Gentry for an hour before 5:30 in the Aldergrove Lake Park for his exercise. John would never expect me to be there as I had said we would be in Oregon, but I did not want to run the risk should he be spying. I disposed of the car and trailer, having taken half of the money from the small bank account the day before I left John. I had to remain patient just a few more days.

On 16th August, my last day in Canada, I borrowed Joanne's car driving over to White Rock to bid my friends Annette and Ernie Kehler goodbye. Ernie was working in an exotic aviary of birds in his front garden, and was so warm to me as I pulled up on the driveway beside him. I could not believe the irony, for as I looked up, there was John glowering, about thirty feet away, behind a massive cedar tree. Ernie saw him too and brusquely called "John we do not need your type here anymore. Joy is staying safely with us. Please go at once."

John replied "I have to talk to her, she cannot leave like this."

Ernie, so much larger that John, answered "Go, or I will call the police." "Joy, go in the house with Annette."

I was received with gentleness and understanding as I shook uncontrollably. We watched from Annette's bathroom window, peering through the delicate sheer drapes, to see Ernie gesticulate firmly, whilst John hovered, looking directly in the window. I was grateful for Ernie's strength, otherwise I know John would have come after me. We stood motionless, fearful for what John might yet do. Ernie glared him down at last, he turned and was gone. Several hours later I left, the Kehler's gardener was to drive Gentry and I down to Seattle the following morning in their Arab horse trailer. How close had been John's detective work!

The break with John was over finally. The legalities would follow. What a terrible waste of twenty years, yet had I not been involved with John I never would have found the Canadian way of life I treasure, or the friends, or Gentry and the incredible career we had together. Gentry would now be safe. I would always regret the financial impossibilities of not taking my beloved horse to The World Quarter Horse Championships after he had qualified in 1974 and 1975. Perhaps the Superhorse Award could have been his.

Flying Tigers had at last made up their mind what currency,

and how much, for our flight they required, along with the date we could fly. Every time I spoke with them I had made it abundantly clear Gentry had to have a double wide crate, for he was too muscular to stand for a long time cramped in a single wide. I put the final gears in motion with frantic phone calls for the Canadian Laboratory test delivery. John Twidale had pulled out all the stops and assured me it would be at the Border Inspection to meet us at 10:00 a.m., but after all the difficulties I found it hard to believe.

There were very sad and tearful goodbyes to the Boyles and Halls for their rescue operations, their support and love had been magnificent. Apart from Gentry himself, I was taking an extraordinary collection of things I could not manage without. The journey in the aircraft was planned for only fifteen hours, but I had learned to be prepared for the unexpected.

There was a succulent bale of green alfalfa hay and a stuffed haynet. A plastic garbage pail holding Gentry's woolen cooler, light cotton sheet, a variety of leg wraps and a padded leather helmet to be attached to his halter in the plane. A clean halter and lead shank with extra long chain, in case the one he wore broke, two large plastic buckets for oats and water were given from the Halls. In my paraphernalia was a 33 lb bucket of Drive, the feed supplement I would never be without, which would relieve stress. My English saddle and bridle in a hessian sack, my own small suitcase of clothing, my tack box with grooming equipment and medication, a briefcase containing the all important papers, my purse, my passport and $6,000 in Travellers checks. Labels had been attached to everything, including my pillow.

A most valuable addition came from dear friend, John Twidale, containing three hypodermics and 10cc of Atravet for use if necessary as a tranquilizer. He had also written a Certificate of Valuation which said:

"This horse has been extremely successful on the Quarter Horse Show Circuit in previous years. However, this year the horse has developed an unsoundness in the wind and is unfit for show. While the sentimental value to the owner is high, the cash value at the present time can be assessed at the rate of 25 cents of 1,200 pounds = $300.00. Signed, J.D.Twidale."

This was to have a tremendous value later. Gentry had shown signs of becoming 'unsound' in his wind during the campaign trail for his AQHA Championship, which ultimately required surgery.

All of these possessions were loaded into the Kehler's trailer. I put bell boots on Gentry to protect his hooves, from which his shoes had been removed only the afternoon before. We did not know if the plane might lurch and he be forced to scramble to remain upright, and possibly tear his legs if the metal shoes had remained. A large bucket of carrots for Gentry came from Joanne Dixon at the last minute. Last, but not least, Gentry squeezed into a trailer too low and tight for him, but obliging as always, he did not complain.

We left for the appointment with the Canadian veterinarian who was to meet us at the U.S. Canada border crossing in Blaine. On arrival I found the negative Piraplosmasis certificate had been waiting less than ten minutes for us after its lengthy journey from Ottawa. Other papers had to be signed, with some retained in my briefcase, and Gentry checked to ensure he was the same horse as listed.

When all was in place, I bade Canada a sad goodbye with a lump in my throat, and we began the two hour journey to Longacres Racetrack in Seattle, Washington State.

Gentry and I were to experience many more adventures ahead, but we would be together, perhaps to gallop into Eternity through the clouds. Just fifteen hours of flying lay before us and we should arrive safely in England. I had not reckoned on the Canadian Controller's strike, but when others followed suit, real problems did arise! Somehow we had to be in England by the end of the month to qualify under the British Agricultural License Permit and I could not believe, strikes or not, we would be travelling for fifteen days.

Kevin, Louisa and my two year old little granddaughter, Victoria, were waiting for us to begin a new life in England.

After paying the airfare I would have three hundred dollars, and a small balance on my Visa card, for unexpected expenses en route. Who the exchange rate favoured most was of no concern to me as long as Gentry and I had safe, efficient passage to a new life on my homeground, away from the fears created by John Richardson.

Upon arrival at the racetrack on the dot of eleven thirty a.m., I was greeted by kindly Earl Brown, who proudly showed me his neat stable block which was fronted by beds of brilliant zinnias in vivid bloom. In checking with Flying Tigers, I was told to expect a fourteen hour delay in takeoff.

Arrangements had been made for Earl Brown, owner of Giddi-Up-Go Horse Transport, to stable Gentry at Longacres where he could wait in comfort. He was, after all, an extremely valuable horse. We were to be at the airport by one-forty-five a.m. for a three forty-five departure that would put us into New York at two p.m. the following day.

Longacres was possibly one of the most beautiful race courses in the world, its infield festooned with immaculately kept flower beds of scarlet geraniums and begonias. More importantly their twenty-four hour security system was excellent.

Given the heat of the day, all the horses were dozing lazily. Gentry and I did the same, Several hours later the Browns kindly invited me to share their supper in their nearby trailer. Shortly after we were at the table, the phone rang and Earl answered. He was told by someone in the Flying Tigers office that I would have to pay an additional nine hundred dollars.

"Blackmail!" Mary and I shouted at the same time.

Earl barely hesitated. He told the party on the other end of the line, that Gentry was not feeling well; he had colic, and would be unable to travel for several days, the vet was with him now. Therefore we were cancelling out on the flight to New York.

For a brief moment I enjoyed feeling victorious for having scorned the Flying Tigers, but knew my situation was precarious. I was now in a foreign country, with precious little money, and appeared to have no way of getting to England. Many phone calls later, Earl connected with a horse agency owned by Alex Nicholls. He agreed to fly us from San Francisco along with eight thoroughbreds from Bay Meadows, to Kennedy Airport in New York. He also said that if I would be willing to take care of a colt enroute to England he would pay me five hundred dollars. He wanted two thousand five hundred dollars fare for Gentry and me.

Giddi-Up-Go were taking a load of horses to California five days later and volunteered to haul Gentry and me nongratis.

During the five day wait at Longacres, I spent most of the time with Gentry, taking meals with the Browns, and helped in their shed row, becoming part of their stable team, helping bathe the horses, wash bandages and rub legs.

The evening racing, with jockeys in their gay silks, the bugle blowing the call to end each race and the sound of thundering hooves passing close by ... all was new and exciting to Gentry. One afternoon I wondered over to the infield to watch the races and ran into leading T. B. Breeder, Russel Bennett, from Westbank, B.C. Russell was the son of the late Social Credit Premier of British Columbia, W.A.C. Bennett. He was amazed to see me, but upon hearing briefly of my story, wished me luck.

It was time to leave the security of Longacres. I did not ride first class to California but Gentry was able to ride in the centre of the twelve horse van, which was usually reserved for provisions. I rode on a mattress in the forward section, where spare tires,oil cans and old blankets were stored, but by standing on tiptoe from time to time I was able to peer through a high, dusty window to note where we were travelling. It was illegal for me to ride up front with the two drivers, although each time they stopped for a brief meal, I was invited out of my prison to join them!

The journey took nineteen hours. Gentry enjoyed visiting with the other horses, but I was soon filthy, exhausted and terrified by thoughts of the immediate future.

We seemed to tour the entire Bay area, dropping off horses along the way, before arriving at Bay Meadows Race Course south of San Francisco. I could not help but remember the last time we had been there for the Nationals Horse Show two years earlier.

My favourite saddle was mislaid somewhere en route, but all else was with me. I had started with eleven possessions, including Gentry, now we were down to ten.

Gentry was smuggled onto the track where only thoroughbreds were allowed, and was soon settled in a stall and fed through the generosity of several trainers, after hearing of our predicament from one of the drivers.

I was taken to a nearby motel where I bathed and washed myself and all my clothing. I hung my clothes in the open window to dry. The weather was humid, the drying was slow, so I remained in a towel until the driver brought my suitcase. Later I joined him for a meal in the restaurant.

Nicholls called many times to change takeoff time, to make additional arrangements, to discuss crating and linkups from Kennedy Airport. Final arrangements were with an American carrier, but Gentry would travel with other horses in a freight plane and I would have to go separately on a passenger flight. Loading time for the horses, all to be tranquilized and bandaged, was 2:00 a.m. from Oakland International.

We adhered to the instructions. The horses were transported to the airport, fourteen miles away, where I was sent off to board the passenger plane. In New York I would be met by a Nicholls agent who would reunite Gentry with me. I was very unhappy to be separated from my horse, but the grooms accompanying eight thoroughbreds would take up the only permitted seating on the plane.

As I was boarding an American Airlines passenger plane for the cross country flight, a special alert was sent out over the loudspeakers, ordering me to call a number in the freight area immediately.....

I stopped breathing. Gentry had fallen from the elevator whilst being loaded! I was totally numb, trembling too much to hold onto a dime to feed into the pay phone. A kindly airport employee did the job for me.

The airline carrier had apparently found a cargo that paid more than the horses, had dumped them and they were on their way back to Bay Meadows. My heart resumed its normal beating.

Miraculously, I was able to collect my suitcase from the plane hold and then parted with a few dollars to take me halfway back to the racetrack by taxi. I hitch hiked the rest of the distance when a kindly couple saw me standing by the roadside and drove me to Bay Meadows.

How grateful I was for the ride, and how angry I felt toward those who had subjected Gentry and I to such unnecessary disruption. The British Quarter Horse Secretary, Sarah Neeld, had warned me to be aware of transporters, but I had been trusting, not knowing how to cope with people who were not. My only option had been to go along with all their suggestions to avoid causing trouble, and look where it had taken me! I had fallen into the trap of scurrilous horse transporters anyway.

Once more Gentry was smuggled into Bay Meadows, and I returned to the same motel. My money was dwindling rapidly! Having no idea of how much longer we would be cursed with treacherous delays, I purchased a large box of dried raisins, ate nothing else during the next four days, and spent as many hours as possible with Gentry. I was not at all certain he was being fed properly, and gave him handfuls of the precious Drive and sneaked alfalfa flakes from the nearby stalls whenever I could.

On the fourth day, the trainer whose stall we were using, told me he needed it back to accommodate a thoroughbred being shipped in for a special race. Gentry would be stalled at a nearby farm.

"He'll have a nice paddock with shade trees," I was told, and there's a running brook close by."

It sounded like a made up pack of lies to me. "If he must leave, then so will I," I said firmly. "I'll not be parted from him."

Other trainers standing around looked rather startled when I said that, making me even more determined not to be separated from my horse. Who knew where they might take him!

"If that's what you want to do", one of the men said, "you'd best take a gun along with you. There's a lot of Mexicans out there on the farm, and they would certainly gang rape you."

That did it. I refused to move an inch from in front of Gentry's stall.

"We're staying right here," I declared.

"Let it be," the trainer finally said, as he and the other walked away, rolling their eyes at each other and in general acting as men are prone to do when they think woman are impossible.

If the thoroughbred did in fact arrive, I do not know what the trainer did with it.

From that time on, I was never away from Gentry for too long at a time, and would call the motel intermittently to see if Alex Nicholls had phoned. Finally, he did. His message indicated that the controller's strike looked as if it would spread into England. More, he was having no luck finding another flight from Oakland Airport near San Francisco to Kennedy Airport in New York.

I received a telephone call from an American veterinarian wanting Gentry hauled to the Cow Palace for a health check! The van that had hauled us south was on its way to Phoenix, but after hearing of my predicament the vet agreed to come to the airport and make his check immediately before takeoff. I never heard from him again.

Bob Oliver, president of Diagnostic Data Inc., makers of the superior horse supplement Drive in Mountain View, heard of our arrival, and wanted to take me out.

Leaving Gentry was so risky, I found it hard to make a definite plan. Eventually we managed breakfast, during which he promised to send letters of introduction to England to the Hon. Teresa Pearson, Lord Cowdray's sister, and also Sy Maxwell from Seyfreids, the grain merchants firm that was initiating importation of Drive. He hoped we would be able to work together, for I had been so successful on the West Coast distributing Drive, I would be able to advise English horsemen for them.

The misery at Bay Meadows continued. On the fourth day I purchased another box of raisins, and took comfort I was now loosing weight quite well and not loosing my energy either, which I knew was essential if Gentry and I were to surmount further trials ahead which this incredible journey continually produced. Gentry was eating reasonably well. I could not do much for him in the daytime, when everyone was around, but at night, when the guards were sleeping, I sequestered the hay and alfalfa I knew he must have.

To add to our misery, the weather grew hotter. The heat factor was sometimes 110 to 115 degrees. A severe water shortage throughout the whole Bay area, and of course Bay Meadows, ensued. We were forbidden to bathe the horses, cherishing every last drop for their drinking pails. Gentry grew filthy, caked with layers of dried fly spray to which all the dust in the barn seemed to cling. I tried to brush him, but the dust was so thick, all I succeeded in doing was barely moving it around.

I was unable to exercise him on the track, or on a hot walker during the day, for fear our cover might me blown. He knew only the duskiness of the barn in daylight hours, but we prowled at night a few times, he and I taking long, cool walks along the shedrow and even venturing onto the track a time or two. With no one around in the night, I cooled the stall roof off a little, spilling a few buckets of water over it, attempting to lower the outside temperature over the horse who could not go outside.

I was forced to curtail even those life saving evening respites. Having removed Gentry's shoes for the flight, treading over the stony ground around Longacres and Bay Meadows, tore his hooves. He was close to thirteen hundred lounds, I could no longer risk giving him his walks no matter how imploringly he nickered. That is the sad part of owning a horse: sometimes one must be cruel, not to punish the horse but to protect it.

Our fifteen hour flight was stretching into an unending motion. I phoned Kevin periodically, who in turn phoned Robin Leyland regarding the horse transport meeting us at Heathrow. They had begun to think they would never see us alive again. Wondering where we would land next. We were only halfway home.

On the sixth day Nicholls was able to place us on lists for New York. The hitch was once again Gentry and I could not travel together, there was no room on the cargo plane for me. He would go with eight other horses via Chicago whilst I would fly direct to New York. I was desperately worried with our being separated. Since he would have to travel without me I gave him a shot of Atravet, a tranquilizer, after accompanying him to the freight area of Oakland International Airport. Unable to forget what had happened the last time we were there, I did not leave until Gentry's plane was safely in the air and I watched it with tears in my eyes, as it swept off in a giant curve over the San Francisco Bay and disappeared over the mountains beyond.

It did not tip, so you had to assume the horses were travelling quietly.

My American Airlines Flight was uneventful, I was even able to sleep the sleep of exhaustion throughout the trip.

An agent was supposed to meet me at Kennedy taking me to the S.P.C.A. shelter where Gentry and I would be housed for the requisite hours of quarantine. Once more precious dollars had to be spent for a taxi ride, which turned out to be less than a quarter mile.

Arriving at the shelter no one knew where my horse was or when he would arrive. A kindly employee, who sensed my distress, patiently put out a tracer and we learned Gentry's plane was still in Chicago, but would probably land at Kennedy in eight hours or so!

Nervous, exhausted, and unable to sleep. I made myself useful in the shelter, where sixty beautiful greyhounds were laying over in horse stalls, en route to some big race meeting. Watering them kept me busy for awhile.

Then two hundred Rhesus monkeys arrived from South Africa, on their way to research facilities. The poor little monkeys were quite wild with terror. We tried filling their water containers in the individual cages, but they dashed them away. I found it so difficult to bear the terrible sadness in their little eyes, and the way their tiny hands gripped the constraining bars of their cages. I gently squeezed water over them hoping to cool them off from the hot and close atmosphere surrounding us.

I had been told a stall was reserved for Gentry, but upon checking, found it was empty - no bedding, hay or grain of any kind was even on the premises! Some was due, but would not arrive in time for us. I put water in the stall, and dispirited, chose one of the examining tables as a resting place, eventually dozing off oblivious to the SPCA staff around me.

Several hours later I was awakened by the attendant who had put out the tracer for Gentry. He took me in his van to the freight area at Kennedy. We arrived just as a huge jet had landed, its engines still roaring while misty rays of area searchlights sparkled across its huge wings and body.

High above me large doors yawned open in the plane's belly. I saw three wooden crates, with three horses in each. Gentry, alert as always, was looking about curiously, but seemed resigned and relaxed for which I was grateful. He did not look in my direction, nor could he hear my frenzied shouts of encouragement.

After what seemed an endless wait, slowly the horses were lowered on the creaking elevator onto a big turntable, then unloaded into a transport van. As soon as all nine horses were loaded it took off, delivering Gentry and I to the SPCA shelter first.

As always, Gentry's large eyes grew brighter when with me and he nudged me repeatedly on the way to his temporary stall. I gave him a handful of my nearly depleted Drive, in lieu of nothing else. He sipped the water and did not seem to mind no hay waiting for him. I assumed he was contented merely with being able to move freely around for the first time in many hours.

Gentry was in no mood to rest. After a flight with strange horses in a machine he had never before encountered, after going through the unloading with searchlight beams streaking wildly across him, and finding himself surrounded by greyhounds and monkeys, he was totally prey to curiosity and adrenaline. He was also elated to be with me again and tried to prove it by repeated nudges harder than usual and loud Gentry little nickers.

In spite of his good spirits I remained worried and kept a close eye on him. Having known him all his life I knew he could easily colic, especially when surroundings were strange, or not to his liking. As a yearling colt in our barn at Heritage he would colic at breakfast time if another horse was fed first. Spoilt maybe, but that is what happened.

Gentry's spirits remained high during the required twenty hours at the SPCA shelter, but mine sank when I remembered Nicholls had originally promised me five hundred dollars for babysitting a colt across the Atlantic. No colt had accompanied Gentry. That deal was off then, and I had been counting on the money for entry expenses into the U.K.

An annoying amount of time during the quarantine stay at the shelter was spent on long distance calls, with all charges reversed, to my doctor son, Kevin, in England. He phoned Sarah Neeld who suggested he employ International Horse Services to try and sort the incredible delays out. As a result, Gentry and I were reserved on a 747 Pan American freight jet that would depart Kennedy Airport at 5:00 am the following morning. They somehow arranged for some of the money I had paid the Nichol's Agency to deliver us into Heathrow, to be transferred to this reputable airline.

"In spite of it all, we're lucky" I told my horse. "We've still a few dollars left, and we're almost there, Gentry, almost there! Be patient just a little longer."

The ESP between Gentry and I had always been incredible, and would continue on. If the plane were to crash I felt confident we would spend the rest of eternity together galloping amongst clouds and glorious sunlight.

Through his tranquil, knowing eyes I had grown strong. His trust in me was absolute. I would not let him down, then or ever.

Gentry's night was peaceful enough, but I hardly slept at all back on the surgical table, and was prepared for the last leg of our journey long before 4:30 a.m.

Five thirty arrived and departed, and still no one had come to fetch us! My nerves had practically gone when the van driver finally appeared. The kindly SPCA attendant who tranquilized Gentry for me noticed my agitation and tried to cheer me with humor:

"I may be tranquilizing the wrong member of this travel team," he smiled, but I was not amused.

My heart lightened as soon as we arrived at the loading bay. The huge silhouette of the 747 on which we were booked, looked safe as well as beautiful. However, my spirit took a nosedive when I saw the crate assigned to Gentry. I had asked for a crate built for a mare and her foal, had asked for it in every conversation with every airline official I had spoken with regarding the flight. Furthermore I had paid for a larger one.

I tried to argue with the ground crew but accomplished nothing. They eluded every point I made with the same excuse: "We're just following orders, Ma'am."

Nothing could be done. Once Gentry was in the crate he had less than two inches to spare all the way around his body.

My next worry was ensuring he remained safe during the elevator ride lifting him to the plane opening. I had never seen such a large plane, the door opening he had to pass through seemed at least forty feet from the ground!

In the end, much to the consternation of the ground crew, I rode with Gentry on that elevator platform, standing in front of him, trying to keep my hands over his eyes. I did not want him to be frightened of the height to which he was being lifted. With one nudge, of course, he could have pushed me over, but I knew he would never do that.

Frightening as it was, we were safely deposited in the vast interior of the plane, where Gentry's crate was locked onto rollers and pushed into a clearing among the rest of the cargo.

"What temperature do you want your horse to have in here?" the Captain inquired as he boarded.

"Seventy degrees will be all right for both of us," I replied, pushing one of my ten pieces of baggage close to Gentry attempting to sit down, but one of the pilot's took me by the arm.

"You'll have to ride up front during the takeoff," he said. "It's regulations," he added, sensing I was about to protest. "You can come back once we've reached cruising altitude," he said comfortingly, leading me the length of the huge plane. We climbed a ladder to the flight deck, and he showed me to a seat directly behind the pilot.

"Fasten your belt," he said, "we'll be moving soon."

I obeyed and found that by craning my neck I could just see Gentry through a small porthole in the door. The tranquilizing shot had taken effect. Gentry was peacefully dozing, and was still dozing when I joined him later. He was not too aware of my arrival, just giving me a sleepy nicker and a nudge on my shoulder.

"All this will pass, Gentry," I told him. "We'll soon be home! England, Gentry!"

He was of course too hot in the 70 degrees. I had chosen far too high a temperature for his comfort. Struggling to undo and remove his blanket, I was useless, for I could not reach down to release the crossed circingles under his stomach, although I did undo the straps in front of his chest. Eventually it slipped down around his padded hind legs, adding more discomfort. He seemed lonely, I would stay with him a while.

I sat beside him on a bucket reflecting on how Gentry's own courage had led him to great strengths during his career, but we had had to pay the price too. During his roping activity, maintained in superb rounded halter condition, through his eagerness he gave his all. Once thoroughly enjoying his work from the Laughlin barn he had roped 97 cows in one day with Bob Avila, taking time out either on the hot walker or briefly in his stall, he had not seemed to tire. As time went by, sadly we noticed he began to make a slight roaring sound when over exerted. All horses are subject to roaring, though it is more common in light breeds. Although no reason has been found for it, roaring is found more in geldings and horses than in mares, and it occurs more at three to six years of age, probably because this age group is asked to do more strenuous work.

Gentry's semi-retirement had not worsened the condition, but I knew at some time in the future, as he grew older, surgery would be necessary to sew up the vocal cords in his throat which were loose and flapping. After which he would have to be kept in a closed stall for a month whilst the throat healed, to prevent his seeing other horses in the yard, to discourage whinnying, which could undo the surgery. Dr. John Twidale had been very well aware of this when he had written the Valuation Certificate to accompany us for entry into England.

I wondered about buttercups in England. They are poisonous and harden the liver, invariably killing the animal. No animals want to eat them, but if nothing else is available, say on a scrub field, they have to. Deadly or woody nightshade, laburnum pods, acorns, yew, bracken and ragwort are all dangerous. I would have to ensure Gentry did not receive dried hay with the poisonous plants in either, for they are just as lethal.

I had been feeding horses under my care for years 6 - 8 dried buccha leaves weekly to clear the kidneys. I hoped they would be easily available. They are especially successful for older horses if they are storing liquid causing an edema. There was a handful with us in my tack box, but I had not used them in England before, and wondered at their availability.

Sitting quietly with my horse I recalled a few of the other things I had learned since leaving England with my youthful horse successes. Experience in Canada had taught me so much, such as adding a tablespoon of paprika, (definitely not cayenne pepper) to the daily feed to redden sorrel and chestnut coats. To prevent proud flesh forming, to coat the wound with Preparation H from a drug store. To float the teeth of young and horses older than nine or ten, at least twice a year, when they grow the most. To be sure and remove wolf teeth which grow by the third year, which can cause serious problems bumping against a bit, the veterinarians can gently ease them out without anesthetic.

Perhaps a special knowledge came to me regarding training young horses. Never to do so without splint boots. If a bump does occur, there will be heat, pain and swelling along the side of the cannon bone. To stop calcification, which would result in a splint, I had found several times, to give a small packet of butozolodin for ten days in the feed. It stopped soft tissue from hardening.

A simple and easy dietary addition had been to add at least a quarter cup of vegetable, preferably canola oil, daily, to keep body parts moving fluidly and giving wonderful coat conditioning.

There were so many issues.

As we flew high above beauteous green Ireland, a message came through to say there was no hope of landing in England, as the controller's strike was heating up. The lights in the cabin flickered more and more with instructions from goodness knew where, as we flew over southern England to the Frankfurt International Airport in Germany!

I was standing beside Gentry when the massive door to 747 Jumbo opened. My brave horse looked around with interest, not at all awed by the near forty-foot drop to the ground below. As he left the plane the pilot told me we would be on the ground for five or six hours at least. There were negotiations to be worked through concerning our entry into England.

The elevator was slotted into position in readiness for our removal. A man spoke in English saying we would be let down very soon, and disappeared. I watched the pilots leaving the plane, feeling very alone yet again. Twenty minutes or so passed, and I became very scared, alone up there with my weary horse, and began calling for help through the doorway, though no one would hear me above the roar of the engines winding down.

After what seemed more interminable waiting, some men did appear, and our platform was guided through the plane to the elevator and slowly lowered to the ground. There were again no sides on the platform. As when we loaded in New York, I rode with Gentry holding my hands over his eyes. The tranquilizer was wearing off, and Gentry, for once, was quite uneasy.

We made it. Upon reaching the ground we were towed swiftly from the noisy landing strip to a large storage shed. The driver of the tractor obviously did not realize he had a valuable animal behind him as he swung back and forth between piles of crates. I was grateful for the leg bandaging I had executed and that the shoes had long since been removed. Gentry's legs would have been seriously lacerated as he tried to maintain his balance.

A large wall clock was just above our heads. I watched the hands wondering what would happen next and when.

Men were scurrying about, towing various-sized crates containing heavy equipment labeled for delivery all over the world. I attempted to speak with several men, but no one appeared to understand the few German words and phrases I knew.

Eventually a coloured man understood and filled my water bucket. Holding it in front of my horse I thought he would gulp it dry, but my smart Gentry new better. He merely slopped his mouth in it and played. He buried his face in above his eyes, blowing refreshing bubbles but would not swallow one drop. Then I remembered he was so tightly confined in his crate he could not stretch out to urinate. I knew he must be suffering, as he had been there more than thirteen hours.

I gave him a small portion of Drive, upturned his bucket, sitting on it in front of his crate. Often he ducked his head to nudge mine.

Finally, almost weeping with frustration and exhaustion from the past fourteen days in transit, we were hitched up, pulled back to the plane and left beneath a huge wing. At least I knew we had not been forgotten. We were close to the main runway, with planes taking off every two minutes, and I shall never forget poor Gentry's head swiveling this way and that as the planes roared by.

I noticed three covered crates with two inch holes punched through the tops, and went to investigate. In two bright pink ones were sad looking zebras and in another a lion. After the machinery had been loaded, in went the sad wild animals, and then us with Gentry safely secured toward the tail of the plane. It was not surprising we would have to wait a little longer for some kind of landing space in Heathrow. When the largest airport in the world is in the throes of a strike, with only a skeleton staff working, confusion was bound to result.

Our careful pilot taxied off, and we were finally on the final leg of our unbelievable journey.

Majestically above us to the east rose a brilliant sun, a thin crimson strip surrounded by darkness, rapidly growing into a fiery ball that soon illuminated a big arc in the sky over Russia. As dawn broke, and we flew on, we noticed the German countryside giving way to that of France -- then the English Channel, and finally England!

As we descended, one side of our vision was engulfed in thick fog of all things. How weird to look down and see only one side of the River Thames winding its way through London. The other was totally lost to us. We would be flying blind! And only sparse controllers on the ground to direct us in safely.

We landed safely with the aid of the automatic pilot. Coming to a final stop, not knowing where to go in the fog until, out in the distance, a tiny, wavering light appeared, slowly coming forward. As it drew closer, we could see that it was a bicycle light. The man riding it guided us to our landing zone. What next?

Due to so many delays we had arrived in England six hours after the Ministry of Agriculture Permit Entry License expired. We were basically being refused entry, and were told to wait for the Minsitry of Agriculture offices to open at nine a.m. five hours away, before Gentry could be released from his prison crate. The taxation department was not to be left out. An agent demanded Value Added Tax on my horse, because he was a gelding. Stallions and mares were not taxed. What an irony. Thank God for the Valuation from Dr. Twidale lodged in my briefcase. International Horse Service's Manager, Malcolm Keogh was waiting. He took my brief case and all the papers ultimately sorting out the final phase of the journey.

Under Malcolm's efforts, after more hours trickling by, the Ministry agreed to admit us. We were free to go at nine a.m. on the 1st of September, 1977.

The crate now on the ground, with the horse van from Leicestershire waiting nearby, I would free Gentry and we could be on our way. We found the spanner to undo the crate bolts had been left behind in New York. Were we to be thwarted even now at the last minute?

No. Someone produced a tire lever, the crate was carefully broken open, and my patient, incredible horse at last touched English soil. Now that his kidneys were at last free to function, he christened it well.

The kind horsevan driver helped me walk Gentry's stiffness away for a few minutes. We gave him fresh water which he gulped down quickly, then raised his beautiful head to look at me with his knowledgeable eyes, conveying his understanding the worst was over. We had survived incredible odds, but we were still together.

We loaded him into the big van, whose interior had been deeply bedded in fresh straw with a fresh haynet of sweet smelling hay hanging by his head. A small window letting in the fresh country air allowed him to breathe and view the countryside as we set off for the ninety miles to Leicestershire.

Sitting beside the patient driver who had waited so long at Heathrow for us, I soon nodded off into worn out snatches of sleep. The relief of having brought my horse from Canada, across America, flying over Ireland into Germany, watching the sun rise over Russia, as we flew back above Belgium, and the tip of France, into England - in fifteen days, was indeed awesome.

Our safe arrival at Robin and Betty Leyland's fine livery stable in Barleythorpe, near Oakham in Leicesterhire, was an anti-climax from the uncertainties of the past weeks. Their warmth in our reception, plus utter knowledge for my horse was what I needed and received. It seemed like a dream after all we had been through.

Old friend, Dr. Richard Watson from the Gibson Horse Clinic closeby, was on hand to help Gentry, expecting to administer reviving medication, which he did not need. I led Gentry from the van. He let out a deep sigh as he looked sharply around, telling me

266

"This is it! We will be alright now!" Robin took him into their riding ring where he trotted off to explore and then crumpled up for a well deserved roll, over and over.

It was time to let Gentry relax, unrestrained, in a cool, well ventilated boxstall, deeply bedded with golden straw. He looked very comfortable and contented as he nibbled sweet hay from a tightly strung haynet, often stopping to sip the fresh water in a large bucket nearby. The thoroughbred hunters on either side of him were in training for the demanding eventing and fox hunting disciplines, making my 'big' Quarter Horse look quite small, although everyone envied his wonderful muscling and 'washerwoman' great hind quarter!

I was more than happy with the competent and professional care Gentry would have until I found a permanent home for us together nearby. If I were not able to ride my horse daily there was no question he would be neglected. Robin undertook to have him shod and 'ride him out' each morning and to see he was properly groomed. It was good to be back where horse's and their daily necessities come first.

The moral of my story is that no horse person should attempt to circumvent a good horse transport travel service. We had taken fifteen days for what should have only been a fifteen hour flight. We could have been in England before the Controller's strikes took off. Frustrations had mounted to horrendous proportions. Gentry's blind trust in me had given me the strength I needed to sustain the increasing odds being stacked against us. Gentry had always, and would continue to, give me reason to live, to fight and to love.

It had been more than three years since I had seen Kevin and Louisa, and in spite of my exhaustion I was anxious to be with them. I was standing in the stable yard as they drove excitedly through the big gates in their car. Louisa climbed from the front seat holding two year old Victoria, the granddaughter I had never met. Kevin rushed to hug me in welcome for the new life lying ahead.

I had fled from the problems of a disastrous husband. I wanted to leave it all behind and begin life anew with my family in the country I had left twenty years before. I had dreamt a quiet life of retirement for Gentry and I lay ahead, but should have known better. With time to reflect, how could I have imagined our future could be far from simple wherever we were. It was not.

Nevertheless, by the Grace of God we were safely home, for now.

Joy Richardson's

HYLINE GENTRY

May 22nd 1970 to June 3rd 1996

1971 Won B.C.'s first (very large) Quarter Horse Futurities B.C. Bred & Open

1971 Hi Colt BCQHA

1972 - 1973 Hi Point Gelding every year shown in Canada, US and England.

Grand Champion Pacific National Exhibition - Vancouver for 4 years.

Grand Champion for 3 years at Pacific International, Portland Oregon.

1973 English Futurity Champion North West International Vancouver

1974 Register of Merit AQHA.

1974 - 1977 qualified for Quarter Horse World Championships in Halter, Hunter under Saddle, Western Pleasure, Roping, Trail.

1972 - 1982 Over 30 Hi Point All Around Show Championships.

1972 - 1982 38 Grand and Reserve Halter Championships.

1975 AQHA Champion and Superior Halter Champion.

1975 Hi Point All Around Horse the State of Jefferson.

1975 Hi Point All Around Horse the State of Oregon.

1972 Movie"A Horse Called Question" with him as fictional star, went to Cannes.

1982 "Barbara Woodhouse's World of Horses" made by BBC with him as feature in Western section (front part was the Queen's horses at the Royal Mews) was shown around the world seven times!

1976 CEF Medium Dressage

1976 Chilliwack International All Around Champion

1977 Fox hunted in Leicestershire, England

1978-1981 British National Supreme Champion Quarter Horse

1981-1982 British Western Horseman National Champion

1982 Winner Small Hunter Classes in England

1986 BC Provincial Dressage Pas de Deux Champion with brother Hyline Paladin.

1986 BCQHA Hi Point Working Hunter

That gives a general idea without all the individual wins! and the many Year Ends. We had such a great time together.